Daniel Wasserrab

From Formal Semantics to Verified Slicing

A Modular Framework with Applications in Language Based Security

From Formal Semantics
to Verified Slicing

A Modular Framework with Applications in Language
Based Security

by
Daniel Wasserrab

KIT Scientific Publishing

Dissertation, Karlsruher Institut für Technologie
Fakultät für Informatik,
Tag der mündlichen Prüfung: 19.10.2010

Impressum

Karlsruher Institut für Technologie (KIT)
KIT Scientific Publishing
Straße am Forum 2
D-76131 Karlsruhe
www.ksp.kit.edu

KIT – Universität des Landes Baden-Württemberg und nationales
Forschungszentrum in der Helmholtz-Gemeinschaft

KIT Scientific Publishing 2011
Print on Demand

ISBN 978-3-86644-594-9

From Formal Semantics to Verified Slicing
A Modular Framework with Applications in Language Based Security

zur Erlangung des akademischen Grads eines

Doktors der Ingenieurswissenschaften/
Doktors der Naturwissenschaften

der Fakultät der Informatik
des Karlsruher Instituts für Technologie (KIT)

genehmigte
Dissertation

von

Daniel Wasserrab

aus Burghausen

Tag der mündlichen Prüfung: 19. Oktober 2010

Erster Gutachter: Prof. Dr.-Ing. Gregor Snelting

Zweiter Gutachter: Prof. Tobias Nipkow, PhD

Acknowledgements

First, I would like to thank my adviser Prof. Gregor Snelting for giving me the freedom and means to carry out this research. His ideas and constant trust in my abilities laid the foundations for this thesis. I thank Prof. Tobias Nipkow not only for the second review of this thesis, but also for helping me with formalization and proof problems, especially in the first part of this work. Dr. Frank Tip was very helpful in the object-oriented details of the first part of this work.

I am very thankful for the many fruitful discussions in the "semantics group", with Andreas Lochbihler and Denis Lohner as co-members. They stopped me several times from running into dead ends or provided me with new perspectives on problems. I know I will miss these discussions. Furthermore, I also thank them and Martin Hecker for reading preliminary drafts of this thesis.

The discussions with my "non-theorem proving" office co-workers in Passau, Christian Hammer and Maximilian Störzer, were helpful to get an unbiased view of things. Also, they have become more than just working colleagues. The same can be said for all other members of our group in Passau and Karlsruhe. In addition to the already mentioned persons these are: Mirko Streckenbach, Dennis Giffhorn, Jürgen Graf, Matthias Braun, Sebastian Buchwald, and Andreas Zwinkau.

I thank the students Martin Dirndorfer, Michael Pisula, and Jan Aidel from Passau and Karlsruhe for their work on the CCCP project.

Last, but not least I thank my wife Karin. Without her love and constant support this thesis would not exist. She confides so strongly in my talent that I cannot doubt myself. I am proud and eager to spend my life with her. Also, I thank my parents and my family for all their assistance. Although they never quite understood what I was doing (I do not blame them), they tried to give me as much help as possible.

Parts of this work were funded by the Deutsche Forschungsgemeinschaft in DFG grant Sn11/10-1.

Zusammenfassung

Statische Programmanalysen sind ein weit verbreitetes Mittel, um aus Programmtexten Informationen über Ausführungen zu erhalten, die für jeden beliebigen Programmlauf gültig sind, ohne das Programm selbst auszuführen. Statische Analysen werden heutzutage in verschiedensten Ber ichen der Informatik eingesetzt, wie z.B. Compiler, Refactoring oder Debugging. Auch für sicherheitskritischen Anwendungen werden statische Analysen inzwischen standardmäßig genutzt.

Viele Eigenschaften von statischen Analysen werden von niemandem bezweifelt werden, für einige existieren sogar formale Beweise (auf Papier). Dennoch stellt sich die Frage, inwiefern damit eine unerschütterliche Vertrauensbasis geschaffen wird, die vor allem für sicherheitskritische Systeme unverzichtbar ist. Maschinengeprüfte Beweise können helfen, diese Vertrauensbasis zu schaffen bzw. zu verstärken, da die Maschine jeden noch so kleinen Fehler in einem Beweis sofort erkennt. Papierbeweise sind dagegen deutlich fehleranfälliger.

An unserem Lehrstuhl wurde eine Sicherheitsanalyse entwickelt [52], die prüft, ob in einem Programm geheime Informationen in öffentliche Ausgaben einfließen können. Solche Probleme werden in der *Informationsflusskontrolle* (Information Flow Control, IFC) betrachtet, einem Teilbereich der *sprachbasierten Softwaresicherheit* (Language Based Security). Die Sicherheitsanalyse basiert auf *Slicing*, einer statischen Analyse auf *Programmabhängigkeitsgraphen* (Program Dependence Graph), die konservativ approximiert, welche Programmpunkte einen spezifischen Programmpunkt beeinflussen können. Der dort betrachtete Ansatz zu Slicing ist komplett graphbasiert und damit unabhängig von einer konkreten Programmiersprache.

Doch kann man den Resultaten dieser Analyse trauen? Oder mit anderen Worten: Wer garantiert, dass die Resultate korrekt sind? An unserem Lehrstuhl wurde das Projekt *Quis custodiet* ins Leben gerufen, mit dem Ziel, die oben genannte und ähnliche Sicherheitsanalysen maschinengeprüft zu verifizieren. Da diese Analysen aber auf Slicing basieren, muss zuallererst einmal bewiesen werden, dass Slicing selbst korrekt ist.

In dieser Arbeit wird ein modulares Framework im Beweisassistenten Isabelle/HOL [81] auf Basis abstrakter Kontrollflussgraphen entwickelt, um die Korrektheit von Slicing zu zeigen. Indem man sich auf solche abstrakten Strukturen stützt, erhält man programmiersprachenunabhängige Korrektheitsresultate, d.h. anstatt eines Beweises für jede Sprache benötigt man im Ganzen nur noch einen Beweis. Um diesen Beweis dann auf eine beliebige Sprache zu übertragen, muss man nur noch für jedes beliebige Programms in dieser Sprache zeigen, dass sein Kontrollflussgraph die erforderlichen Eigenschaften des Frameworks erfüllt.

Dazu benötigt man eine formale Semantik der Sprache in Isabelle/HOL. Der erste Teil dieser Arbeit zeigt, dass dies selbst für Kerne von komplexen Hochsprachen machbar ist, indem eine formale Semantik einer C++-Kernsprache definiert wird. Diese ist vollständig objektorientiert und beinhaltet die komplizierte Mehrfachvererbung von C++ mit ihren zwei Vererbungsarten. Ein bedeutendes Resultat dieser Arbeit ist der erste Beweis [134], dass diese besondere Mehrfachvererbung die Typsicherheit nicht verletzt, was lange Jahre zwar angenommen, aber nie bewiesen wurde. Typsicherheit und damit die Abwesenheit von Laufzeitfehlern zu garantieren ist ein anderer wichtiger Bereich der sprachbasierten Softwaresicherheit.

Im zweiten Teil dieser Arbeit wird die Korrektheit von Slicing in Isabelle/HOL bewiesen. Diese Programmanalyse berechnet eine konservative Approximation der Menge aller Programmpunkte, die einen bestimmten Programmpunkt beeinflussen können. Deshalb sollte es für die verwendeten Variablen an diesem Programmpunkt keinen Unterschied machen, ob man ein Programm durchläuft, in dem alle Punkte entfernt wurden, die nicht in der Slicingmenge sind, oder das ursprüngliche Programm. Wenn diese Eigenschaft gilt, ist Slicing korrekt. Die vorliegende Arbeit beschränkt sich nicht nur auf intraprozedurales Slicing – wie alle früheren Ergebnisse –, sondern betrachtet auch den ausgefeilten interprozeduralen Algorithmus von Horwitz, Reps und Binkley [57]. Dieser Algorithmus ist kontextsensitiv, d.h. er unterscheidet verschiedene Aufrufstellen von Prozeduren, weshalb er genauer als andere Algorithmen ist. Aufgrund der dafür benötigten *Summarykanten* und interprozeduralen Besonderheiten wie Parameterübergabe etc. war es nicht trivial, diesen Algorithmus zu formalisieren und zu verifizieren. Durch diese Verifikation wird in dieser Arbeit zum ersten Mal formal die Korrektheit des Horwitz-Reps-Binkley-Algorithmus nachgewiesen.

Dass die Resultate tatsächlich auf verschiedenste Programmiersprachen anwendbar sind, zeigen zwei Instantiierungen des Frameworks:

(i) eine einfache While-Sprache und (ii) die objektorientierte Bytecode-sprache von Jinja [61], einer weit entwickelten Kernsprache für Java.

Zuletzt wird noch ein erstes Resultat für die Anwendbarkeit von Slicing für IFC gezeigt, ein wichtiger Schritt für die Ziele des Projekts *Quis custodiet*. Aufgrund der Korrektheitsresultate für Slicing konnte gezeigt und bewiesen werden, wie klassische Nichtinterferenz mittels Slicing garantiert werden kann. Diese verlangt, dass geheime Informationen keine öffentlich einsehbaren Variablen beeinflussen. Da Slicing fluss- und (bei Verwendung des Horwitz-Reps-Binkley-Algorithmus) auch kontextsensitiv ist, liefert dieses Verfahren weniger Fehlalarme als die üblichen Sicherheitstypsysteme [96], die weder kontext- noch (bis auf wenige Ausnahmen) flusssensitiv sind.

Abstract

Static program analyses gain information from programs without executing them. They are commonly used in various areas such as compilers, refactoring, or debugging, even in safety-critical applications. While many program analyses are intuitively correct and some even accompanied with manual proofs, machine-checked proofs can help to verify complex analyses for which correctness is not so easy to see.

Our group developed a security analysis which determines if secret information may leak to public output. *Information flow control*, a subarea of *language based security* considers such problems. This approach bases on *slicing*, a program analysis which conservatively determines which program points potentially influence a certain statement. The slicing approach applied builds on (dependence) graphs, hence is language-independent. But are the results of this analysis trustworthy? Our group initiated the project *Quis custodiet* to verify this and similar security analyses in theorem provers. But to achieve this, slicing needs to be proved correct first.

This thesis presents a modular framework for slicing in the proof assistant Isabelle/HOL which is based on abstract control flow graphs. Building on such abstract structures renders the correctness results in the framework language-independent. To prove that they hold for a specific language, it remains to instantiate the framework with this language, i.e., show that the control flow graph of a program fulfills the properties of the framework.

This requires a formal semantics of this language in Isabelle/HOL. The first part of this thesis shows that formal semantics even for sophisticated high-level languages are realizable. I formalize the formal semantics of a C++ kernel language focusing on C++'s inheritance mechanisms. Inheritance in C++ is complex as it allows (i) multiple inheritance and (ii) two different kinds of inheritance relations. An important result of this work is the first proof that inheritance à la C++ does not compromise type safety.

In the second part, this thesis provides correctness proofs for dynamic as well as static intra- and interprocedural slicing. Prior works only examine intraprocedural slicing and are restricted to simple imperative languages. In contrast, this thesis also proves the context-sensitive interprocedural slicing algorithm by Horwitz, Reps, and Binkley correct; this is the first formal correctness result on this standard algorithm.

By instantiating the framework with two different languages, I show that the abstraction chosen in the framework are indeed sensible. Finally, via the correctness of slicing, this thesis proves that slicing can guarantee classical noninterference, an important result for the *Quis custodiet* project. All proofs in this thesis are carried out in the proof assistant Isabelle/HOL.

Contents

Contents

1

Introduction

Today, huge program developments in high-level languages are ubiquitous. Therefore, we need the means to handle such big projects. This includes the potential to guarantee that the program has some properties, be it by design or via analysis. Safety properties are of particular interest: type safe languages can help to avoid certain run-time errors during programming, whereas static program analyses help to guarantee that the finished code fulfills some properties. Thus, deciding this is shifted from the concrete program to the type system or analysis. By verifying that a language is type safe or proving that the program analysis result is indeed correct, one increases confidence in these techniques significantly.

This thesis positions itself in this area of research. In its first part, it presents a formalization of a formal semantics of C++, which focuses on multiple inheritance, in a theorem prover, namely Isabelle/HOL [81]. Multiple inheritance in C++ is dreaded mostly because of its combination of virtual and non-virtual inheritance. In combination with diamond-shaped inheritance relations, this may lead to quite unintuitive behaviour. This thesis also provides a machine-checked correctness proof that the semantics – and thus C++'s multiple inheritance concept – is indeed type safe.

In the second part, this thesis formalizes a framework for a program analysis called *program slicing* – or short slicing – based on dependence graphs. Weiser introduced slicing some thirty years ago [135, 136] to determine which program points may influence the execution at a certain statement. This is an important task in various areas of computer science. Weiser's work initiated a whole new research area, in which a wealth of different slicing techniques and applications has been designed and published.

Slicing based on dependence graphs is not restricted to specific languages. I provide a language-independent framework for slicing with correctness proofs for dynamic, static intra- and interprocedural slicing. This includes a proof that the context-sensitive slicing algorithm by Horwitz, Reps, and Binkley [57] is indeed correct. I also instantiate the framework with two different languages to show its applicability. All of the proofs are again machine-checked in Isabelle/HOL.

Finally, this thesis proves that slicing guarantees classical information flow noninterference. Information flow control [96] checks if secret information can leak to public outputs. This result shows that verifying sophisticated information flow algorithms such as [52] is no longer out of reach.

1.1 Context

Information flow control (IFC), a subset of *language based security* (LBS) [101], checks if secret information can leak to public output in a program. Following years of research on dependence graphs and slicing, our group developed a software security analysis for IFC which can handle full Java byte code [52]. The security analysis builds on slicing to gain information on which program points can influence others. As it is flow-, context-, and object-sensitive, this analysis triggers fewer false alarms than standard type system approaches [96]. It can handle programs with up to 50kLoC.

Yet, as a security algorithm this work suffers from a severe drawback: it has no correctness proof. To eliminate this deficiency, our group initiated the *Quis custodiet* project[1]. It aims at formally verifying such information flow security analyses in theorem provers. Being machine-checked, the correctness results will provide a new level of confidence, as manual proofs for such complex algorithms are notoriously error-prone.

As the security analyses under consideration use slicing to determine if information flows between program points, their verification requires to prove slicing correct first. The complex interprocedural context-sensitive algorithm by Horwitz, Reps, and Binkley [57] (usually with an improvement by Reps et al. [91]) is standard, as the trade-off between slice size and runtime is very good. Yet, every result in this area prior to this thesis [92, 7, 90, 3] restricts itself to the intrapro-

---

[1]*Quis custodiet ipsos custodes?* Who is guarding the guards?, Juvenal.

cedural case. There is to our knowledge no work on the correctness of context-sensitive interprocedural slicing.

Also, all of the correctness results mentioned above only consider simple imperative languages. Yet, slicing algorithms such as the one by Horwitz, Reps, and Binkley are based on dependence – and thus on control flow – graphs, not on a concrete programming language. Therefore, we aim for a language-independent framework which axiomatizes these graph structures to prove slicing correct. Instantiating it with a semantics and concrete control flow graph formalization transfers these results to a concrete language.

1.2 State of the Art

I briefly summarize the situation today in formal semantics and type safety as well as in program analysis, focusing on IFC. More on these topics can be found in Sec. 7.

1.2.1. Formal Semantics

Formal semantics is the standard mechanism to describe *what* a program does without referring to prosaic descriptions or examples. There are several ways to formalize semantics, e.g. axiomatic, denotational, or operational. Whereas the denotational approach, which describes programs as partial functions between initial and final states, was initially more common, operational semantics, which consider execution on an abstract machine, became standard in the last years. Wright and Felleisen [140] devised the now widely used approach to prove type safety of operational semantics: *progress* and *preservation*, i.e., the semantics does not get "stuck" and types are preserved by semantic evaluation.

Today, formal semantics on paper exist even for realistic high-level languages, e.g. for Eiffel [6], Java [42], Scala [85] and C# [45]. All of these works formalize semantics operationally (or using related concepts, such as abstract state machines), the last three also include a type safety proof.

Recently, proof assistants attracted attention as a means to formalize semantics and prove type safety machine-checked. The work by Gordon [47] about formalizing the axiomatic semantics of Hoare [54] can be considered a door-opener in this area. Jinja [61] and the preceding Bali project was another significant milestone. Other impressive works that describe the language semantics on a very detailed level, yet do not contain type safety proofs, include the C [82] and C++ [83] semantics by Norrish in HOL [48], and the JVM semantics formalized in Coq [18], called Bicolano [36].

1.2.2. Program Analysis and Information Flow Control

Program analysis has made significant progress in the last years, not least because object-oriented languages demand for complex analyses. Points-to Analysis, for which efficient [112] and context-sensitive [43] variants have been developed, and Shape Analysis [98] may serve as examples. However, such analyses have become so elaborate that it is hard to provide a correctness result that is more than just an intuitive argument. In theorem provers in particular, correctness proofs of analyses that go beyond simple dataflow analyses or compiler optimizations are rare; the works on a Java byte code verifier [61, 17] and a context sensitive points-to analysis [39] represent notable exceptions.

Nevertheless, IFC still disregards the cutting edge of modern program analysis, despite its potential. Its standard approach are flow types systems [96], for which advanced tools for Java [75] and OCaml [105] exist. A big advantage of type systems is that they are compositional, i.e., smaller program parts can be checked independently, whereas program analysis in this area still requires to analyze programs as a whole. Also, verifying flow type systems is in general more easy, even in theorem provers, as techniques for formalizing and verifying such type systems in them is common knowledge. For some correctness results regarding flow type systems in theorem provers, see Sec. 7.5.1.

In general, type systems may suffer from false alarms, a problem which no approach at all can eliminate completely due to decidability problems. However, we expect precision to increase when the slicing based algorithm developed in our group [52, 109] is used, as it is context-, object-, and flow-sensitive; recent research presented a flow type system [58] that fulfills the latter. But this precision comes at a cost: (i) the algorithm is not trivial to understand, (ii) although it can handle large programs, in general, it only scales well for smallish and less complex examples, and (iii) verification is much harder. Prior to this thesis, only one correctness statement existed [109], but it assumed the correctness of slicing instead of proving it.

1.3 Contributions

This thesis revolves around the following two statements:

- The multiple-inheritance of C++ is type safe.

- Dynamic as well as static intra- and interprocedural slicing is correct, independent of the underlying language.

To show that both propositions are valid, I formalized them in the proof assistant Isabelle/HOL [81] and verified them. Both formalizations are substantial and the accompanying proofs nontrivial.

While having been assumed for a long time, no formal proof showed that multiple inheritance as realized in C++ is type safe. I formalize a small but fully object-oriented core language which mirrors all multiple inheritance features of C++ precisely. Thus, it extends previous work, e.g. [61, 126], which either does not consider multiple inheritance at all or deviates from C++ in subtle but significant details. I show that this semantics is type safe in the sense of Cardelli [33], i.e., no untrapped errors may occur at runtime, but controlled exceptions are allowed. Hence, this constitutes the first proof that C++'s multiple inheritance is type safe.

The framework for slicing provides the first formalization of dependence graphs as real graph structures in a proof assistant. I define dynamic as well as static intra- and interprocedural slicing directly on these structures, hence do not depend on a specific language; a limitation, which restrains all the existing correctness proofs for slicing based on dependence graphs. In the dynamic and static intraprocedural case, I was also able to eliminate the need for a concrete control dependence definition. Instead, the correctness proofs hold for any dependence relation which fulfills a certain criterion. By providing language instantiations for the framework I demonstrate that I axiomatized the abstract graph structures sensibly. Via this modularization, no language or control dependence instantiation has to reprove any part of the slicing correctness proof.

No prior work addressed the correctness of context-sensitive interprocedural slicing, hence the correctness proof of the Horwitz-Reps-Binkley slicing algorithm presented in this thesis is the first of its kind. It comes with a precision proof, which guarantees that the slice respects context-sensitivity. These proofs require to significantly adapt the intraprocedural framework, but still retain language independence.

5

Again, two language instantiations show the validity of the framework requirements.

Finally, I use these correctness results to prove that slicing can safely guarantee classical information flow noninterference. This is the first machine-checked correctness proof for IFC based on dependence graphs [108, 109]. While this proof demands some adaptions to the graphs, I also show that every valid framework graph can be easily lifted to meet these requirements.

Since IFC as well as type safety are important areas of LBS, this thesis provides significant contributions to this area. Finally, this work demonstrates that it is indeed possible to formalize and verify intricate properties on elaborate structures in proof assistants such as Isabelle, since they have now become powerful and user-friendly enough for such tasks. This work extends the applicability of formal semantics and theorem prover technology to a new level of complexity. Still, all the formalizations and proofs are written in a declarative style, which is easily understandable for human readers, instead of cryptic tactic application. None of the results presented in this thesis would have been realizable some ten years ago.

1.4 Isabelle

Isabelle is a generic interactive theorem prover (or *proof assistant*), instantiable with different object logics, most widespread is *Higher Order Logic* (HOL), which is also used in this work. Proof assistants are in general not able to prove lemmas automatically, even when provided with the definitions and statements necessary. Thus, formal proofs still require much effort by an expert user, a limitation Isabelle shares with all such proof systems. A proof is an interactive process, a dialogue where the user has to provide the overall proof structure and the system checks its correctness but also offers a number of tools for filling in missing details. Chief among these tools are the simplifier (for simplifying formulas) and the logical reasoner (for proving predicate calculus formulas automatically).

Isabelle allows one to define functions in a way analogous to functional programming languages (e.g. ML). Most of the proofs in this paper are written in *Isar* [137], a language of structured and stylized mathematical proofs understandable to both machines and humans. This proof language is invaluable when constructing, communicating and maintaining large proofs like the ones presented in this thesis. Definitions and lemmas taken from Isabelle are typeset *small and slanted*. In few cases, the presentation is simplified w.r.t. the actual formalization to achieve a better readability.

1.4.1. Notation

Types include the basic types of truth values, natural numbers and integers, which are called *bool*, *nat*, and *int* respectively. The space of total functions is denoted by $\Rightarrow$. Type variables are written $'a$, $'b$, etc. $t{::}\tau$ means that the HOL term t has HOL type τ.

Pairs come with the two projection functions *fst* $:: 'a \times 'b \Rightarrow 'a$ and *snd* $:: 'a \times 'b \Rightarrow 'b$. We identify tuples with pairs nested to the right: (a, b, c) is identical to $(a, (b, c))$ and $'a \times 'b \times 'c$ is identical to $'a \times ('b \times 'c)$.

Sets (type $'a\ set$) follow the usual mathematical convention. Function *card* returns the cardinality of a finite set; such sets fulfil the predicate *finite*. $\emptyset$ is the empty set.

Lists (type $'a\ list$) come with the empty list $[]$, the infix constructor $\cdot$, the infix @ that appends two lists, and the conversion function *set* from lists to sets. Variable names ending in "s" usually stand for lists and $|xs|$ is the length of *xs*. If $i < |xs|$ then $xs_{[i]}$ denotes the i-th element of *xs*. Functions *hd* and *tl* are standard, returning the first element and the remainder of the list, respectively. Also *last* and *butlast* are defined as usual, the former returns the last element, the latter chops off the last element of the list. The standard functions *map*, which applies a function to every element in a list, and *filter*, where $[x \leftarrow xs.\ P]$ filters all elements from *xs* which fulfil P, are also avilable.

Function update is defined as: $f(a := b) \equiv \lambda x.\ if\ x = a\ then\ b\ else\ f\ x$, where $f :: 'a \Rightarrow 'b$ and $a :: 'a$ and $b :: 'b$. If we have a list of values *as*, which should be updated to values *bs* element by element in f, we write $f(as\ [:=]\ bs)$.

datatype $'a\ option = None\ |\ Some\ 'a$ adjoins a new element *None* to a type $'a$. All existing elements in type $'a$ are also in $'a\ option$, but are prefixed by *Some*. For succinctness we write $\lfloor a \rfloor$ instead of *Some a*. Hence *bool option* has the values $\lfloor True \rfloor$, $\lfloor False \rfloor$ and *None*.

Case distinctions on data types use guards, where every guard must be followed by a data type constructor. E.g. *case x of* $\lfloor y \rfloor \Rightarrow f\ y\ |\ None \Rightarrow g$ means that if x is some y then the result is $f\ y$ where f may refer to value y, and if x is *None*, then the result is g.

Partial functions are modeled as functions of type $'a \Rightarrow 'b\ option$, where *None* represents undefinedness and $fx = \lfloor y \rfloor$ means x is mapped to y. Instead of $'a \Rightarrow 'b\ option$ we write $'a \rightharpoonup 'b$, call such functions **maps**, and abbreviate $f(x := \lfloor y \rfloor)$ to $f(x \mapsto y)$. The latter notation extends to lists: $f([x_1, \ldots, x_m] \ [\mapsto] \ [y_1, \ldots, y_n])$ means $f(x_1 \mapsto y_1) \ldots (x_i \mapsto y_i)$, where i is the minimum of m and n. The notation works for arbitrary list expressions on both sides of $[\mapsto]$, not just enumerations. Multiple updates like $f(x \mapsto y)(xs [\mapsto] ys)$ can be written as $f(x \mapsto y, xs [\mapsto] ys)$. The map $\lambda x.\ None$ is written *empty*, and $empty(\ldots)$, where $\ldots$ are updates, abbreviates to $[\ldots]$. For example, $empty(x \mapsto y, xs[\mapsto]ys)$ becomes $[x \mapsto y, xs\ [\mapsto]\ ys]$. The domain of a map is defined as $dom\ m = \{a \mid m\ a \neq None\}$. Function *map-of* turns a list of pairs into a map:

$$map\text{-}of\ [] = empty$$
$$map\text{-}of\ (p {\cdot} ps) = map\text{-}of\ ps(fst\ p \mapsto snd\ p)$$

1.4.2. Locales

Locales in Isabelle [8] provide the means to modularize proofs, using self-defined proof contexts. Within a locale, one introduces (**fixes**) definitions and functions by stating their signature which may also contain type variables. To impose certain constraints on these definitions one **assumes** that the respective statement holds. When defining new functions or proving lemmas within the locale one can then use these fixed definitions and the assumed constraints.

One or multiple locales can also be extended by a new locale (using +) with additional definitions and constraints. All the definitions and lemmas proved in the base locales are available in the extended locale.

As a short example, consider the following definition of semigroups where we fix an operator $\odot$, whose signature depends on the type variable $'a$, and assume that this operator is associative by the fact named *assoc*. Defining a new locale *semi-comm* which extends *semi* and requires that operator $\odot$ is commutative (see rule *comm*) is also straightforward.

locale *semi* =
    fixes $\odot :: 'a \Rightarrow 'a \Rightarrow 'a$
    assumes *assoc*: $(x \odot y) \odot z = x \odot (y \odot z)$

locale *semi-comm* = *semi* +
    assumes *comm*: $x \odot y = y \odot x$

Well-typed programs cannot go
wrong.

        R. Milner

Type Safe Semantics for C++

In [126], I showed how to integrate C++-like multiple inheritance, including both repeated and shared (virtual) inheritance, in a formal semantics and type system. However, the typing and semantics rules presented there deviate in some cases from the actual behaviour of C++. This chapter fills the last gaps and answers the final questions by presenting the language *CoreC++* [134], in which we reformulated some rules such that the semantics and type system model exactly the multiple inheritance of C++ in all its complexity.

Casting in the presence of multiple inheritance is a non-trivial operation, even more so as C++ provides two recommended casting operators, **static_cast** and **dynamic_cast**, whose behaviours can differ significantly in some situations. Modeling dynamic dispatch and covariant return types posed the biggest challenge, as ambiguities may occur at run-time which have to be resolved. The resulting semantics enables one – for the first time – to fully understand and express the behaviour of operations such as method calls, field accesses, and casts in C++ programs without referring to compiler data structures such as virtual function tables (v-tables) as usual in the standard [116].

I also present a type safety proof for the CoreC++ language. This proof not only guarantees that C++'s multiple inheritance is no impediment to type safety, but also shows that proof assistants are finally powerful enough to machine-check formalizations of high-level programming languages and to provide enough support to verify utterly non-trivial properties on them.

This part of the thesis is joint work with Tobias Nipkow, Gregor Snelting, and Frank Tip. They provided me with detailed insight in the way C++ works and helped me in finding the right abstractions for the formalization. Hence, in most parts of this chapter I use the notion "we" instead of "I".

The whole project, i.e., all the formalizations and the type safety proof, is available online [127]. In a few cases I changed the syntax in this thesis for readability.

2.1 The Story so far...

More than ten years ago, the group of Tobias Nipkow initiated the project BALI[1]. It strived to formalize a large sequential subset of the Java source and byte code semantics in the proof assistant Isabelle/HOL and to prove both type safe. Java had already been regarded as type safe at that time [42], however this consensus lacked the rigid formal proof in a theorem prover. Furthermore, BALI aimed for the verification of a compiler between the source and byte code language together with a byte code verifier. All these objectives were achieved and the project culminated in the presentation of *Jinja* [61]. This work demonstrated for the first time that machine-checking realistic high-level programming languages has become reality.

Naturally, the question arose if C++, the other wide-spread object-oriented programming language, also guarantees type safety. Of course, one has to leave out of consideration things like pointer arithmetic or templates, as these are inherently not type safe. But there is another big difference between C++ and Java. One of the main sources of complexity in C++ is a complex form of multiple inheritance, in which a combination of shared ("virtual") and repeated ("nonvirtual") inheritance is permitted. Because of this complexity, the behaviour of operations on C++ class hierarchies has traditionally been defined informally [116], and in terms of implementation-level constructs such as v-tables. In 1996, Rossie, Friedman, and Wand [94] stated that "In fact, a provably-safe static type system [...] is an open problem" and there was no real progress in this question the following years.

In my diploma thesis [126], I tackled the task of extending the *Jinja* source code language with multiple inheritance à la C++. The sub-object model by Rossie and Friedman [93] that formalizes the object model of C++ was used as a starting point. Rossie and Friedman defined the behaviour of method calls and member access using this model, but their definitions do not follow C++ behaviour precisely. Hence, the semantics and type system rules in [126] represent just a

---

[1]http://isabelle.in.tum.de/bali/

first step towards an accurate description of the behaviour of C++-like multiple inheritance.

The next two sections – first an introduction to the multiple inheritance mechanisms of C++, then an overview of the existing formalization – recapitulate the work of [126], thus are no contribution of this thesis. In Sec. 2.4, I discuss some problems of the existing semantics and show how to rewrite some rules so that their semantics mirror those of C++ to the maximum extent possible. Basing on these new rules, the type safety of C++-like multiple inheritance is then be proved in Sec. 2.5. Finally, I present a tool for interpreting real C++ programs in the CoreC++ semantics (Sec. 2.6), discuss related work and conclude.

2.2 Multiple Inheritance in C++

2.2.1. An Intuitive Introduction to Subobjects

C++ features both *nonvirtual* (or *repeated*) and *virtual* (or *shared*) multiple inheritance. The difference between the two flavors of inheritance is subtle, and only arises in situations where a class Y indirectly inherits from the same class X via more than one path in the hierarchy. In such cases, Y will contain *one* or *multiple* X-"subobjects", depending on the kind of inheritance that is used. More precisely, if only shared inheritance is used, Y will contain a single, shared X-subobject, and if only repeated inheritance is used, the number of X-subobjects in Y is equal to N, where N is the number of distinct paths from X to Y in the hierarchy. If a combination of shared and repeated inheritance is used, the number of X-subobjects in a Y-object will be between 1 and N (a more precise discussion follows). C++ hierarchies with only single inheritance (the distinction between repeated and shared inheritance is irrelevant in this case) are semantically equivalent to Java class hierarchies.

Fig. 2.1(a) shows a small C++ class hierarchy. In these and subsequent figures, a solid arrow from class C to class D denotes the fact that C repeated-inherits from D, and a dashed arrow from class C to class D denotes the fact that C shared-inherits from D. Here, and in subsequent examples, all methods are assumed to be `virtual` (i.e., dynamically dispatched), and all classes and inheritance relations are assumed to be `public`.

```
class Top { int x, y; ... };
class Left : Top { ... };
class Right : Top { int y; ... };
class Bottom : Left, Right { int x; ... };
```

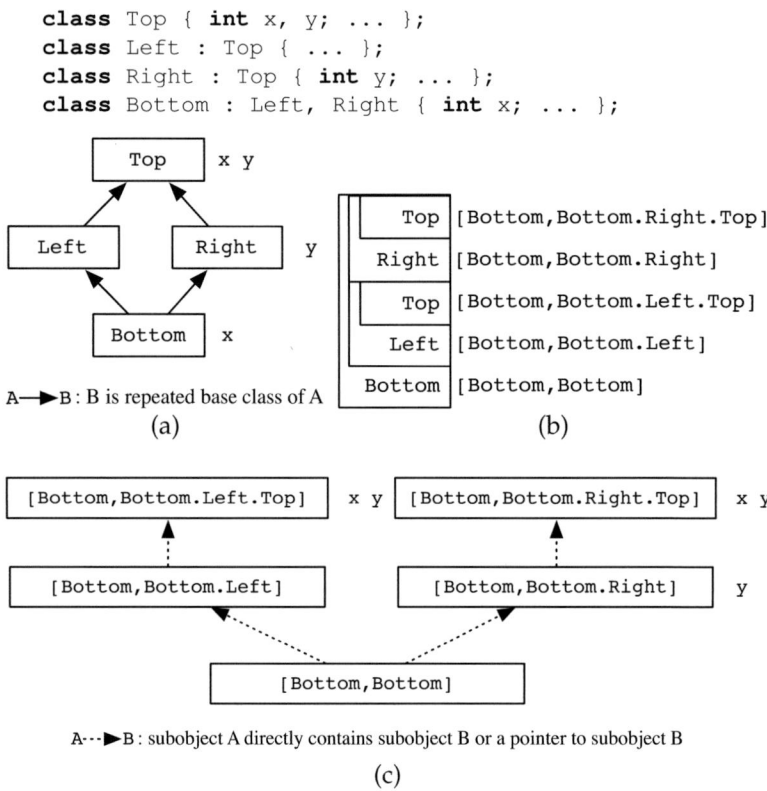

Figure 2.1.: The repeated diamond

In Fig. 2.1(a), all inheritance is repeated. Since class Bottom repeated-inherits from classes Left and Right, a Bottom-object has one subobject of each of the types Left and Right. As Left and Right each repeated-inherit from Top, (sub)objects of these types contain distinct subobjects of type Top. Hence, for the C++ hierarchy of Fig. 2.1(a), an object of type Bottom contains *two distinct subobjects* of type Top. Fig. 2.1(b) shows the layout used for a Bottom object by a typical compiler, given the hierarchy of Fig. 2.1(a). Each subobject has local copies of the subobjects that it contains, hence it is possible to lay out the object in a contiguous block of memory without indirections.

Fig. 2.2(a) shows a similar C++ class hierarchy in which the inheritance between Left and Top and between Right and Top is *shared*.

12

```
class Top { void f() { ... }; ... };
class Left : virtual Top { ... };
class Right : virtual Top { void f() { ... }; ... };
class Bottom : Left, Right { ... };
```

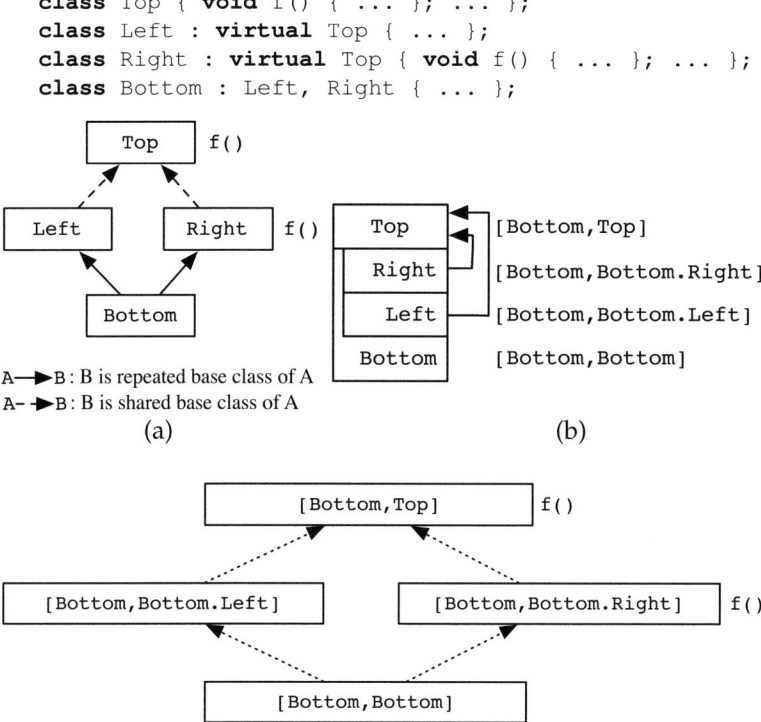

A——▶B : B is repeated base class of A
A--▶B : B is shared base class of A

(a)

(b)

A···▶B : subobject A directly contains subobject B or a pointer to subobject B

(c)

Figure 2.2.: The shared diamond

Again, a `Bottom`-object contains one subobject of each of the types `Left` and `Right`, due to the use of repeated inheritance. However, since `Left` and `Right` both shared-inherit from `Top`, the `Top`-subobject contained in the `Left`-subobject is *shared* with the one contained in the `Right`-subobject. Hence, for this hierarchy, a `Bottom`-object will contain *a single subobject* of type `Top`. In general, a shared subobject may be shared by arbitrarily many subobjects, and requires an object layout with indirections (typically in the form of *virtual-base pointers*) [115, p.266]. Fig. 2.2(b) shows a typical object layout for an object of type `Bottom` given the hierarchy of Fig. 2.2(a). Observe that the `Left`-subobject and the `Right`-subobject each contain a pointer to the single shared `Top`-subobject.

2.2.2. The Rossie-Friedman Subobject Model

Rossie and Friedman [93] proposed a subobject model for C++-style inheritance, and used that model to formalize the behaviour of method calls and field accesses. Informally, one can think of the Rossie-Friedman model as an abstract representation of object layout. Intuitively, a *subobject*[2] identifies a component of type D that is embedded within a complete object of type C. However, simply defining a subobject type as a pair (C, D) would be insufficient, because, as we have seen in Fig. 2.1, a C-object may contain multiple D-components in the presence of repeated multiple inheritance. Therefore, a subobject is identified by a pair $[C, Cs]$, where C denotes the type of the "complete object", and where the *path* Cs consists of a sequence of class names $C_1. \ldots .C_n$ that encodes the transitive inheritance relation between C_1 and C_n. There are two cases here: For *repeated* subobjects we have that $C_1 = C$, and for *shared* subobjects, we have that C_1 is the least derived (most general) shared base class of C that contains C_n. This scheme is sufficient because shared subobjects are unique within an object (i.e., there can be at most one *shared* subobject of type S within any object). More formally, for a given class C, the set of its subobjects, along with a containment ordering on these subobjects, is inductively defined as follows:

---

[2] In this thesis, we follow the terminology of [93] and use the term "subobject" to refer both to the label that uniquely identifies a component of an object type, as well as to components within concrete objects that are identified by such labels. In retrospect, the term "subobject label" would have been better terminology for the former concept.

1. $[C, C]$ is the subobject that represents the "full" C-object.

2. if $S_1 = [C, Cs.X]$ is a subobject for class C where Cs is any sequence of class names, and X shared-inherits from Y, then $S_2 = [C, Y]$ is a subobject for class C that is accessible from S_1 through a pointer.

3. if $S_1 = [C, Cs.X]$ is a subobject for class C where Cs is any sequence of class names, and X repeated-inherits from Y, then $S_2 = [C, Cs.X.Y]$ is a subobject for class C that is directly contained within subobject S_1.

Fig. 2.1(c) and Fig. 2.2(c) show *subobject graphs* for the class hierarchies of Fig. 2.1 and Fig. 2.2, respectively. Here, an arrow from subobject S to subobject S' indicates that S' is directly contained in S or that S has a pointer leading to S'. For a given subobject $S = [C, Cs.D]$, we call C the *dynamic class* of subobject S and D the *static class* of subobject S. Associated with each subobject are the members that occur in its static class. Hence, if an object contains multiple subobjects with the same static class, it will contain multiple copies of members declared in that class. For example, the subobject graph of Fig. 2.1(c) shows two subobjects with static class `Top`, each of which has distinct fields x and y.

Intuitively, a subobject's dynamic class represents the type of the "full object" and is used to resolve dynamically dispatched method calls. A subobject's static class represents the declared type of a variable that points to an (subobject of the full) object and is used to resolve field accesses. In this thesis, we use the Rossie-Friedman subobject model to define the behaviour of operations such as method calls and casts as functions from subobjects to subobjects. As we shall see shortly, it will be necessary in our semantics to maintain full subobject information even for "static" operations such as casts and field accesses.

Multiple inheritance can easily lead to situations where multiple members with the same name are visible. In C++, many member accesses that are seemingly ambiguous are resolved using the notion of *dominance* [116]. A member m in subobject S' *dominates* a member m in subobject S if S is contained in S' (i.e., S' has a path leading to S in the subobject graph). Member accesses are resolved by selecting the unique dominant member m if it exists; otherwise an access is ambiguous[3]. For example, in Fig. 2.2, a `Bottom`-object sees two declarations of `f()`, one in class `Right` and one in class `Top`. Thus a call (**new** `Bottom())->f())` seems ambiguous. But it is not, because in the subobject graph for `Bottom` shown in Fig. 2.2(c), the definition of `f()` in [`Bottom,Bottom.Right`] dominates the one in [`Bottom,Top`]. On the other hand, the subobject graph in Fig. 2.1(c) contains three definitions of `y` in [`Bottom,Bottom.Right`], [`Bottom,Bottom.Right.Top`], and [`Bottom,Bottom.Left.Top`]. As there is no unique dominant definition of `y` here, a field access (**new** `Bottom())->y)` is ambiguous.

2.2.3. Examples

We will now discuss some examples to illustrate the subtleties that arise in the C++ inheritance model; more can be found in the subsequent sections.

Example 1.   Dynamic dispatch behaviour can be counterintuitive in the presence of multiple inheritance. One might expect a method call always to dispatch to a method definition in a superclass or subclass of the type of the receiver expression. Consider, however, the shared diamond example of Fig. 2.2, where a method `f()` is defined in classes `Right` and `Top`. Now assume that the following C++ code is executed (note the implicit up-cast to `Left` in the assignment):

```
Left* b = new Bottom(); b->f();
```

One might expect the method call to dispatch to `Top::f()`. But in fact it dispatches to `f()` in class `Right`, which is neither a superclass nor a subclass of `Left`. The reason is that up-casts do not switch off dynamic dispatch, which is based on the receiver object's dynamic class. The dynamic class of `b` remains `Bottom` after the cast, and since `Right::f()` dominates `Top::f()`, the former is called.

This makes sense from an application viewpoint: Imagine the top class to be a "Window", the left class to be a "Window with menu", the right class to be a "Window with border", the bottom class to be a "Window with border and menu", and `f()` to compute the available window space. Then, a "Window with border and menu" object which is casted to "Window with menu" pretends not to have a border

---

[3] In some cases, C++ uses the static class of the receiver for further disambiguation. This will be discussed shortly.

anymore (border methods cannot be called). But for the area computation, the hidden border must be taken into account, thus f() from "Window with border" must be called.

Example 2. The next example illustrates the need to track some subobject information at run-time, and how this complicates the semantics. Consider the program fragment in Fig. 2.3(a), where b points to a B-subobject. This subobject occurs in two different "contexts", namely either as a [D,D.B] subobject (if the then-case of the **if** statement is executed), or as an [E,E.B] subobject (if the else-case is executed). Note that executing the assignments b = **new** D() and b = **new** E() involves an implicit up-cast to type B. Depending on the context, the call b->f() will dispatch to D::f() or E::f(). Now, executing the body of this f() involves an implicit assignment of b to its this pointer. Since the static type of b is B, and the static type of this is the class containing its method, an implicit down-cast (to D or to E, depending on the context) is needed. At compile time it is not known which cast will happen at run-time, which implies that the compiler must keep track of some additional information to determine the cast that must be performed.

In a typical C++ implementation, a cast actually implies changing the pointer value in the presence of multiple inheritance, as is illustrated in Fig. 2.3(b). The up-cast from D to B (then-case, upper part of Fig. 2.3(b)) is implemented by adding the offset $delta(B)$ of the [D,D.B]-subobject within the D object to the pointer to the D object. Afterwards, the pointer points to the [D,D.B]-subobject. As we discussed, the subsequent call b->f() requires that the pointer be down-casted to D again. This cast is implemented by adding the negative offset $-delta(B)$ of the [D,D.B]-subobject to the pointer. The else-case (lower part of Fig. 2.3(b)) is analogous, but involves a different offset, which happens to be 0. In other words, the offsets in the then- and else-cases are different, and we do not know until run-time which offset has to be used. To this end, C++ compilers typically extend the virtual function table (v-table) [115] with "delta" values that, for each v-table entry, record the offset that has to be added to the this-pointer in order to ensure that it points to the correct subobject after the cast (Fig. 2.3(b)).

Our semantics correctly captures the information needed for performing casts, without referring to compiler data structures such as v-table entries and offsets.

```
class A {...};
class B {void f();};
class C {...};
class D : A,B {void f();};
class E : B,C {void f();};

B* b;
if (...)
 b = new D();
else
 b = new E();
b->f();
```

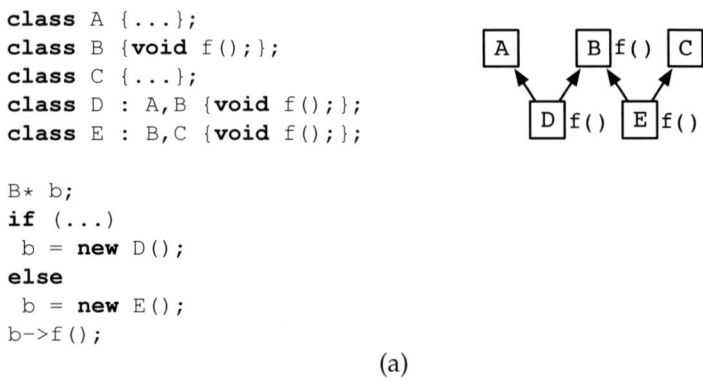

(a)

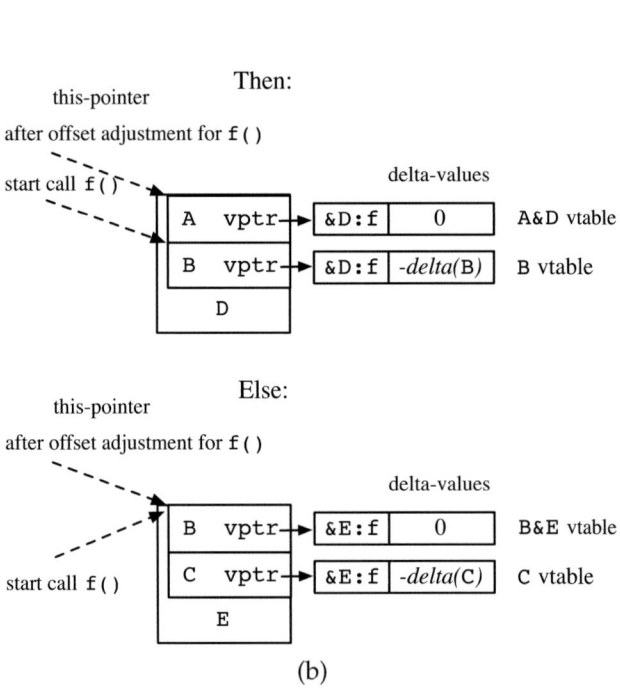

(b)

Figure 2.3.: C++ fragment demonstrating dynamically varying sub-object context

Example 3. This example is taken from [89]. It shows that many compilers treat dominance incorrectly and thus have problems with field access/assignment (as well as method call):

```
class A { int x; };
class B { int x; };
class C : virtual A, virtual B { int x; };
class D : virtual A, virtual B, C {};

(new D())->x = 42;
```

The g++ compiler rejects the left hand side of (**new** D())->x = 42 as ambiguous, whereas the Intel® C++ compiler correctly accepts this program.

Clearly, the semantics of method calls, field accesses, and casts are quite complicated in the presence of shared and repeated multiple inheritance. Typical C++ compilers rely on implementation-level artifacts such as v-tables and subobject offsets to define the behaviour of these constructs. In the next sections, we present a formalization that relies solely on subobjects and paths, which enables us to demonstrate type safety.

2.3 The Present Situation of CoreC++

In the following, we will give a short introduction how the semantics has been formalized in [61, 126] before we go into the details of the relevant object-oriented constructs.

2.3.1. Formalization

Names, paths, and base classes. Type *cname* is the (HOL) type of class names. The (HOL) variables C and D will denote class names, Cs and Ds are paths. We introduce the type abbreviation *path = cname list*.

Programs are denoted by P. For the moment we do not need to know what programs look like. Instead we assume the following predicates describing the class structure of a program:

- $P \vdash C \prec_R D$ means D is a direct repeated base class of C in P.
- $P \vdash C \prec_S D$ means D is a direct shared base class of C in P.
- $\preceq^*$ means $(\prec_R \cup \prec_S)^*$.
- *is-class* $P\,C$ means class C is defined in P.

Subobjects. We slightly changed the appearance of subobjects in comparison with Rossie-Friedman style: we use a tuple with a class and a path component where a path is represented as a list of class names. For example, a Rossie-Friedman subobject [Bottom,Bottom.Left] is translated into (Bottom,[Bottom,Left]).

The subobject definitions are parameterized by a program P. First we define $Subobjs_R\ P$, the subobjects whose path consists only of repeated inheritance relations:

$$\frac{\text{is-class } P\ C}{(C, [C]) \in Subobjs_R\ P} \qquad \frac{P \vdash C \prec_R D \qquad (D, Cs) \in Subobjs_R\ P}{(C, C{\cdot}Cs) \in Subobjs_R\ P}$$

Now we define $Subobjs\ P$, the set of all subobjects:

$$\frac{(C, Cs) \in Subobjs_R\ P}{(C, Cs) \in Subobjs\ P}$$

$$\frac{P \vdash C \preceq^* C' \qquad P \vdash C' \prec_S D \qquad (D, Cs) \in Subobjs_R\ P}{(C, Cs) \in Subobjs\ P}$$

We have shown that this definition and the one by Rossie and Friedman (see Sec. 2.2.2) are equivalent. Ours facilitates proofs because paths are built up following the inductive nature of lists.

Path functions. We need a concatenation of paths $@_p$ such that the following property holds under the assumption that program P is well-formed[4]:

If $(C, Cs) \in Subobjs\ P$ and $(last\ Cs, Ds) \in Subobjs\ P$
then $(C, Cs\ @_p\ Ds) \in Subobjs\ P$.

If the second path only contains repeated inheritance, then it starts with the same class the first one ends with, so we can append both of them via @ (taking care to just use the common class once). If the second path begins with a shared class, the first path just disappears (because we lose all information below the shared class).

Thus, function $@_p$ appends two paths assuming the second one is starting where the first one ends with:

$$Cs\ @_p\ Cs' \equiv if\ last\ Cs = hd\ Cs'\ then\ Cs\ @\ tl\ Cs'\ else\ Cs'$$

---

[4]A well-formed program requires certain natural constraints of the program such as the class hierarchy relation to be irreflexive (see Sec. 2.4.4).

An ordering on paths $\sqsubset^1$ is defined as follows:

$$\frac{(C, Cs) \in Subobjs\ P \qquad (C, Ds) \in Subobjs\ P \qquad Cs = butlast\ Ds}{P,C \vdash Cs \sqsubset^1 Ds}$$

$$\frac{(C, Cs) \in Subobjs\ P \qquad P \vdash last\ Cs \prec_S D}{P,C \vdash Cs \sqsubset^1 [D]}$$

The reflexive and transitive closure of $\sqsubset^1$ is written $\sqsubseteq$. The intuition of this ordering is subobject containment: $P,C \vdash Cs \sqsubseteq Ds$ means that subobject (C,Ds) lies below (C,Cs) in the subobject graph. For example, it is not hard to derive $P,Bottom \vdash [Bottom] \sqsubseteq [Bottom,Left,Top]$ (in the repeated diamond) from these definitions.

2.3.2. Abstract Syntax of CoreC++

We do not define a concrete syntax for CoreC++, just an abstract syntax. The translation of the C++-subset corresponding to CoreC++ into abstract syntax is straightforward and will not be discussed here.

In the sequel, we use the following (HOL) variable conventions: V is a (CoreC++) variable name, F a field name, M a method name, e an expression, v a value, and T a type.

In addition to *cname* (class names) there are also the (HOL) types *vname* (variable and field names), and *mname* (method names). We do not assume that these types are disjoint, e.g. all of them may be *strings*.

References. A **reference** refers to a subobject within an object. Hence it is a pair of an **address** that identifies the object on the heap (see Sec. 2.3.4 below) and a path identifying the subobject. Formally:

$$reference = addr \times path$$

The path represents the dynamic context of a subobject as a result of previous casts (as explained in Sec. 2.2.3), and corresponds to the result of adding "delta" values to an object pointer in the standard "v-table" implementation. Our semantics does not emulate the standard implementation, but is more abstract.

Note: CoreC++ references are not equivalent to C++ references, but are more like C++ pointers.

As an example, consider Fig. 2.3. If we assume that the **else** statement is executed, then b will have the reference value $(a, [E, B])$ where a is the memory address of the new E object, and path $[E, B]$ represents the fact that this object has been up-cast to B and b in fact points to the B subobject.

Values and Expressions.   A CoreC++ **value** (abbreviated *val*) can be

- a boolean *Bool b*, where $b :: bool$, or

- an integer *Intg i*, where $i :: int$, or

- a reference *Ref r*, where $r :: reference$, or

- the null reference *Null*, or

- the dummy value *Unit*.

CoreC++ is an imperative but expression-based language where statements are expressions that evaluate to *Unit*. The following **expressions** (of HOL type *expr*) are supported by CoreC++:

- creation of a new object: new C

- static casting: stat_cast $C\,e$

- dynamic casting: dyn_cast $C\,e$

- literal value: Val v

- binary operation: e_1 «*bop*» e_2 (where *bop* is one of + or ==)

- variable access Var V and variable assignment $V := e$

- field access $e.F\{Ds\}$ and field assignment $e_1.F\{Ds\} := e_2$
  (where Ds is the path to the subobject where F is declared)

- method call $e.M(es)$ and qualified method call $e.C::M(es)$

- block with a locally declared variable: $\{V:T; e\}$

- sequential composition: $e_1;;\ e_2$

- conditional: if $(e)\ e_1$ else e_2
  (do not confuse with HOL's *if b then x else y*)

- while loop: while $(e)\ e'$

- throwing arbitrary exceptions *throw e*

$$
\begin{array}{llll}
\textit{prog} & = \textit{cdecl list} & \textit{cdecl} & = \textit{cname} \times \textit{class} \\
\textit{class} & = \textit{base list} \times \textit{fdecl list} \times \textit{mdecl list} \\
\textit{fdecl} & = \textit{vname} \times \textit{ty} & \textit{mdecl} & = \textit{mname} \times \textit{method} \\
\textit{method} & = \textit{ty list} \times \textit{ty} \times \textit{vname list} \times \textit{expr}
\end{array}
$$

datatype *base* = *Repeats cname* | *Shares cname*

Figure 2.4.: Abstract program syntax

The constructors `Val` and `Var` are needed in our meta-language to disambiguate the syntax. Binary operators are evaluated left-to-right, in C++ this order is unspecified. There is no return statement because everything is an expression and returns a value.

The annotation {*Ds*} in field access and assignment is not part of the input language but is something that a preprocessor, e.g., the type checking phase of a compiler, must add.

To ease notation we introduce some abbreviations:

- *ref r* ≡ `Val`(*Ref r*)

- *null* ≡ `Val` *Null*

- *true* ≡ `Val`(*Bool True*)

- *false* ≡ `Val`(*Bool False*)

- *unit* ≡ `Val` *Unit*

Programs.   The abstract syntax of programs is given by the type definitions in Fig. 2.4, where *ty* is the HOL type of CoreC++ types (see Sec. 2.3.3).

A CoreC++ program is a list of class declarations. A **class declaration** consists of the name of the class and the class itself. A **class** consists of the list of its direct superclass names (marked *Shares* or *Repeats*), a list of field declarations and a list of method declarations. A **field declaration** is a pair of a field name and its type. A **method declaration** consists of the method name and the method itself, which consists of the parameter types, the result type, the parameter names, and the method body.

Note that CoreC++ (like Java, but unlike C++) does not have global variables. Method bodies can access only their *this*-pointer and parameters, and return a value.

We refrain from showing the formal definitions (see [61]) of the predicates like $P \vdash C \prec_R D$ introduced in Sec. 2.3.1 as they are straightforward. Instead we introduce one more access function:

class P C: the class (more precisely: *class option*) associated with *C* in *P*

2.3.3. Type System

CoreC++ types are either primitive (*Boolean* and *Integer*), class types *Class C*, *NT* (the type of *Null*), or *Void* (the type of *Unit*). The set of these types (i.e., the corresponding HOL type) is called *ty*. Function *typeof* returns the type of a value (except for references, which return *None*):

$$typeof\ (Bool\ b) = \lfloor Boolean \rfloor, \quad typeof\ (Int\ i) = \lfloor Integer \rfloor,$$
$$typeof\ (Ref\ r) = None, \quad typeof\ Null = \lfloor NT \rfloor, \quad typeof\ Void = \lfloor Unit \rfloor$$

The first two rules of the subtype relation $\le$ are straightforward:

$$P \vdash T \le T \qquad P \vdash NT \le Class\ C$$

To relate two classes, we have to take care that we can use an object of the smaller type wherever an object of the more general type can occur. This property can be guaranteed by requiring that a static cast between these two types can be performed, resulting in the premise[5]:

$$P \vdash path\ C\ to\ D\ unique \equiv \exists!Cs.\ (C,\ Cs) \in Subobjs\ P \wedge last\ Cs = D$$

This property ensures that the path from class *C* leading to class *D* exists and is unique ($\exists!$ is unique existence). This leads to the third subtyping rule:

$$\frac{P \vdash path\ C\ to\ D\ unique}{P \vdash Class\ C \le Class\ D}$$

The point-wise extension of $\le$ to lists is written $[\le]$.

The core of the type system is the judgment $P,E \vdash e :: T$, , where *E* is an **environment**, i.e., a map from variables to their types. We call *T* the **static** type of *e*. [::] lifts :: to lists.

Fig. 2.5 shows the typing rules for the imperative constructs of CoreC++ together with object creation and exception throwing. All

---

[5]For more information about static casts, see Sec. 2.4.1.

WTNew: $\dfrac{is\text{-}class\ P\ C}{P,E \vdash \texttt{new}\ C :: Class\ C}$ WTVal: $\dfrac{typeof\ v = \lfloor T \rfloor}{P,E \vdash \texttt{Val}\ v :: T}$

WTVar: $\dfrac{E\ V = \lfloor T \rfloor}{P,E \vdash \texttt{Var}\ V :: T}$ WTBlock: $\dfrac{is\text{-}type\ P\ T \qquad P,E(V \mapsto T) \vdash e :: T'}{P,E \vdash \{V{:}T;\ e\} :: T'}$

WTBinOp: $\dfrac{\begin{array}{c} P,E \vdash e_1 :: T_1 \qquad P,E \vdash e_2 :: T_2 \\ case\ bop\ of == \Rightarrow T_1 = T_2 \wedge T = Boolean \\ |\ + \Rightarrow T_1 = Integer \wedge T_2 = Integer \wedge T = Integer \end{array}}{P,E \vdash e_1\ \ll bop \gg e_2 :: T}$

WTSeq: $\dfrac{P,E \vdash e_1 :: T_1 \qquad P,E \vdash e_2 :: T_2}{P,E \vdash e_1 \texttt{;;}\ e_2\ ::\ T_2}$

WTCond: $\dfrac{P,E \vdash e :: Boolean \qquad P,E \vdash e_1 :: T \qquad P,E \vdash e_2 :: T}{P,E \vdash \texttt{if}\ (e)\ e_1\ \texttt{else}\ e_2 :: T}$

WTWhile: $\dfrac{P,E \vdash e :: Boolean \qquad P,E \vdash c :: T}{P,E \vdash \texttt{while}\ (e)\ c :: Void}$

WTThrow: $\dfrac{P,E \vdash e :: Class\ C}{P,E \vdash \texttt{throw}\ e :: Void}$

WTNil: $P,E \vdash [] \ [::] \ []$ WTCons: $\dfrac{P,E \vdash e :: T \qquad P,E \vdash es [::] Ts}{P,E \vdash e{\cdot}es [::] T{\cdot}Ts}$

Figure 2.5.: Typing rules for sequential constructs, object creation and exception throwing

these rules are standard and an exhaustive discussion of them can be found elsewhere [61, 126]. Note that rule WTVal guarantees via *typeof* that references are not typed, since the type system should reject programs with explicit references. The rules for the remaining expressions can be found in Sec. 2.4.

2.3.4. Semantics

The big step semantics is a (deterministic) relation between an initial expression-state pair ⟨e,s⟩ and a final expression-state pair ⟨e′,s′⟩. The syntax of the relation is $P,E \vdash \langle e,s \rangle \Rightarrow \langle e',s' \rangle$ and we say that e *evaluates* to e′. The need for E will be explained in Sec. 2.4.3. The rules will be such that *final* expressions are always values (Val) or thrown exceptions (throw), i.e., final expressions are completely evaluated. Again, [⇒] lifts the evaluation to lists of expressions, e.g. parameter lists.

$$
\begin{array}{llllll}
state & = & heap \times locals & locals & = & vname \rightharpoonup val \\
heap & = & addr \rightharpoonup obj & obj & = & cname \times subo\ set \\
subo & = & path \times (vname \rightharpoonup val)
\end{array}
$$

Figure 2.6.: The type of CoreC++ program states

We proved that the big step rules are deterministic, i.e., an expression-state pair always evaluates to the same result.

State. The set of states is defined in Fig. 2.6. A **state** is a pair of a **heap** and a **store** (*locals*). A store is a map from variable names to values. A heap is a map from addresses to objects. An **object** is a pair of a class name and its subobjects. A **subobject** (*subo*) is a pair of a path (leading to that subobject) and a field table mapping variable names to values.

The naming convention is that h is a heap, l is a store (the *l*ocal variables), and s a state.

Note that CoreC++, in contrast to C++, does not allow stack-allocated objects: variable values can only be pointers (CoreC++ references), but not objects. Objects are only on the heap (as in Java). We do not expect stack based objects to interfere with multiple inheritance.

Remember further that a reference contains not only an address but also a path. This path selects the current subobject of an object and is modified by casts (see below).

Exceptions. CoreC++ supports exceptions. They are essential to prove type soundness as certain problems can occur at run-time (e.g., a failing cast) which we cannot prevent statically. In these cases we throw an exception so the semantics does not get stuck. Three exceptions are predefined in CoreC++: *OutOfMemory*, if there is no more space on the heap, *ClassCast* for a failed cast and *NullPointer* for null pointer access. Some semantic rules concerning exception throwing can be found in Fig. 2.7, the remaining ones are explained in Sec. 2.4. *THROW C* is syntactic sugar for *throw* (*Ref* (*addr-of-sys-xcpt C*,[*C*])), where *addr-of-sys-xcpt* is a fixed address on the heap for each of the predefined exceptions.

Evaluation. Recall that $P,E \vdash \langle e,s \rangle \Rightarrow \langle e',s' \rangle$ is the evaluation judgment, where P denotes the program and E the type environment. For

NewFail:
$$\frac{\textit{new-Addr } h = \textit{None}}{P,E \vdash \langle \texttt{new } C,(h,l)\rangle \Rightarrow \langle \textit{THROW OutOfMemory},(h,l)\rangle}$$

BinOpThrow1:
$$\frac{P,E \vdash \langle e_1,s_0\rangle \Rightarrow \langle \texttt{throw } e,s_1\rangle}{P,E \vdash \langle e_1 \ll bop \gg e_2,s_0\rangle \Rightarrow \langle \texttt{throw } e,s_1\rangle}$$

BinOpThrow2:
$$\frac{P,E \vdash \langle e_1,s_0\rangle \Rightarrow \langle \texttt{Val } v_1,s_1\rangle \quad P,E \vdash \langle e_2,s_1\rangle \Rightarrow \langle \texttt{throw } e,s_2\rangle}{P,E \vdash \langle e_1 \ll bop \gg e_2,s_0\rangle \Rightarrow \langle \texttt{throw } e,s_2\rangle}$$

SeqThrow:
$$\frac{P,E \vdash \langle e_0,s_0\rangle \Rightarrow \langle \texttt{throw } e,s_1\rangle}{P,E \vdash \langle e_0\texttt{;; } e_1,s_0\rangle \Rightarrow \langle \texttt{throw } e,s_1\rangle}$$

CondThrow:
$$\frac{P,E \vdash \langle e,s_0\rangle \Rightarrow \langle \texttt{throw } e',s_1\rangle}{P,E \vdash \langle \texttt{if } (e) \ e_1 \texttt{ else } e_2,s_0\rangle \Rightarrow \langle \texttt{throw } e',s_1\rangle}$$

WhileCondThrow:
$$\frac{P,E \vdash \langle e,s_0\rangle \Rightarrow \langle \texttt{throw } e',s_1\rangle}{P,E \vdash \langle \texttt{while } (e) \ c,s_0\rangle \Rightarrow \langle \texttt{throw } e',s_1\rangle}$$

WhileBodyThrow:
$$\frac{P,E \vdash \langle e,s_0\rangle \Rightarrow \langle \textit{true},s_1\rangle \quad P,E \vdash \langle c,s_1\rangle \Rightarrow \langle \texttt{throw } e',s_2\rangle}{P,E \vdash \langle \texttt{while } (e) \ c,s_0\rangle \Rightarrow \langle \texttt{throw } e',s_2\rangle}$$

Throw:
$$\frac{P,E \vdash \langle e,s_0\rangle \Rightarrow \langle \textit{ref } r,s_1\rangle}{P,E \vdash \langle \texttt{throw } e,s_0\rangle \Rightarrow \langle \textit{Throw } r,s_1\rangle}$$

ThrowThrow:
$$\frac{P,E \vdash \langle e,s_0\rangle \Rightarrow \langle \texttt{throw } e',s_1\rangle}{P,E \vdash \langle \texttt{throw } e,s_0\rangle \Rightarrow \langle \texttt{throw } e',s_1\rangle}$$

ThrowNull:
$$\frac{P,E \vdash \langle e,s_0\rangle \Rightarrow \langle \textit{null},s_1\rangle}{P,E \vdash \langle \texttt{throw } e,s_0\rangle \Rightarrow \langle \textit{THROW NullPointer},s_1\rangle}$$

ConsThrow:
$$\frac{P,E \vdash \langle e,s_0\rangle \Rightarrow \langle \texttt{throw } e',s_1\rangle}{P,E \vdash \langle e\cdot es,s_0\rangle \ [\Rightarrow] \ \langle \texttt{throw } e'\cdot es,s_1\rangle}$$

Figure 2.7.: Big step rules concerning exception throwing

a better understanding of the evaluation rules it is helpful to realize that they preserve the following heap invariant: for any object (C, S) on the heap we have

- S contains exactly the paths starting from C:
  $\{Ds \mid \exists fs.\ (Ds, fs) \in S\} = \{Ds \mid (C, Ds) \in Subobjs\ P\}$,

- S is a (finite) function: $\forall (Cs,fs), (Cs',fs') \in S.\ Cs = Cs' \longrightarrow fs = fs'$

Furthermore, if an expression e evaluates to $ref\ (a, Cs)$ then the heap maps a to $\lfloor(C, S)\rfloor$ such that

- Cs is the path of a subobject in S: $(Cs, fs) \in S$ for some fs.

- $last\ Cs$ is equal to the class of e inferred by the type system.

New:
$$\frac{\textit{new-Addr } h = \lfloor a \rfloor \quad h' = h(a \mapsto (C, \{(Cs, fs) \mid \textit{init-obj } P\ C\ (Cs, fs)\}))}{P,E \vdash \langle \texttt{new } C,(h, l)\rangle \Rightarrow \langle \textit{ref } (a, [C]),(h', l)\rangle}$$

Val:
$$P,E \vdash \langle \texttt{Val } v,s\rangle \Rightarrow \langle \texttt{Val } v,s\rangle$$

Var:
$$\frac{l\ V = \lfloor v \rfloor}{P,E \vdash \langle \texttt{Var } V,(h, l)\rangle \Rightarrow \langle \texttt{Val } v,(h, l)\rangle}$$

BinOp:
$$\frac{P,E \vdash \langle e_1,s_0\rangle \Rightarrow \langle \texttt{Val } v_1,s_1\rangle}{P,E \vdash \langle e_2,s_1\rangle \Rightarrow \langle \texttt{Val } v_2,s_2\rangle \quad binop\ (bop,\ v_1,\ v_2) = \lfloor v \rfloor}{P,E \vdash \langle e_1 \ll bop \gg e_2,s_0\rangle \Rightarrow \langle \texttt{Val } v,s_2\rangle}$$

Block:
$$\frac{P,E(V \mapsto T) \vdash \langle e_0,(h_0, l_0(V := None))\rangle \Rightarrow \langle e_1,(h_1, l_1)\rangle}{P,E \vdash \langle\{V{:}T;\ e_0\},(h_0, l_0)\rangle \Rightarrow \langle e_1,(h_1, l_1(V := l_0\ V))\rangle}$$

Seq:
$$\frac{P,E \vdash \langle e_0,s_0\rangle \Rightarrow \langle \texttt{Val } v,s_1\rangle \quad P,E \vdash \langle e_1,s_1\rangle \Rightarrow \langle e_2,s_2\rangle}{P,E \vdash \langle e_0;; \ e_1,s_0\rangle \ \Rightarrow \ \langle e_2,s_2\rangle}$$

CondT:
$$\frac{P,E \vdash \langle e,s_0\rangle \Rightarrow \langle \textit{true},s_1\rangle \quad P,E \vdash \langle e_1,s_1\rangle \Rightarrow \langle e',s_2\rangle}{P,E \vdash \langle \texttt{if } (e)\ e_1 \texttt{ else } e_2,s_0\rangle \Rightarrow \langle e',s_2\rangle}$$

CondF:
$$\frac{P,E \vdash \langle e,s_0\rangle \Rightarrow \langle \textit{false},s_1\rangle \quad P,E \vdash \langle e_2,s_1\rangle \Rightarrow \langle e',s_2\rangle}{P,E \vdash \langle \texttt{if } (e)\ e_1 \texttt{ else } e_2,s_0\rangle \Rightarrow \langle e',s_2\rangle}$$

WhileT:
$$\frac{P,E \vdash \langle e,s_0\rangle \Rightarrow \langle \textit{true},s_1\rangle}{P,E \vdash \langle c,s_1\rangle \Rightarrow \langle \texttt{Val } v_1,s_2\rangle \quad P,E \vdash \langle \texttt{while } (e)\ c,s_2\rangle \Rightarrow \langle e_3,s_3\rangle}{P,E \vdash \langle \texttt{while } (e)\ c,s_0\rangle \Rightarrow \langle e_3,s_3\rangle}$$

WhileF:
$$\frac{P,E \vdash \langle e,s_0\rangle \Rightarrow \langle \textit{false},s_1\rangle}{P,E \vdash \langle \texttt{while } (e)\ c,s_0\rangle \Rightarrow \langle \textit{unit},s_1\rangle} \qquad \text{Nil: } P,E \vdash \langle [],s\rangle \ [\Rightarrow] \ \langle [],s\rangle$$

Cons:
$$\frac{P,E \vdash \langle e,s_0\rangle \Rightarrow \langle \texttt{Val } v,s_1\rangle \quad P,E \vdash \langle es,s_1\rangle \ [\Rightarrow] \ \langle es',s_2\rangle}{P,E \vdash \langle e{\cdot}es,s_0\rangle \ [\Rightarrow] \ \langle \texttt{Val } v{\cdot}es',s_2\rangle}$$

Figure 2.8.: Big step rules of sequential constructs and object creation

The imperative subset of the big step semantic rules and the ones for object creation are presented in Fig. 2.8. In rule New, by using *init-obj* we require that all object fields are initialized with default values (see also Sec. 2.5.2). Note that C++ does not initialize fields. Our desire for type safety requires us to deviate from C++ in this minor aspect; for more details, see Sec. 2.5.2. The interested reader can find more information on these standard rules in [61, 126].

Small Step Semantics Big step rules are easy to understand but cannot distinguish nontermination from being stuck. Hence we also have a *small step* semantics where expression-state pairs are gradually reduced. The reduction relation is written $P,E \vdash \langle e,s \rangle \rightarrow \langle e',s' \rangle$ and its transitive reflexive closure is $P,E \vdash \langle e,s \rangle \rightarrow^* \langle e',s' \rangle$. The rules can be found in appendix A.

We have proven the equivalence of the big and small step semantics (for well-formed programs, see Sec. 2.4.4):

$$P,E \vdash \langle e,s \rangle \Rightarrow \langle e',s' \rangle = (P,E \vdash \langle e,s \rangle \rightarrow^* \langle e',s' \rangle \wedge \textit{final } e').$$

2.4 Improving the Semantics towards real C++

In this section, we concentrate on the adaptions to the existing semantics necessary to model C++-like multiple inheritance precisely.

2.4.1. Static and Dynamic Casts

In contrast to Java, casting is a non-trivial operation in C++, as it adjusts the object's `this`-pointer to reference the actual subobject. This adjustment is necessary as for field accesses (and even dispatch) it may be of importance via which path we reached the subobject (e.g., to distinguish the accessed `x` variable in the `Top` subobject in the repeated diamond Fig. 2.1). Hence, casting in C++ is a frequent source of errors and obtaining the desired result requires much care and experience.

C++ has three cast operators for traversing class hierarchies, each of which has significant limitations[6]. Most commonly used are so-called C-style casts. C-style casts may be used to cast between arbitrary unrelated types, although some static checking is performed on up-casts (e.g., a C-style up-cast is statically rejected if the receiver's static type does not contain a unique subobject whose static class is the type being cast to), but no run-time checks. C-style casts cannot be used to down-cast along a shared inheritance relation, as it is not possible to "go back" along the indirection pointers in the object. When used incorrectly, C-style casts may cause run-time errors. We do not model C-style casts as they are regarded as "old-style" and should be replaced with the "new-style" casting operators described in the following.

---

[6] The remaining two cast operators in C++, **reinterpret_cast** and **const_cast** are out of scope of this work: the former is inherently non type safe, as it allows casting even between unrelated pointer types, and the latter just sets the **const** attribute of its parameter, i.e., is concerned with mutability of objects.

The **static_cast** operator only performs compile-time checks (e.g., to ensure that a unique subobject of the target type exists) and disallows casting between unrelated types. **static_cast** cannot be used to down-cast along a shared inheritance relation. When used incorrectly, **static_cast** may cause run-time errors.

The **dynamic_cast** operator is the recommended cast operator in C++. It has the desirable property that failing casts result in controlled exceptions (when the target of the cast is a reference) or the special value NULL (when the target is a pointer). Unlike the previous two operators, down-casting along shared inheritance relations is allowed, and **dynamic_cast** may be used to cast between unrelated types. However, a subtle limitation exists: A **dynamic_cast** is statically incorrect when applied to an expression whose declared type does not declare virtual methods.

The following examples will be used to elucidate the different behaviour of **static_cast** and **dynamic_cast**. For this purpose, we will make use of the repeated and shared diamond as shown in Fig. 2.1 and Fig. 2.2.

Example 1.

```
Top* t = static_cast<Top*>(new Bottom());
Top* t = dynamic_cast<Top*>(new Bottom());
```

Both casts fail in the repeated diamond due to two different paths leading to possible subobjects: [Bottom, Left, Top] and [Bottom, Right, Top]. So there is no unique path, the cast is ambiguous and the compiler rejects it. But the same cast in the shared diamond is possible, as there is only one possible path, namely [Top].

Example 2. Let us assume that we have a field **int** z in class Left in the repeated diamond which is initialized with the value 42. Now, we cast from Bottom via Right to Top:

```
Top* t = static_cast<Top*>
         (static_cast<Right*>(new Bottom()));
```

A dynamic down-cast to Left and accessing z returns the correct value 42:

```
Left* l = dynamic_cast<Left*>(t);
l->z; // returns the value 42
```

Since a real down-cast from `t` to a class `Left` is not possible here, the dynamic cast builds the new casted object "bottom-up" by casting the "full" `Bottom` subobject up to `Left`.

A static down-cast from `t` to `Left` should however not be possible, as no `Left` class is in the current subobject path. However, this program compiles and even accessing field `z` is allowed, although the result of the field access is unspecified:

```
Left* l = static_cast<Left*>(t);
l->z; // can return any value
```

What happens here is that the C++ implementation just reduces the `this`-pointer by the "delta" for `Left`, resulting in a `this`-pointer pointing to an arbitrary point in the object. Of course, this breaks type safety. Thus, in our semantics, we decided to throw a *ClassCast* exception to report that something went wrong, instead of carrying on with undefined behaviour as C++ does.

Example 3. In any of the two diamonds, a **dynamic_cast** allows so called "cross-casts", casts between classes where one class is not a (direct or indirect) super class of the other. For **static_cast**s, the compiler rejects "cross-casts":

```
Left* l = static_cast<Left*>(new Bottom());
Right* r = dynamic_cast<Right*>(l); //compiles&executes
Right* r = static_cast<Right*>(l); //compiler rejects
```

The **static_cast** is rejected as there is no path between `Left` and `Right`. The **dynamic_cast** can again work "bottom-up" and cast the "full" `Bottom` subobject up to `Left`. However, as the compiler allows "cross-casts" for **dynamic_cast**, it also allows casting between completely unrelated classes:

```
Right* r = dynamic_cast<Right*>(new Left()); //compiles
```

As a `Left` object has no `Right` subobject, this cast cannot be performed at run-time. Thus, **dynamic_cast** returns the special value `NULL`.

Example 4. In the last two examples we saw that a dynamic down-cast can be resolved "bottom-up", via up-casts on the "full" `Bottom` subobject. However, the **dynamic_cast** does not always work this way, as we can see in the repeated diamond:

```
Left* l = static_cast<Left*>(new Bottom());
Top* t = dynamic_cast<Top*>(l);
```

WTStaticCast:

$$\frac{P,E \vdash e :: Class\ D \qquad is\text{-}class\ P\ C \qquad P \vdash path\ D\ to\ C\ unique \lor}{P,E \vdash \mathtt{stat\_cast}\ C\ e :: Class\ C}$$

$P \vdash C \preceq^* D \land (\forall Cs.\ P \vdash path\ C\ to\ D\ via\ Cs \longrightarrow (C, Cs) \in Subobjs_R\ P)$

StaticUpCast:
$$\frac{P,E \vdash \langle e,s_0 \rangle \Rightarrow \langle ref\ (a, Cs),s_1 \rangle}{P,E \vdash \langle \mathtt{stat\_cast}\ C\ e,s_0 \rangle \Rightarrow \langle ref\ (a, Ds),s_1 \rangle}$$
$$P \vdash path\ last\ Cs\ to\ C\ via\ Cs' \qquad Ds = Cs\ @_p\ Cs'$$

StaticDownCast:
$$\frac{P,E \vdash \langle e,s_0 \rangle \Rightarrow \langle ref\ (a, Cs\ @\ [C]\ @\ Cs'),s_1 \rangle}{P,E \vdash \langle \mathtt{stat\_cast}\ C\ e,s_0 \rangle \Rightarrow \langle ref\ (a, Cs\ @\ [C]),s_1 \rangle}$$

StaticCastNull:
$$\frac{P,E \vdash \langle e,s_0 \rangle \Rightarrow \langle null,s_1 \rangle}{P,E \vdash \langle \mathtt{stat\_cast}\ C\ e,s_0 \rangle \Rightarrow \langle null,s_1 \rangle}$$

StaticCastThrow:

$$\frac{P,E \vdash \langle e,s_0 \rangle \Rightarrow \langle ref\ (a, Cs),s_1 \rangle \qquad \neg P \vdash last\ Cs \preceq^* C \qquad C \notin set\ Cs}{P,E \vdash \langle \mathtt{stat\_cast}\ C\ e,s_0 \rangle \Rightarrow \langle THROW\ ClassCast,s_1 \rangle}$$

Figure 2.9.: Type and semantic rules for static cast

If the **dynamic_cast** again looked "bottom-up" from the basic `Bottom` subobject, it would see two different `Top` subobjects, one via `Right` the other one via `Left`. Hence, the cast would be ambiguous. However, the **dynamic_cast** behaves just like a **static_cast** and casts to the `Top` subobject in the `Left` subobject. Actually, **dynamic_cast** always mimics **static_cast**, only in cases where the **static_cast** would be rejected, the "bottom-up" technique is used.

Remember that any object reference contains a path component identifying the current subobject which is referenced. A cast changes this path, thus selects a different subobject. Hence casting must adjust the path component of the reference. This mechanism corresponds to Stroustrup's adjustment of pointers by "delta" values. We consider this a prime example of the fact that our semantics does not rely on run-time data structures but on abstract concepts.

The semantics of the cast operator presented in [126] (there called simply *Cast*) meets the behaviour of C++'s **static_cast**; thus, we use the syntax `stat_cast` in this thesis. To recapitulate, we show its typing rule and big step semantic rules in Fig. 2.9. (the small step rules are completely analogous and can be found in the appendix). Typing static casts is non-trivial in CoreC++ because the type system needs to prevent ambiguities at run-time (although it cannot do so completely). When evaluating `stat_cast C e`, the object that e evaluates to may have multiple subobjects of class C. If it is an up-cast, i.e., if $P,E \vdash e :: Class\ D$ and D is a subclass of C, we have to check if there is a unique path from D to C. For down-casts we need to remember (cf. Example 2) that we have chosen to model a type safe variant of **static_cast** (which means we throw an exception where C++ produces undefined behaviour), for which C++ has fixed the rules as follows: down-casts may only involve repeated inheritance. To enforce this restriction we introduce the predicate

$$P \vdash path\ C\ to\ D\ via\ Cs\ \equiv (C, Cs) \in Subobjs\ P \wedge last\ Cs = D.$$

Combining the checks for up- and down-casts in one rule while requiring the class to be known we obtain WTStaticCast. Recall that $(C, Cs) \in Subobjs_R\ P$ means that Cs involves only repeated inheritance.

For the semantics, let us first look at the static up-cast rule Static-UpCast: After evaluating e to a reference with path Cs, that path is extended (upward) by a (unique, if the cast is well-typed, WTStatic-Cast) path Cs' from the end of Cs up to C, which we get by predicate *path-via*. Rule StaticDownCast models the static down-cast which forbids down-casts involving shared inheritance. This means that class C must occur in the path component of the reference, or the cast is "wrong". If neither of these two rules applies, the static cast throws a *ClassCast* exception (StaticCastThrow).

Let us now concentrate on the dynamic cast operator, written `dyn_cast`; this cast was not regarded in [126]. Its type and semantic rules can be found in Fig. 2.10. Dynamic casts are non-trivial operations at run-time but statically they are quite simple: rule WTDynCast only requires that the expression is well-typed, the class is known and not more than one path between the static class and the cast target class exists (there is either a unique path or none at all). This liberality is not just admissible (because dynamic casts detect type mismatches at run-time) but even necessary.

Semantically, if possible, `dyn_cast` tries to behave like the static cast. Rules StaticUpDynCast and StaticDownDynCast are the analogues of StaticUpCast and StaticDownCast, except that StaticUpDyn-Cast has the additional premise $P \vdash path\ last\ Cs\ to\ C\ unique$. This uniqueness property is not necessary for the type safety proof, but for the de-

WTDynCast:
$$\frac{P,E \vdash e :: Class\ D \qquad is\text{-}class\ P\ C \qquad P \vdash path\ D\ to\ C\ unique \vee (\forall\ Cs.\ \neg\ P \vdash path\ D\ to\ C\ via\ Cs\ )}{P,E \vdash \texttt{dyn\_cast}\ C\ e :: Class\ C}$$

StaticUpDynCast:
$$\frac{P,E \vdash \langle e,s_0 \rangle \Rightarrow \langle ref\ (a,\ Cs),s_1 \rangle \qquad P \vdash path\ last\ Cs\ to\ C\ unique \qquad P \vdash path\ last\ Cs\ to\ C\ via\ Cs' \qquad Ds = Cs\ @_p\ Cs'}{P,E \vdash \langle \texttt{dyn\_cast}\ C\ e,s_0 \rangle \Rightarrow \langle ref\ (a,\ Ds),s_1 \rangle}$$

StaticDownDynCast:
$$\frac{P,E \vdash \langle e,s_0 \rangle \Rightarrow \langle ref\ (a,\ Cs\ @\ [C]\ @\ Cs'),s_1 \rangle}{P,E \vdash \langle \texttt{dyn\_cast}\ C\ e,s_0 \rangle \Rightarrow \langle ref\ (a,\ Cs\ @\ [C]),s_1 \rangle}$$

DynCast:
$$\frac{P,E \vdash \langle e,s_0 \rangle \Rightarrow \langle ref\ (a,\ Cs),(h,\ l) \rangle \qquad h\ a = \lfloor (D,\ S) \rfloor \qquad P \vdash path\ D\ to\ C\ via\ Cs' \qquad P \vdash path\ D\ to\ C\ unique}{P,E \vdash \langle \texttt{dyn\_cast}\ C\ e,s_0 \rangle \Rightarrow \langle ref\ (a,\ Cs'),(h,\ l) \rangle}$$

DynCastNull:
$$\frac{P,E \vdash \langle e,s_0 \rangle \Rightarrow \langle null,s_1 \rangle}{P,E \vdash \langle \texttt{dyn\_cast}\ C\ e,s_0 \rangle \Rightarrow \langle null,s_1 \rangle}$$

DynCastFail:
$$\frac{P,E \vdash \langle e,s_0 \rangle \Rightarrow \langle ref\ (a,\ Cs),(h,\ l) \rangle \qquad h\ a = \lfloor (D,\ S) \rfloor \qquad \neg\ P \vdash path\ D\ to\ C\ unique \qquad \neg\ P \vdash path\ last\ Cs\ to\ C\ unique \qquad C \notin set\ Cs}{P,E \vdash \langle \texttt{dyn\_cast}\ C\ e,s_0 \rangle \Rightarrow \langle null,(h,\ l) \rangle}$$

Figure 2.10.: Type and semantic rules for dynamic cast

terminism of the semantics. It is also possible that a legal down-cast cannot be performed by rule StaticDownDynCast because C does not occur in the path. Assume B is a shared subclass of A. Then a term which is statically of class A and evaluates to $ref\ (b,\ [A])$ but points to an object of class B can be cast to $ref\ (b,\ [B])$, but not by Static-DownDynCast. Both cross-casts and such dynamic down-casts are performed by rule DynCast. This is the "bottom-up" technique we already mentioned in the examples: after evaluating e to a reference to address a, we look up the class D of the object at address a. If D has a unique C subobject, that is the one the reference must now point to.

As $\texttt{dyn\_cast}$ allows more casts than $\texttt{stat\_cast}$, the premises for rule DynCastFail for failing casts differ from StaticCastFail. Both have to assure that class C is not in the current path Cs (otherwise a down-cast would be possible). While for failing static casts, it is sufficient to assure that the static class *last Cs* is no subclass of *C*, for failing dynamic casts there may not be a unique path between the dynamic class *D* and class *C* (otherwise rule DynCast could be applied). The fourth premise, denying a unique path between *last Cs* and *C* is not needed for type safety, but for determinism of the semantics. If rule DynCastFail holds, i.e., `dyn_cast` fails, we return the null pointer, i.e., the value *null*. This is exactly how C++ handles failing **dynamic_cast**s.

2.4.2. Dynamic (and Static) Dispatch

Dynamic dispatch in the presence of multiple inheritance is highly non-trivial. The typing rule WTCall, however, is no source of complications (cf. Fig. 2.11). The class *C* of *e* is used to collect all declarations of *M* and select the least one. The set of all definitions of method *M* from class *C* upwards is defined as

MethodDefs P C M ≡ {(*Cs, mthd*) | (*C, Cs*) ∈ *Subobjs P* ∧
(∃ *Bs fs ms*. *class P* (*last Cs*) = ⌊(*Bs, fs, ms*)⌋ ∧ *map-of ms M* = ⌊*mthd*⌋)}

This set pairs the method (of type *method*, see Fig. 2.4) with the path *Cs* leading to the defining class. Among all definitions the least one (w.r.t. the ordering on paths) is selected:

P ⊢ *C has least M* = *mthd via Cs* ≡ (*Cs, mthd*) ∈ *MethodDefs P C M* ∧
(∀ (*Cs', mthd'*)∈*MethodDefs P C M*. *P*,*C* ⊢ *Cs* ⊑ *Cs'*)

Unfortunately, the absence of static ambiguity of method lookup is not sufficient to avoid ambiguities at run-time. Even for a well-typed call, *e* may evaluate to a class below *C* from which there is no least declaration of *M*. As already observed in [126], the semantic rule for call presented there is flawed, as it does not take care of these run-time ambiguities. The following example shows how C++ resolves such ambiguities by exploiting static types.

Example 1. In the repeated diamond of Fig. 2.1, let us assume that we have declared a method `f()` in class `Top` and execute the following code:

```
Left* b = new Bottom(); b->f();
```

Note that the assignment performs an implicit up-cast to type `Left`, and that the method call is statically correct because a single definition of `f()` is visible. However, at run-time the dynamic class of the subobject (`Bottom`,[`Bottom`,`Left`]) associated with `b` is used to resolve the dynamic dispatch. The dynamic class of `b` is `Bottom`, and `b` has *two* `Top` subobjects containing `f` (and `x`). As neither definition of `f()` dominates the other, the call to `b->f()` appears to be ambiguous.

Note that the code for `f` exists only once, but this code will be called with an ambiguous `this`-pointer at run-time: is it the one pointing to the (`Bottom`,[`Bottom.Left.Top`]) subobject, or the one pointing to the (`Bottom`,[`Bottom.Right.Top`]) subobject? Each of these subobject has its own field `x`, and these `x`'s may have different values at run-time when referenced by `f()`, leading to ambiguous program behaviour.

C++ uses the static type of `b` to resolve the ambiguity and generate a unique v-table entry for `f()`. As `b`'s static type is `Left`, the "delta" part of the v-table entry will cause the dynamic object of type `Bottom` (and thus the `this`-pointer) to be cast to (`Bottom`,[`Bottom.Left.Top`]), and *not* to (`Bottom`,[`Bottom.Right.Top`]).

While this may seem to be a "natural" way to resolve the ambiguity, it makes the result of dynamic dispatch—which, intuitively, is based *solely* on an object's *dynamic* type—additionally dependent on the object's static type. During the evolution of our semantics, for a long time we considered this a flaw in the design of C++, and our first semantics [133] (for a language then called C+) did not resolve the ambiguity using the static type, but threw a *MemberAmbiguousException* exception instead:

$$
\frac{
\begin{array}{c}
P \vdash \langle e, s_0 \rangle \Rightarrow \langle ref\ (a, Cs), s_1 \rangle \\
P \vdash \langle ps, s_1 \rangle\ [\Rightarrow]\ \langle map\ Val\ vs, (h_2, l_2) \rangle \qquad h_2\ a = Some(C, S) \\
\forall\ Ts\ T\ pns\ body\ Cs'.\ \neg\ P \vdash C\ \textit{has least}\ M = (Ts, T, pns, body)\ \textit{via}\ Cs'
\end{array}
}{
P \vdash \langle e \cdot M(ps), s_0 \rangle \Rightarrow \langle THROW\ MemberAmbiguous, (h_2, l_2) \rangle
}
$$

This viewpoint was inspired by Rossie and Friedman, who also treated this situation as ambiguous.

As now we want to stick exactly to C++ – even though this makes the semantics more complex –, we reformulate the semantic rule for call. The resulting rule Call (cf. Fig. 2.11) is lengthy:

- evaluate e to a reference (a, Cs) and the parameter list ps to a list of values vs;

- look up the dynamic class C of the object in the heap at a;

WTCall:
$$\frac{\begin{array}{c} P,E \vdash e :: Class\ C' \\ P \vdash path\ C'\ to\ C\ unique \qquad P \vdash C\ has\ least\ M = (Ts,\ T,\ m)\ via\ Cs \\ P,E \vdash es\ [::]\ Ts' \qquad P \vdash Ts'\ [\leq]\ Ts \end{array}}{P,E \vdash e.M(es) :: T}$$

Call:
$$\frac{\begin{array}{c} P,E \vdash \langle e,s_0 \rangle \Rightarrow \langle ref\ (a,\ Cs),s_1 \rangle \qquad P,E \vdash \langle ps,s_1 \rangle\ [\Rightarrow]\ \langle map\ \texttt{Val}\ vs,(h_2,\ l_2) \rangle \\ h_2\ a = \lfloor (C,\ S) \rfloor \qquad P \vdash last\ Cs\ has\ least\ M = (Ts',\ T',\ pns',\ body')\ via\ Ds \\ P \vdash (C,Cs\ @_p\ Ds)\ selects\ M = (Ts,\ T,\ pns,\ body)\ via\ Cs' \qquad |vs| = |pns| \\ P \vdash Ts\ Casts\ vs\ to\ vs' \qquad l_2' = [this \mapsto Ref\ (a,\ Cs'),\ pns \mapsto vs'] \\ new\text{-}body = (case\ T'\ of\ Class\ D \Rightarrow \texttt{stat\_cast}\ D\ body\ |\ \text{-} \Rightarrow body) \\ P,E(this \mapsto Class\ (last\ Cs'),\ pns \mapsto Ts) \vdash \langle new\text{-}body,(h_2,\ l_2') \rangle \Rightarrow \langle e',(h_3,\ l_3) \rangle \end{array}}{P,E \vdash \langle e.M(ps),s_0 \rangle \Rightarrow \langle e',(h_3,\ l_2) \rangle}$$

Figure 2.11.: Type and semantic rules for (dynamic) method call

- look up the method definition used at type checking time (*last Cs* is the static class of *e*) and note its return type T' and the path *Ds* from *last Cs* to this definition;

- select the dynamically appropriate method (see below) and note its parameter names *pns*, parameter types *Ts*, body *body*, and path Cs' from *C* to this definition;

- check that there are as many actual as formal parameters;

- cast the parameter values *vs* up to their static types *Ts* by using $P \vdash Ts$ *Casts vs to vs'*, the point-wise extension of casts to lists (see the next section for details), yielding vs';

- evaluate the body (with an up-cast to T', if T' is a class) in an updated type environment where *this* has type *Class* (*last Cs'*) (the class where the dynamically selected method lives) and the formal parameter names have their declared types, and where the local variables are *this* and the parameters, suitably initialized.

The need to cast the parameters and the return value of the method body will be discussed in the next section.

The final store is the one obtained from the evaluation of the parameters; the one obtained from the evaluation of *body* is discarded – remember that CoreC++ does not have global variables.

```
class Top { void f(); };
class Right2 : Top { ... };
class Right : virtual Right2 { void f(); };
class Left : Top { void f(); };
class Bottom : Left, Right { ... };

((Right2*)(new Bottom()))->f();
```

Figure 2.12.: Example illustrating static resolution of dynamically ambiguous method calls

Method selection is performed by the judgment $P \vdash (C, Cs)$ *selects* $M = mthd$ *via* Cs' , where (C,Cs) is the subobject where the method lives that was used at type checking time. Hence there is at least one definition of M visible from C. There are two possible cases. If we are lucky, we can select a unique method definition based solely on C:

$$\frac{P \vdash C \text{ has least } M = mthd \text{ via } Cs'}{P \vdash (C, Cs) \text{ selects } M = mthd \text{ via } Cs'}$$

Otherwise we need static information to disambiguate the selection as Example 1 already demonstrated. But before we state the appropriate rule, let us again look at an example:

Example 2. To appreciate the full intricacies of this mechanism, let us consider the example in Fig. 2.12, where a subobject (Bottom,[Right2]) calls method f: the path components in *MethodDefs* P *Bottom* f are [Bottom,Left], [Bottom,Left,Top], [Bottom, Right] and [Right2,Top]. None of these paths is smaller than all of the others, so we cannot resolve the method call purely dynamically. So another approach is taken: we select the minimal paths in *MethodDefs P Bottom f*, which leaves us with [Bottom,Left] and [Bottom,Right]. Now we have to find out which of these two paths will select the method to call. This is done by considering the statically selected method call (i.e., the least one seen from the static class Right2), yielding path [Right2,Top], which is guaranteed to be unique by the type system. Now we append this "static" path to the path component of the subobject, which results in the path where the dynamic class sees the statically selected method definition, namely [Right2] $@_p$ [Right2,Top] = [Right2,Top]. Finally we select a path from the above set of minimal paths that is smaller than the composed path, which results in [Bottom,Right]. Well-formedness of the program guarantees the uniqueness of this path (see Sec. 2.4.4 (iii)).

Abstractly, $P \vdash (C, Cs)$ *selects* $M = mth$ *via* Cs' selects that Cs' from the set of minimal paths from C to definitions of M that lies on Cs, i.e., that lies below the statically selected method definition Cs. The minimal elements are collected by *MinimalMethodDefs*,

MinimalMethodDefs P C M $\equiv \{(Cs, mth) \in MethodDefs\ P\ C\ M\ |$
$(\forall (Cs', mth') \in MethodDefs\ P\ C\ M.\ P,C \vdash Cs' \sqsubseteq Cs \longrightarrow Cs' = Cs)\}$

the ones that override the definition at Cs, i.e., are below Cs, are selected by *OverriderMethodDefs*,

OverriderMethodDefs P (C, Ds) M $\equiv$
$\{(Cs, mth) \in MinimalMethodDefs\ P\ C\ M\ |$
$\exists Cs'\ mth'.\ P \vdash last\ Ds$ *has least* $M = mth'$ *via* $Cs' \wedge P,C \vdash Cs \sqsubseteq Ds\ @_p\ Cs'\}$

and selection of a least overrider is performed as follows:

$P \vdash (C, Ds)$ *has overrider* $M = mth$ *via* $Cs \equiv$
OverriderMethodDefs P (C, Ds) M $= \{(Cs, mth)\}$

Note that *OverriderMethodDefs* returns a singleton set if the program is well-formed (see Sec. 2.4.4 (iii)). Hence the second defining rule for *selects* is

$$\frac{\forall mth\ Cs'.\ \neg\ P \vdash C\ \textit{has least}\ M = mth\ \textit{via}\ Cs' \quad P \vdash (C, Cs)\ \textit{has overrider}\ M = mth\ \textit{via}\ Cs'}{P \vdash (C, Cs)\ \textit{selects}\ M = mth\ \textit{via}\ Cs'}$$

WTStaticCall:

$$\frac{\begin{array}{c} P,E \vdash e :: Class\ C' \\ P \vdash path\ C'\ to\ C\ unique \qquad P \vdash C\ has\ least\ M = (Ts,\ T,\ m)\ via\ Cs \\ P,E \vdash es\ [::]\ Ts' \qquad P \vdash Ts'\ [\leq]\ Ts \end{array}}{P,E \vdash e.C::M(es) :: T}$$

StaticCall:

$$\frac{\begin{array}{c} P,E \vdash \langle e,s_0 \rangle \Rightarrow \langle ref\ (a,\ Cs),s_1 \rangle \qquad P,E \vdash \langle ps,s_1 \rangle\ [\Rightarrow]\ \langle map\ \mathtt{Val}\ vs,(h_2,\ l_2) \rangle \\ P \vdash path\ last\ Cs\ to\ C\ unique \qquad P \vdash path\ last\ Cs\ to\ C\ via\ Cs'' \\ P \vdash C\ has\ least\ M = (Ts,\ T,\ pns,\ body)\ via\ Cs' \\ Ds = (Cs\ @_p\ Cs'')\ @_p\ Cs' \qquad |vs| = |pns| \\ P \vdash Ts\ Casts\ vs\ to\ vs' \qquad l_2' = [this \mapsto Ref\ (a,\ Ds),\ pns \mapsto vs'] \\ P,E(this \mapsto Class\ (last\ Ds),\ pns \mapsto Ts) \vdash \langle body,(h_2,\ l_2') \rangle \Rightarrow \langle e',(h_3,\ l_3) \rangle \end{array}}{P,E \vdash \langle e.C::M(ps),s_0 \rangle \Rightarrow \langle e',(h_3,\ l_2) \rangle}$$

Figure 2.13.: Type and semantic rules for qualified call

We also allow method calls to be qualified, a feature that was not present in [126]. A qualified method call $e.C::M(es)$ states that the method found in C should be called, a technique often used to disambiguate between method calls. In this thesis, we also use the term "static call", as explicitly given static information is used to disambiguate; however, it has nothing to do with methods qualified with the **static** modifier in C++.

The typing as well as the semantics rules, which can be found in Fig. 2.13, differ considerably from those of the standard call. The typing rule WTStaticCall assures that the static class of the expression C' has a unique path leading to class C, which qualifies the call. This is also the class that is used to perform the static method lookup (instead of the static class of the expression, as would be the case for "normal" method call).

For the semantic rule StaticCall we again evaluate e to a reference (a, Cs) and the parameter list ps to a list of values vs. The qualifying class C is used for the method lookup, thus the result is the same as in the typing rule. Now, we need to adjust the path to the called subobject. This path is composed of three components, combined with $@_p$:

- Cs, the current subobject path;
- Cs'', the unique path between $last\ Cs$ and C;
- Cs', the path from the method lookup.

CallObjThrow:
$$\frac{P,E \vdash \langle e,s_0 \rangle \Rightarrow \langle \texttt{throw } e',s_1 \rangle}{P,E \vdash \langle \textit{Call e Copt M es},s_0 \rangle \Rightarrow \langle \texttt{throw } e',s_1 \rangle}$$

CallParamsThrow:
$$\frac{P,E \vdash \langle e,s_0 \rangle \Rightarrow \langle \texttt{Val } v,s_1 \rangle \qquad P,E \vdash \langle es,s_1 \rangle \; [\Rightarrow] \; \langle \textit{map } \texttt{Val } vs \; @ \; \texttt{throw } ex \cdot es',s_2 \rangle}{P,E \vdash \langle \textit{Call e Copt M es},s_0 \rangle \Rightarrow \langle \texttt{throw } ex,s_2 \rangle}$$

CallNull:
$$\frac{P,E \vdash \langle e,s_0 \rangle \Rightarrow \langle \textit{null},s_1 \rangle \qquad P,E \vdash \langle es,s_1 \rangle \; [\Rightarrow] \; \langle \textit{map } \texttt{Val } vs,s_2 \rangle}{P,E \vdash \langle \textit{Call e Copt M es},s_0 \rangle \Rightarrow \langle \textit{THROW NullPointer},s_2 \rangle}$$

Figure 2.14.: Exceptional semantic rules for calls

The premise that requires the uniqueness of the path between *last Cs* and *C* is again not necessary for the type safety proof (as it is also guaranteed by the typing rule), but for the determinism of the semantics. The remaining premises for StaticCall are completely equivalent to the ones in Call. The whole problem of dynamic ambiguities does not occur with qualified calls, as the uniqueness of the method lookup from the explicitly qualified class is guaranteed from the typing rule, i.e., the method lookup in type and semantic rule dispatch to the same target.

The exception throwing rules are the same for both qualified and unqualified method calls. To this end, we introduce the syntax *Call e Copt M es*, where *Copt::cname option* is *None* for the dynamic call and *Some C* for the call qualified with *C*. Fig. 2.14 shows that a *NullPointer* exception is thrown if the expression evaluates to *null*, and the exception propagation rules.

2.4.3. Covariance and Contravariance

C++ allows method overriding with *covariant* (i.e., more specific) return types. Unrestricted covariance can however lead to ambiguities.

Example 1. In the context of the repeated diamond of Fig. 2.1, consider:

```
class A { Top* f(); };
class B : A { Bottom* f(); }; //not allowed

A* a = new B();
Top* t = a->f();
```

Statically, everything seems fine: because the type of a is A, the type of a->f() is Top. However, if we allowed the redefinition of f(), at run-time a->f() evaluates to a Bottom object. C++ implicitly casts to the return type of the statically selected method (which would be Top); but this cast is ambiguous, as a Bottom object has two different Top subobjects in the repeated diamond. Hence this redefinition is statically incorrect. C++ requires *unique covariance*: if the return type of the statically selected method is C and the return type of the dynamically selected one is D, then there must exist a unique path from D back to C.

However, in the presence of overridden methods with covariant return types, special care needs to be exercised (a topic that I was not aware of in [126]). To illustrate this, we alter Example 1 slightly:

Example 2. Again, we make use of the repeated diamond of Fig. 2.1:

```
class A { Top* f() {return new Top();} };
class B : A { Left* f() {return new Bottom();} };

A* a = new B();
(a->f())->x = 42;
```

In a previous version of the semantics [133], we did not perform any implicit casts. Hence, a->f() evaluated at runtime to a Bottom object. Remember that field access and assignment contain path annotations from the static type of the referenced object to the static class that contains the field and is statically seen. In our case, with (a->f())->x = 42;, this annotation would be Top, since the static type of a->f() is Top and field x can be found in class Top. Yet, the last class of the path component of the reference of a->f() is Bottom, since it evaluated to an (uncasted) Bottom object. This means that the semantic rules for field access and assignment have to provide a path to fill this "gap" between the last class of the path component of the evaluated object and the static class in such cases; this is what we did in [133]. However, in the above situation, there is no unique path between class Bottom and Top. Hence, the semantic rule could not fill the "gap" without introducing nondeterminism; analogously to ambiguous dynamic dispatch, we threw a *MemberAmbiguousException* in such cases.

But C++ does not require such an exception. To get rid of it and close the "gap" between the last class of a reference and the class computed by the type system we extend method call rules with explicit casts to the static type; this is also what C++ does. In the semantic rule for call, cf. Fig. 2.11, the 9th premise takes care of this[7]:

$$new\text{-}body = (\textbf{case } T' \textbf{ of } Class\ D \Rightarrow \texttt{stat\_cast}\ D\ body \mid \text{-} \Rightarrow body)$$

We statically cast the return value of the method body *body* to the return type determined from the method lookup from the static class (as this is the expected return type for the type system) – this cast is of course only necessary if no primitive value is returned –, obtaining the new method body *new-body*. Because of this explicit cast, the value dynamically returned from a method call has exactly the type the type system expects, thus no "gaps" can occur. C++ itself uses so called "thunks" [41, §2.1.1] to adjust the `this`-pointer in such cases, which can only occur in the presence of multiple inheritance.

CoreC++ allows, just as C++, the assignment of values with covariant types to variables and fields. In these cases, the semantic rules must take care of the implicit casts necessary. These are done via *casts to*, whose rules are as follows:

$$\frac{\forall C.\ T \neq Class\ C}{P \vdash T\ \textit{casts}\ v\ \textit{to}\ v} \qquad P \vdash Class\ C\ \textit{casts Null to Null}$$

$$\frac{P \vdash \textit{path last Cs to C via Cs'} \qquad Ds = Cs\ @_p\ Cs'}{P \vdash Class\ C\ \textit{casts Ref}\ (a, Cs)\ \textit{to Ref}\ (a, Ds)}$$

Let us now look what this means for local assignment. The typing rule WTLAss, see Fig. 2.15, is completely straightforward as the expression on the right hand side has to be a subtype of the variable type on the left hand side, which we get by consulting the typing environment. The semantics rule LAss then requires an up-cast of the expression to the static type T of the variable. Hence we need the environment E to look up T (by $E\ V = \lfloor T \rfloor$). The up-cast is inserted implicitly by the semantics.

Assignment of values with covariant types is also possible for fields. For the sake of completeness, we will now not only discuss field assignment but also field access.

---

[7]Qualified calls are not affected by this, as for them, the static lookup of the type system and the lookup of the semantic rule agree, as both use the qualified class as source.

WTLAss:
$$\frac{E\ V = \lfloor T \rfloor \qquad P,E \vdash e :: T' \qquad P \vdash T' \leq T}{P,E \vdash V := e :: T}$$

LAss:
$$\frac{E\ V = \lfloor T \rfloor \qquad P,E \vdash \langle e,s_0 \rangle \Rightarrow \langle \texttt{Val } v,(h,\ l) \rangle \qquad P \vdash T \text{ casts } v \text{ to } v' \qquad l' = l(V \mapsto v')}{P,E \vdash \langle V := e,s_0 \rangle \Rightarrow \langle \texttt{Val } v',(h,\ l') \rangle}$$

LAssThrow:
$$\frac{P,E \vdash \langle e,s_0 \rangle \Rightarrow \langle \texttt{throw } e',s_1 \rangle}{P,E \vdash \langle V := e,s_0 \rangle \Rightarrow \langle \texttt{throw } e',s_1 \rangle}$$

Figure 2.15.: Type and semantic rules for local assignment

WTFAcc:
$$\frac{P,E \vdash e :: \textit{Class } C \qquad P \vdash C \textit{ has least } F : T \textit{ via } Cs}{P,E \vdash e.F\{Cs\} :: T}$$

WTFAss:
$$\frac{P,E \vdash e_1 :: \textit{Class } C}{P \vdash C \textit{ has least } F : T \textit{ via } Cs \qquad P,E \vdash e_2 :: T' \qquad P \vdash T' \leq T}{P,E \vdash e_1.F\{Cs\} := e_2 :: T}$$

FAcc:
$$\frac{P,E \vdash \langle e,s_0 \rangle \Rightarrow \langle \textit{ref } (a,\ Cs'),(h,\ l) \rangle}{h\ a = \lfloor (D,\ S) \rfloor \quad Ds = Cs' @_p\ Cs \quad (Ds,\ fs) \in S \quad fs\ F = \lfloor v \rfloor}{P,E \vdash \langle e.F\{Cs\},s_0 \rangle \Rightarrow \langle \texttt{Val } v,(h,\ l) \rangle}$$

FAccNull:
$$\frac{P,E \vdash \langle e,s_0 \rangle \Rightarrow \langle \textit{null},s_1 \rangle}{P,E \vdash \langle e.F\{Cs\},s_0 \rangle \Rightarrow \langle \textit{THROW NullPointer},s_1 \rangle}$$

FAccThrow:
$$\frac{P,E \vdash \langle e,s_0 \rangle \Rightarrow \langle \texttt{throw } e',s_1 \rangle}{P,E \vdash \langle e.F\{Cs\},s_0 \rangle \Rightarrow \langle \texttt{throw } e',s_1 \rangle}$$

FAss:
$$\frac{\begin{array}{c} P,E \vdash \langle e_1,s_0 \rangle \Rightarrow \langle \textit{ref } (a,\ Cs'),s_1 \rangle \\ P,E \vdash \langle e_2,s_1 \rangle \Rightarrow \langle \texttt{Val } v,(h_2,\ l_2) \rangle \qquad h_2\ a = \lfloor (D,\ S) \rfloor \\ P \vdash \textit{last } Cs' \textit{ has least } F : T \textit{ via } Cs \qquad P \vdash T \textit{ casts } v \textit{ to } v' \\ Ds = Cs' @_p\ Cs \qquad (Ds,\ fs) \in S \qquad fs' = fs(F \mapsto v') \\ S' = S - \{(Ds,\ fs)\} \cup \{(Ds,\ fs')\} \qquad h_2' = h_2(a \mapsto (D,\ S')) \end{array}}{P,E \vdash \langle e_1.F\{Cs\} := e_2,s_0 \rangle \Rightarrow \langle \texttt{Val } v',(h_2',\ l_2) \rangle}$$

FAssNull:
$$\frac{P,E \vdash \langle e_1,s_0 \rangle \Rightarrow \langle ,s_1 \rangle \qquad P,E \vdash \langle e_2,s_1 \rangle \Rightarrow \langle \texttt{Val } v,s_2 \rangle}{P,E \vdash \langle e_1.F\{Cs\} := e_2,s_0 \rangle \Rightarrow \langle \textit{THROW NullPointer},s_2 \rangle}$$

FAssThrow1:
$$\frac{P,E \vdash \langle e_1,s_0 \rangle \Rightarrow \langle \texttt{throw } e',s_1 \rangle}{P,E \vdash \langle e_1.F\{Cs\} := e_2,s_0 \rangle \Rightarrow \langle \texttt{throw } e',s_1 \rangle}$$

FAssThrow2:
$$\frac{P,E \vdash \langle e_1,s_0 \rangle \Rightarrow \langle \texttt{Val } v,s_1 \rangle \qquad P,E \vdash \langle e_2,s_1 \rangle \Rightarrow \langle \texttt{throw } e',s_2 \rangle}{P,E \vdash \langle e_1.F\{Cs\} := e_2,s_0 \rangle \Rightarrow \langle \texttt{throw } e',s_2 \rangle}$$

Figure 2.16.: Type and semantic rules for field access and assignment

The typing rule for field access WTFAcc (see Fig. 2.16) is straight-forward. It can either be seen as a rule that takes an expression where field access is already annotated (by $\{Cs\}$), and the rule merely checks that the annotation is correct. Or it can be seen as a rule for computing the annotation. The latter interpretation relies on the fact that predicate $P \vdash C$ *has least* $F : T$ *via* Cs can compute T and Cs from P, C and F. So it remains to explain $P \vdash C$ *has least* $F : T$ *via* Cs: it checks if Cs is the least (w.r.t. $\sqsubseteq$) path leading from C to a class declaring an F. First we define the set *FieldDecls P C F* of all (Cs, T) such that Cs is a valid path leading to a class with an F of type T:

FieldDecls P C F $\equiv \{(Cs, T) \mid (C, Cs) \in Subobjs\ P\ \wedge$
$(\exists Bs\ fs\ ms.\ class\ P\ (last\ Cs) = \lfloor(Bs, fs, ms)\rfloor \wedge map\text{-}of\ fs\ F = \lfloor T \rfloor)\}$

Then we select a least element from that set:

$P \vdash C$ *has least* $F : T$ *via* $Cs \equiv$
$(Cs, T) \in FieldDecls\ P\ C\ F \wedge (\forall\,(Cs', T') \in FieldDecls\ P\ C\ F.\ P,C \vdash Cs \sqsubseteq Cs')$

If there is no such least path, field access is ambiguous and hence not well-typed. We give an example. Once again we concentrate on the re-peated diamond in Fig. 2.1 and assume that a field x is defined in class `Bottom` and class `Top`. When type checking $e.x$, where e is of class `Bottom`, the path components in *FieldDecls P Bottom x* are [`Bottom`], [`Bottom,Left,Top`] and [`Bottom,Right,Top`]. The least element of the path components in this set is [`Bottom`], so the x in class `Bottom` will be accessed. Note that if no x in `Bottom` is declared, then there is no el-ement with a least path in *FieldDecls* and the field access is ambiguous and hence illegal.

Field assignment works equally as shown in WTFAss in Fig. 2.16.

For the semantics, let us first look at field access in rule FAcc in Fig. 2.16. There are two paths involved. Cs is (if the expression is well-typed, see WTFAcc), the path from the class of e to the class where F is declared. Cs' is the path component of the reference that e evaluates to. As we have discussed in Sec. 2.3.4, *last Cs'* is equal to the static class of e. To obtain the complete path leading to the subobject in which F lives, we just have to concatenate the two paths via $@_p$. The resulting path Ds is the path to the subobject we are looking for. If e does not evaluate to a reference, but to a null pointer, we throw a *NullPointer* exception, see FAccNull.

45

Field assignment (rule FAss, see Fig. 2.16) is similar, except that we now have to update the heap at a with a new set of subobjects. The up-cast is inserted implicitly, analogously to LAss. Note that the functional nature of this set is preserved.

C++ does not allow method overriding with *contravariant* (i.e., less specific) parameter types; neither does Java, while Jinja [61] allows them. However, as parameter passing in method calls can be regarded equivalent to assignment w.r.t. typing, we also need explicit casts, as we allow values with covariant types in the parameters (cf. WTCall in Fig. 2.11 and WTStaticCall in Fig. 2.13). As the whole parameter list needs to be implicitly casted, we lift *casts to* to lists, obtaining *Casts to*:

$$P \vdash [] \; Casts \; [] \; to \; [] \qquad \frac{P \vdash T \; casts \; v \; to \; v' \qquad P \vdash Ts \; Casts \; vs \; to \; vs'}{P \vdash T \cdot Ts \; Casts \; v \cdot vs \; to \; v' \cdot vs'}$$

In the local variables of the state in which the method body is executed the formal parameters are now initialized with the values after this cast.

2.4.4. Well-formed Programs

A well-formed CoreC++ program (*wf-C-prog P*) must obey all the usual requirements (every method body is well-typed and of the declared result type, the class hierarchy is acyclic, etc. — for details see [61]). Additionally, there are CoreC++-specific conditions concerning method overriding:

(i) covariance in the result type combined with the uniqueness of paths from the new result class to *all* result classes in previous definitions of the same method (see Example 1 in Sec. 2.4.3). This requirement is easily formalized by means of the *path unique* predicate;

(ii) invariance in the argument types;

(iii) for every method definition a class C sees via path Cs, the corresponding subobject (C, Cs) must have a least overrider as explained in Sec. 2.4.2 (otherwise the corresponding C++ program would not be able to construct a unique v-table entry for this method call and the program would be rejected at compile time).

2.5 Type Safety Proof

Type safety, one of the hallmarks of a good language design, means that the semantics is sound w.r.t. the type system: *well-typed expressions cannot go wrong*. Going wrong does not mean throwing an exception but arriving at a genuinely unanticipated situation. The by now standard formalization of this property [140] requires proving two properties: *progress* (well-typed expressions can be reduced w.r.t. the small step semantics if they are not final yet — the small step semantics does not get stuck) and *preservation* or *subject reduction*: reducing a well-typed expression results in another well-typed expression whose type is $\leq$ the original type.

In the remainder, we concentrate on the specific technicalities of the CoreC++ type safety proof. We do not even sketch the actual proof, which is routine enough, but all the necessary invariants and notions without which the proof is very difficult to reconstruct. For a detailed exposition of the Jinja type safety proof, our starting point, see [61]. For a tutorial introduction to type safety see, for example, [87].

2.5.1. Run-time Type System

The main complication in many type safety proofs is the fact that well-typedness w.r.t. the static type system is *not* preserved by the small step semantics. The fault does not lie with the semantics, but the type system: for pragmatic reasons it requires properties that are not preserved by reduction and are irrelevant for type safety. Thus, a second type system is needed which is more liberal but closed under reduction. This is known as the *run-time type system* [42] and the judgment is $P,E,h \vdash e : T$. Please note that there is no type checking at run-time: this type system is merely the formalization of an invariant which is not checked but whose preservation we prove. Many of the rules of the run-time type system are the same as in the static type system. The ones which differ are shown in Fig. 2.17.

Rule WTrtVal takes care of the fact that small step reduction may introduce reference values into an expression (although the static type system forbids them, see Sec. 2.3.3). The premise $P \vdash typeof_h\ v = \lfloor T \rfloor$ expresses that the value is of the right type; if $v = Ref\ (a, Cs)$, its type is $Class\ (last\ Cs)$ provided $h\ a = \lfloor (C, \_) \rfloor$ and $(C, Cs) \in Subobjs\ P$.

The main reason why static typing is not preserved by reduction is that the type of subexpressions may decrease from a class type to a

WTrtStaticCast:

$$\frac{P,E,h \vdash e : T \qquad \textit{is-refT } T \qquad \textit{is-class } P\,C}{P,E,h \vdash \texttt{stat\_cast } C\,e : \textit{Class } C}$$

WTrtDynCast:

$$\frac{P,E,h \vdash e : T \qquad \textit{is-refT } T \qquad \textit{is-class } P\,C}{P,E,h \vdash \texttt{dyn\_cast } C\,e : \textit{Class } C}$$

WTrtVal:

$$\frac{P \vdash \textit{typeof}_h\, v = \lfloor T \rfloor}{P,E,h \vdash \texttt{Val } v : T}$$

WTrtFAccNT:

$$\frac{P,E,h \vdash e : NT}{P,E,h \vdash e.F\{Cs\} : T}$$

WTrtFAssNT:

$$\frac{P,E,h \vdash e_1 : NT \qquad P,E,h \vdash e_2 : T' \qquad P \vdash T' \leq T}{P,E,h \vdash e_1.F\{Cs\} := e_2 : T}$$

WTrtCallNT:

$$\frac{P,E,h \vdash e : NT \qquad P,E,h \vdash es\ [:]\ Ts}{P,E,h \vdash \textit{Call } e\ Copt\ M\ es : T}$$

Figure 2.17.: Run-time type system

null type with reduction. Because of this, both cast rules only require the expression to cast to have a reference type (*is-refT T*), which means either a class or the null type. None of the checks that are needed for the static cast are important for the run-time type system.

Rule WTrtFAccNT takes care of $e.F\{Cs\}$ where the type of e has reduced to *NT*. Since this is going to throw an exception, and exceptions can have any type, this expression can have any type, too. Rules WTrtFAssNT and WTrtCallNT work similarly for field assignment and method call.

We have proved that $P,E \vdash e :: T$ implies $P,E,h \vdash e : T$. Heap h is unconstrained as the premise implies that e does not contain any references.

2.5.2. Conformance and Definite Assignment

Progress and preservation require that all semantic objects *conform* to the type constraints imposed by the syntax. We say that a value v conforms to a type T (written $P,h \vdash v :\leq T$) if the type of v equals type T or, if T is a class type, v has type *NT*. A heap conforms to a program if for every object (C, S) on the heap

- if $(Cs, fs) \in S$ then $(C, Cs) \in Subobjs\ P$[8] and if F is a field of type T declared in class *last Cs* then $fs\ F = \lfloor v \rfloor$ for some v, whose type (in the sense of rule WTrtVal) conforms to type T.

- if $(C, Cs) \in Subobjs\ P$ then $(Cs, fs) \in S$ for exactly one fs.

In this case we write $P \vdash h\ \sqrt{}$. A store l conforms to a type environment E iff $l\ V = \lfloor v \rfloor$ implies $E\ V = \lfloor T \rfloor$ such that v conforms to T. In symbols: $P,h \vdash l\ (:\leq)_w\ E$. We also need conformance concerning the type environment: $P \vdash E\ \sqrt{}$ states that for every variable that maps to a type in environment E, the type is a valid type in program P.

$$P \vdash E\ \sqrt{} \equiv \forall\ V\ T.\ E\ V = \lfloor T \rfloor \longrightarrow \textit{is-type}\ P\ T$$

If $P \vdash h\ \sqrt{}$, $P,h \vdash l\ (:\leq)_w\ E$ and $P \vdash E\ \sqrt{}$ then we write $P,E \vdash (h,l)\ \sqrt{}$ and say that state (h,l) conforms to the program and the environment.

For the proof we need another conformance property, which we call *type-conf*. It simply describes that given a certain type, an expression has that type in the run-time type system. However, if this given type is a class type, the run-time type system may also return the null type for the expression.

$$P,E,h \vdash e :_{NT} Class\ C\ =\ P,E,h \vdash e : Class\ C \lor P,E,h \vdash e : NT$$
$$P,E,h \vdash e :_{NT} Void\ \ \ =\ P,E,h \vdash e : Void$$

The rules for *Boolean*, *Integer* and *NT* are analogous to the *Void* rule.

From Jinja we have inherited the notion of *definite assignment*, a static analysis that checks if in an expression every variable is initialized before it is read. This constraint is essential for proving type safety. Definite assignment is encoded as a predicate $\mathcal{D}$ such that $\mathcal{D}\ e\ A$ (where A is a set of variables) asserts the following property: if initially all variables in A are initialized, then execution of e does not access an uninitialized variable. For technical reasons A is in fact of type *vname set option*. That is, if we want to execute e in the context of a store l we need to ensure $\mathcal{D}\ e\ \lfloor dom\ l \rfloor$. Since $\mathcal{D}$ is completely orthogonal to multiple inheritance we have omitted all details and refer to [61] instead.

In C++, accessing the value of a not previously assigned variable is unspecified; most compilers just return the contents of the respective location.

---

[8]Cf. the heap invariants presented in Sec. 2.3.4, **Evaluation**.

2.5.3. Progress

Progress means that any (run-time) well-typed expression which is not yet not fully evaluated (i.e., final) can be reduced by a rule of the small step semantics. To prove this we need to assume that the program is well-formed, the heap and the environment conform, and the expression passes the definite assignment test:

Theorem 2.1 *Progress:*

If *wf-C-prog P* and $P,E,h \vdash e : T$ and $P \vdash h \sqrt{}$ and $P \vdash E \sqrt{}$
and $\mathcal{D} \, e \, \lfloor dom \, l \rfloor$ and $\neg \, final \, e$ then $\exists e' s'. \, P,E \vdash \langle e,(h, l) \rangle \to \langle e',s' \rangle$.

Proof. This theorem is proved by a quite exhausting rule induction on the (run-time) typing rules, where most cases consist of several case distinctions, like *e* being final or not. So some cases can get quite long (e.g., the proof for method call has about 150 lines of proof script). □

2.5.4. Preservation

To achieve type safety we have to show that all of the assumptions in the Progress theorem above are preserved by the small steps rules.

First, we consider heap conformance:

Lemma 2.2 *Heap Conformance:*

If *wf-C-prog P* and $P,E \vdash \langle e,(h, l) \rangle \to \langle e',(h', l') \rangle$ and
$P,E,h \vdash e : T$ and $P \vdash h \sqrt{}$ then $P \vdash h' \sqrt{}$.

We proof this by induction on the small step rules. Most cases are straightforward, the only work lies in the rules which alter the heap, namely the ones for creation of new objects and field assignment.

Next, we need a similar rule for the conformance of the store. To prove this, we need to assume that the program is well-formed, the environment conforms to it and the expression is well typed in the run-time type system:

Lemma 2.3 *Store Conformance:*

If *wf-C-prog P* and $P,E \vdash \langle e,(h, l) \rangle \to \langle e',(h', l') \rangle$ and
$P,E,h \vdash e : T$ and $P,h \vdash l \, (:\leq)_w E$ and $P \vdash E \sqrt{}$ then $P,h' \vdash l' \, (:\leq)_w E$.

Here, the interesting cases from the small step rule induction are those that change the locals, namely variable assignment and blocks with locally declared variables.

Furthermore, also definite assignment needs to be preserved by the semantics. The corresponding lemma is easily proved by induction on the small step rules:

Lemma 2.4 *Definite Assignment Conformance:*

If *wf-C-prog P* and $P,E \vdash \langle e,(h,l)\rangle \to \langle e',(h',l')\rangle$ and $\mathcal{D}\ e\ \lfloor dom\ l\rfloor$ then $\mathcal{D}\ e'\ \lfloor dom\ l'\rfloor$.

Finally we have to show that the semantics preserves well-typedness. Preservation of well-typedness here means that the type of the reduced expression is equal to that of the original expression or, if the original expression had a class type, the type may reduce to the null type. This is formalized via the *type-conf* property from Sec. 2.5.2, *hp s* is the heap component of *s*:

Theorem 2.5 *Preservation:*

If *wf-C-prog P* and $P,E \vdash \langle e,s\rangle \to \langle e',s'\rangle$ and $P,E \vdash s\ \sqrt{}$ and $P,E,hp\ s \vdash e : T$ then $P,E,hp\ s' \vdash e' :_{NT} T$.

Proof. This proof by rule induction is quite lengthy because the most complicated cases (mostly method call and field assignment) of the 61 small step rules can have up to 80 lines of proof script each. $\square$

2.5.5. The Type Safety Proof

All the preservation lemmas only work 'one step'. We have to extend them from $\to$ to $\to^*$, which is done by induction (because of the equivalence of big and small step semantics mentioned in Sec. 2.3.4, all these lemmas now also hold for the big step rules). Now combining type preservation with progress yields the main theorem:

Theorem 2.6 *Type Safety:*

If *wf-C-prog P* and $P,E \vdash s\ \sqrt{}$ and $P,E \vdash e :: T$ and $\mathcal{D}\ e\ \lfloor dom\ (lcl\ s)\rfloor$ and $P,E \vdash \langle e,s\rangle \to^* \langle e',s'\rangle$ and $\nexists e''\ s''.\ P,E \vdash \langle e',s'\rangle \to \langle e'',s''\rangle$ then $(\exists v.\ e' = \texttt{Val}\ v \wedge P,hp\ s' \vdash v :\leq T) \vee$ $(\exists r.\ e' = Throw\ r \wedge the\text{-}addr\ (Ref\ r) \in dom\ (hp\ s'))$.

If the program is well-formed, state *s* conforms to it, *e* has type *T* and passes the definite assignment test w.r.t. *dom (lcl s)* (where *lcl s* is the store component of *s*) and its $\to$-normal form is *e'*, then the following property holds: either *e'* is a value of type *T* (or *NT*, if *T* is of type class) or an exception *Throw r* such that the address part of *r* is a valid address in the heap.

2.6 Interpreting Real C++ Programs in the Semantics

To further enhance the trust in our formalization, and to narrow the "formalization gap" between C++ and the semantics, we implemented a tool called *CCCP*[9], which allows us to evaluate real C++ programs in the semantics. We implemented this tool as a plugin for the Eclipse framework[10]. As the underlying concept is a completely formal semantics, it is an ideal basis for checking if concrete implementations, e.g. of compilers, are correct.

Fig. 2.18 shows an overview of the tool as a plugin in Eclipse. It basically shows Eclipse in its C/C++ development view, however, a new button starting CCCP can be found. Pressing this button triggers the tool, whose functionality can be divided in two phases, *Translation* and *Evaluation*, which we will now describe in more detail.

2.6.1. Translation

We use the *Eclipse C/C++ Development Tooling*[11] – or short CDT – to generate an abstract syntax tree of the given program. This syntax tree is then translated in a program representation in ML that the CoreC++ semantics can understand.

We have seen in the previous sections that the syntax of CoreC++ is quite restricted, many standard constructs are not supported. Instead of incorporating them in CoreC++ – and thus bloating the semantics –, we opted for the parser to translate such constructs into the kernel language of CoreC++:

Operators: CoreC++ itself supports only addition on integers and equality checks. Considering them as syntactic sugar, we also parse the following operators: ++, +=, -=, &&, ||, ?: (the last three using the functional if provided from CoreC++), and !.

---

[9]C++ to CoreC++ **Plugin**
[10]www.eclipse.org
[11]www.eclipse.org/cdt

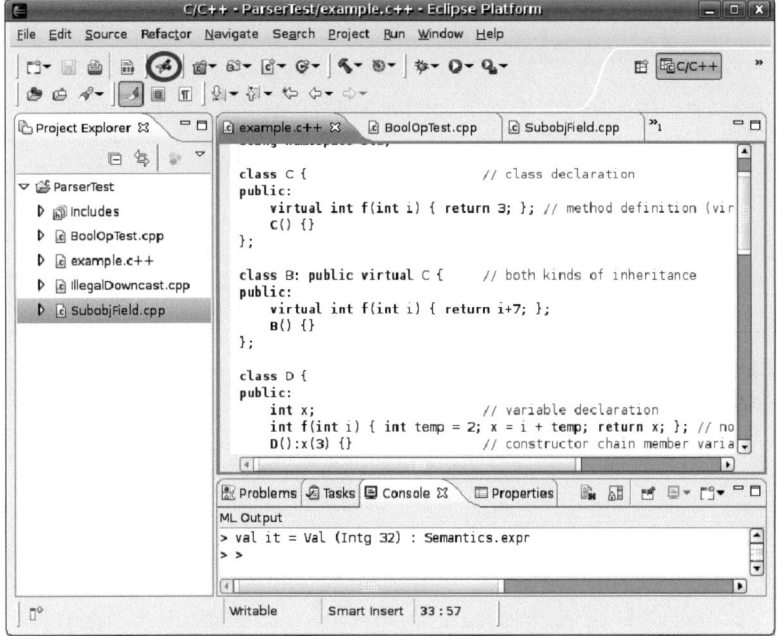

Figure 2.18.: CCCP in Eclipse, the tool start button is highlighted

Simple `for`-loops: We translate `for`-loops into `while`-loops, which are supported by CoreC++.

Constructors: CoreC++ only allows object creation with default values in their fields. However, we can fully handle constructors with parameters, constructor chains with member variable initialization and super constructor calls, etc. This is highly non-trivial due to the two kinds of inheritance, as the constructors of all shared base classes have to be called (only once!) before the constructors of the other base classes are called. This guarantees that every subobject is initialized. We have implemented an algorithm by Frank Tip [118], which emulates correct C++ constructor behaviour using the default constructor and method calls. The algorithm does the following: in each class `C`

- a default constructor is introduced,
- the user-defined constructors are replaced with initC_L, a new method with the same body, and returning **this**,

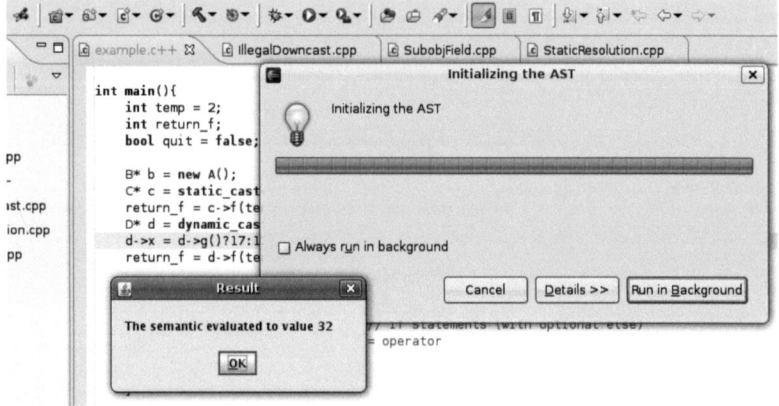

Figure 2.19.: Result popup

- when the class has **virtual** base classes (e.g. B), a method initC_S is introduced, containing qualified calls to the initB_L methods of each virtual super class B in a left-first, depth-first manner,

- a method initC is added, calling its initC_S method (if it exists), then returning the pointer returned from the call to its initC_L method.

Finally, we replace constructor calls of class C with the result of calling method initC on its default constructor. This algorithm preserves C++ constructor calling order. For an example, see appendix B, where we show a program before and after applying this algorithm.

Note that the translator itself cannot be verified; however, as it only performs small translation steps, the possibility for introducing errors can be neglected.

2.6.2. Evaluation

Isabelle enables one to automatically create ML files from theories ("rapid prototyping") by using its built-in code generator [15]. We have done so for the semantics and the type system, hence obtaining an interpreter for CoreC++ programs given in ML syntax. CCCP now calls Poly/ML[12] to run the semantics interpreter on the ML program representation resulting from the translation phase. This interpretation of the program in the semantics returns the final value (or exception) of the evaluation in a popup window, see Fig. 2.19; as CoreC++ is purely functional, direct input and output are not possible.

---

[12]www.polyml.org

3

Correctness of Static Intraprocedural Slicing

Nowadays, slicing algorithms using dependence graphs are standard and can be found in various areas of computation [21, 37], even in safety-critical applications [52]. Hence, it is surprising that correctness proofs for such slicing algorithms [92, 7, 90, 3] are always restricted to simple imperative programming languages. Yet, as the idea of slicing is independent of a concrete programming language, a correctness proof should reflect this property. Furthermore, these proofs consider each only one specific definition of control dependence. In [90], Ranganath et al. present several control dependence definitions, each capturing a different intuition. The elements in the slice will differ, depending on which control dependence is used. The existing correctness results, inflexible to such changes, need to be reproved, which is nontrivial.

After introducing slicing and its basic notions in Sec. 3.1, I present a machine-checked modular framework for intraprocedural slicing based on CFGs and PDGs (see Sec. 3.2) together with a correctness proof for static intraprocedural slicing in Sec. 3.3. The framework (see also [132]) is not restricted to a specific programming language, but builds on abstract structural and well-formedness properties the CFG of a program has to fulfil. It is also independent of a specific control dependence definition, but requires it to have one particular property. A profitable feature of this structure is the separation of language-dependent parts from language-independent ones.

As I showed in the previous chapter, formalizing kernels of realistic high-level programming languages is no longer out of reach. Thus, the abstractions in the framework pose no insurmountable obstacle for rich language formalizations like CoreC++ [134] or Jinja [61]. In Sec. 3.4, I present instantiations of the framework with two formalizations of different languages to show the validity and applicability of my work. The framework is available online [128], together with the instantiations presented in this chapter.

3.1 What is Slicing?

Given a certain point in a program, a slice collects all statements that may influence this point. Slicing proved to be useful for many applications, e.g. debugging [111], testing [14], reducing specifications [141, 66], and software security algorithms [52, 109]. Today, commercial slicing tools such as Codesurfer [4] are routinely used for some of these tasks.

Most slicing tools are based on the program dependence graph (PDG) [56, 92] which is computed from the control flow graph (CFG). The PDG reuses the CFG nodes, which correspond to the program statements, and connects them with *data dependences* and *control dependences*. The *static intraprocedural backward slice* of a given program point (i.e., a specific PDG node, called the *slicing criterion* or *slicing node*) is defined as the set of all nodes on which the point is transitively data or control dependent.[1] This set conservatively approximates all statements that may influence the slicing node's statement. Note that for realistic languages, PDG generation and precise slicing is absolutely non-trivial. Hundreds of papers on slicing have been published in the last three decades, for an overview, see the surveys by Tip [117] and Krinke [64].

3.1.1. Dependences in Program Dependence Graphs

Data Dependence

The data dependence definition is based on *Def* and *Use* sets for every node. All variables defined (e.g. assigned) in a statement are in the Def set of the respective node, those which are used (e.g. in a calculation or predicate) in its Use set. A node n' is data dependent on a node n, if there is a variable V in the Def set of n which is also in the Use set of

---

[1] Also for dependence relations that do not constitute a PDG, e.g. because they are not binary, the backward slice is computed this way.

n' and there is a CFG *path* (sequence of edges) from n to n' such that V is not defined in any other node on this path.

Control Dependence

Control dependence captures the effect that nodes can influence whether the control flow reaches other nodes. The definition by Ferrante et al. [44] – one of the first formal definitions – is most widespread and considered standard.

Nevertheless, this is an area of active research, see Ranganath et al. [90] for a recent overview. Each control dependence definition serves a different purpose, so the choice of control dependence affects the semantics of the slice. In this chapter we focus on three different kinds of control dependences:

(i) *standard control dependence* as it has been in use for years,

(ii) *weak control dependence* as defined by Podgurski and Clarke [88], and

(iii) *weak order dependence* as defined by Amtoft [3].

The first two are binary relations, so we get program dependence graphs with them; for the third one, a ternary relation, this does not hold.

We now look more closely at each of these three dependence relations, state their definitions informally and illustrate them using the CFG in Fig. 3.1, where E denotes the entry and X the exit node. Note that the subgraph built of nodes 2 to 5 does not describe the control flow of a *structured* program; however, it still is a valid CFG in our framework.

Standard Control Dependence.   In the usual understanding, a node n' is control dependent on node n if selecting an outgoing edge of n in the CFG affects whether n' is reached; e.g. all nodes in the branches of an if-statement are dependent on the node representing the if-predicate. To define standard control dependence (SCD) we first need to define *postdomination* using a unique reachable exit node: a node n' postdominates node n if every path from n to the exit node contains n'; the exit node itself, however, must not be a postdominator for any node. In the table in Fig. 3.1 we list the postdominators for every node n, i.e., the set of all nodes n' which postdominate n.

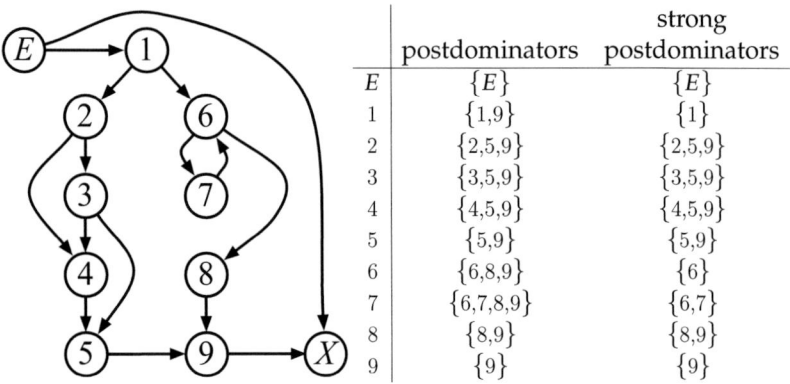

	postdominators	strong postdominators
E	$\{E\}$	$\{E\}$
1	$\{1,9\}$	$\{1\}$
2	$\{2,5,9\}$	$\{2,5,9\}$
3	$\{3,5,9\}$	$\{3,5,9\}$
4	$\{4,5,9\}$	$\{4,5,9\}$
5	$\{5,9\}$	$\{5,9\}$
6	$\{6,8,9\}$	$\{6\}$
7	$\{6,7,8,9\}$	$\{6,7\}$
8	$\{8,9\}$	$\{8,9\}$
9	$\{9\}$	$\{9\}$

Figure 3.1.: Example CFG and postdominators

Ferrante et al. [44] defined that a node n' is control dependent on a node n (written $n \longrightarrow_{scd} n'$), if n' postdominates all nodes on a path in the CFG between n and n' but not n. However, we consider an equivalent definition (see the lemma in Sec. 3.2.2) by Wolfe [139] as more suitable for the formalization and the proofs in the framework: a node n' is control dependent on a node n, if n has at least two successors, one postdominated by n', while the other one is not. Thus, the example in Fig. 3.1 contains the following SCDs:

$$E \longrightarrow_{scd} 1, E \longrightarrow_{scd} 9, 1 \longrightarrow_{scd} 2, 1 \longrightarrow_{scd} 5, 1 \longrightarrow_{scd} 6,$$
$$1 \longrightarrow_{scd} 8, 2 \longrightarrow_{scd} 3, 2 \longrightarrow_{scd} 4, 3 \longrightarrow_{scd} 4, 6 \longrightarrow_{scd} 7$$

Weak Control Dependence. Nonterminating loops prevent nodes after the loop from being executed, a fact that SCD ignores. To capture this effect, control dependence edges between those nodes and the loop predicate are often desired; this is the concept of weak control dependence (WCD). It uses the notion of *strong postdomination*, where no loops[2] on any path between a node and its postdominator are allowed. Otherwise, there would be an infinite path always running through the loop but never reaching the postdominator. Therefore, I define that n' strongly postdominates n if n' postdominates n and there is no loop on any path between n and n'.

---

[2]Statically, we must assume that any loop may be nonterminating.

WCD itself is then defined analogously to SCD, just replacing post-domination with strong postdomination in Wolfe's or Ferrante's definition. We write $n \longrightarrow_{wcd} n'$ if n' is weakly control dependent on n. In Fig. 3.1, the following holds:

$$E \longrightarrow_{wcd} 1, 1 \longrightarrow_{wcd} 2, 1 \longrightarrow_{wcd} 5, 1 \longrightarrow_{wcd} 6, 1 \longrightarrow_{wcd} 9,$$
$$2 \longrightarrow_{wcd} 3, 2 \longrightarrow_{wcd} 4, 3 \longrightarrow_{wcd} 4, 6 \longrightarrow_{wcd} 7, 6 \longrightarrow_{wcd} 8, 6 \longrightarrow_{wcd} 9$$

Note that 8 and 9 now depend on nodes other than before. Since they immediately follow the loop at node 6, they are now dependent on 6. If we assume that above example does not contain any data dependences, the backward slice of node 8 using SCD would be $\{E, 1, 8\}$, for WCD however we get $\{E, 1, 6, 8\}$.

Weak Order Dependence. The advantage of weak order dependence (WOD) is that there is no need for a unique reachable end node, as is the case in e.g. reactive systems. Unlike the former two, WOD is not a binary relation, but a set of triples of nodes. Intuitively, two nodes are weak order dependent on another node, if the latter node controls the order in which the other two nodes are executed (which includes that one of these nodes may never be executed). However, the definition is a bit more complicated: we say that two nodes n_1 and n_2 are weak order dependent on node n (all three nodes distinct), written $n \longrightarrow_{wod} n_1, n_2$, if

(i) n can reach n_1 in the CFG without visiting n_2,

(ii) n can reach n_2 in the CFG without visiting n_1 and

(iii) there exists an immediate successor m of n, such that either
    a) m can reach n_1 and all paths from m to n_2 contain n_1 or
    b) m can reach n_2 and all paths from m to n_1 contain n_2.

Since there are many WOD triples for the example CFG in Fig. 3.1, we present them as a set of node pairs which are weak order dependent on the node preceding this set, leaving out all tuples where the two components are swapped or where one component is the exit node:

$1: \{(2, 6), (2, 7), (2, 8), (2, 9), (3, 6), (3, 7), (3, 8), (3, 9),$
$\quad (4, 6), (4, 7), (4, 8), (4, 9), (5, 6), (5, 7), (5, 8), (5, 9),$
$\quad (6, 9), (7, 9), (8, 9)\},$
$2: \{(3, 4), (3, 5), (3, 9), (4, 5), (4, 9)\},$
$3: \{(4, 5), (4, 9)\},$
$6: \{(7, 8), (7, 9)\},$

While the number of node triples that are weak order dependent in this example is huge compared to the cardinality of the former two dependence relations, the slice computed using WOD may be smaller. For example, if we again compute the slice for node 8, the slice is a singleton set which consists only of the element 8. We may only include a WOD predecessor in this set, if the pair of its successors would be in the slice. As only node 8 is in the slice, but neither 2, 3, 4, nor 5, node 1 is not part of the slice; analogously, as 7 is not in the slice, node 6 is not included either.

Whereas slices w.r.t. SCD and WCD have well understood semantics, this seems not to be the case for WOD. Omitting the exit node from a slice can result in slices smaller than one would expect. However, I consider this orthogonal to my work, as the correctness properties in this thesis still hold.

3.1.2. A Running Example

The program presented in this section, which serves as a running example throughout this chapter, is used to clarify the notions introduced in the previous section. Fig. 3.2 on the right shows the program code; for simplicity, we assume that all variables are initialized to a default value.

Fig. 3.3 (a) shows the corresponding CFG where the node numbers correspond to the line numbers in the code above. The corresponding PDG with standard control dependence is shown in Fig. 3.3 (b). Solid arrows denote control, dashed ones data dependence (data dependence edges are labelled with the variable that triggers this dependence). The nodes corresponding to the then- and else-branches (4 and 5, resp.) are control dependent on the node for the if-predicate (3), just like the nodes that represent the loop body (7 and 8) are control dependent on the node for the while-predicate (6). All other nodes that do not explicitly have a control dependence predecessor are control dependent on the entry node E; to force this, an edge between E and X is introduced, a standard trick for de-

```
1    y := 7;
2    b := a && d;
3    if (b) {
4        x := 5 + y;
     } else {
5        c := 4;
     }
6    while (c < 3) {
7        w := w + v;
8        c := c + 1;
     }
9    z := 3 * w;
10   z := x + y;
```

Figure 3.2.: Example code

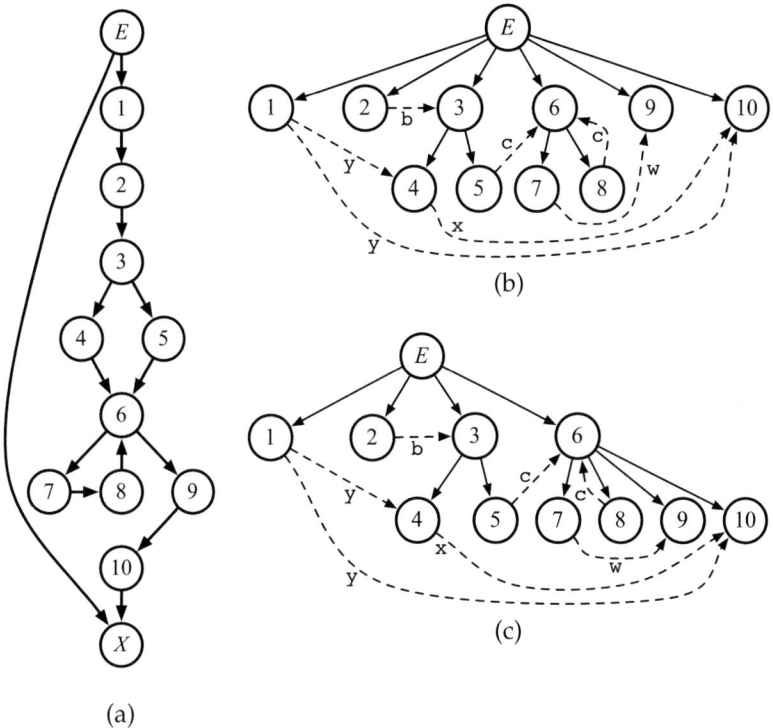

(a)

(b)

(c)

Figure 3.3.: The CFG and PDGs for the code example

pendence calculation. Hence X is the second successor of E which is not postdominated by any other node. The data dependences should be clear from the program code.

The PDG looks different (see Fig. 3.3 (c)) when using weak control dependence, as now the nodes after the while loop (9 and 10) depend on this loop, as it is treated as potentially nonterminating. The remaining data and control dependences are the same as before.

As weak order dependence is no binary relation, edges cannot represent this dependence, so building a PDG is impossible (at least in the common understanding). Hence, I write the weak order dependence triples for this example as in the section above; however, this time including pairs containing the exit node X:

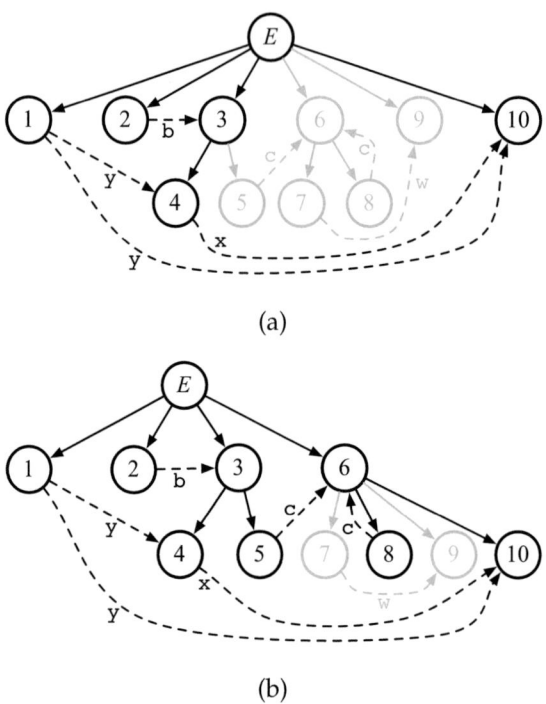

(a)

(b)

Figure 3.4.: The "sliced PDGs" of node 10

E: $\{(1, X), (2, X), (3, X), (6, X), (9, X), (10, X)\}$
3: $\{(4, 5), (4, 6), (4, 7), (4, 8), (4, 9), (4, 10), (4, X),$
$\quad (5, 6), (5, 7), (5, 8), (5, 9), (5, 10), (5, X)\}$,
6: $\{(7, 8), (7, 9), (7, 10), (7, X), (8, 9), (8, 10), (8, X)\}$

Computing the slice of a node in the intraprocedural case is a mere matter of transitive closure: every node on which the slicing node transitively depends is part of the slice set. Fig. 3.4 (a) and (b) again show the PDGs for standard and weak control dependence, respectively, but only nodes that contribute to the slice of node 10 are in black, those not occurring in the slice are grey. As one can immediately see, the slices differ: the slice for 10 in the PDG using standard control dependence is $BS_{SCD} = \{E,1,2,3,4,10\}$, the one using weak control dependence is $BS_{WCD} = \{E,1,2,3,4,5,6,8,10\}$. So taking non-termination of

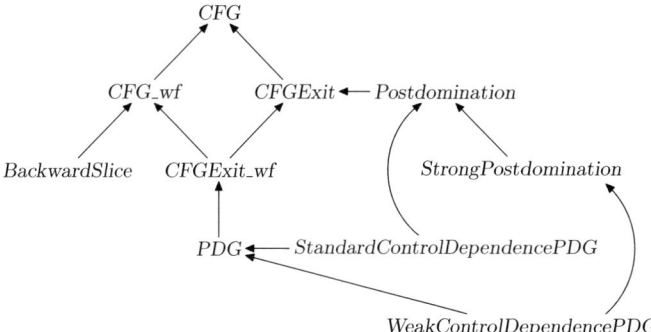

Figure 3.5.: Locale hierarchy of the framework

the while loop into account, slicing for node 10 yields a much bigger slice, even in this small example.

Remember that for weak order dependence, we have a dependence predecessor and a pair of successors. The predecessor is only included in the slice, if it contains already *both* successors. When computing the slice for node 10, first 10 itself is included. As no other node is part of the slice, no node can be included due to weak order dependence, so we first consider data dependences. This leads to nodes 1 and 4 being in the slice. Now, we can add node 3, as (4, 10) is a dependence successor pair for this node. The next step inserts node 2 in the slice, as 3 is data dependent on it. No other node can be included, not even E, as this would require X to be in the slice. Thus, the slice for weak order dependence is $BS_{WOD} = \{1,2,3,4,10\}$

3.2 The Formalization

The framework for slicing presented in this thesis is based on an abstract control flow graph (CFG) containing semantic information. This abstract CFG is defined using locales (see Sec. 1.4.2), which state certain structural and well-formedness properties; thus there is no need for a concrete underlying programming language. Also the concrete definition of control dependence used in the correctness proof (see Sec. 3.3) for slicing is not fixed; I merely state one condition this definition has to fulfil and demonstrate that for three quite distinct control dependence definitions, which are formalized in Sec. 3.2.2, this condition holds.

locale *CFG* =
fixes *valid-edge* :: *'edge* $\Rightarrow$ *bool*
fixes *src* :: *'edge* $\Rightarrow$ *'node*
fixes *trg* :: *'edge* $\Rightarrow$ *'node*
fixes *kind* :: *'edge* $\Rightarrow$ *'state edge-kind*
fixes (*-Entry-*) :: *'node*
assumes *Entry-target*: *valid-edge a* $\Longrightarrow$ *trg a* $\neq$ (*-Entry-*)
and *no-multi-edges*:
⟦*valid-edge a*; *valid-edge a'*; *src a* = *src a'*; *trg a* = *trg a'*⟧ $\Longrightarrow$ *a* = *a'*

locale *CFGExit* = *CFG* +
fixes (*-Exit-*) :: *'node*
assumes *Exit-source*: *valid-edge a* $\Longrightarrow$ *src a* $\neq$ (*-Exit-*)
and *Entry-Exit-edge*:
$\exists$*a*. *valid-edge a* $\wedge$ *src a* = (*-Entry-*) $\wedge$ *trg a* = (*-Exit-*) $\wedge$ *kind a* = (λ*s. False*)$_\sqrt{}$

Figure 3.6.: Locale defining the structure of the abstract CFG

Fig. 3.5 shows the locales present in the framework and their dependences. A locale that extends another one has an arrow pointing to this locale. All the locales will be explained in the following two sections.

3.2.1. The Abstract Intraprocedural Control Flow Graph

The abstract CFG, defined via the locale depicted in Fig. 3.6, consists of nodes of type *'node* and edges of type *'edge*. An edge *a* is in the set of CFG edges if the predicate *valid-edge a* holds, a parameter of the instantiating language. In the proof context of the locale, the set of CFG nodes is defined via its characteristic function *valid-node n*: *n* must be the source or target node of a *valid-edge*. Formally: *valid-node n* $\equiv$ $\exists$*a*. *valid-edge a* $\wedge$ (*n* = *src a* $\vee$ *n* = *trg a*). Assumed functions *src*, *trg* and *kind* determine the source node, target node and edge kind of an edge, respectively.

Edges carry semantic information (thus the abstract CFG is more like a *control flow automata*, see [53, Sec. 3.1]), the edge kind states the action taken when traversing this edge. There are two edge kinds of type *'state edge-kind*, both parameterized with a state type variable *'state*: (i) updating the current state with a function *f*::*'state* $\Rightarrow$ *'state*, written ⇑*f*, or (ii) assuring that a predicate *Q*::*'state* $\Rightarrow$ *bool* in the current state holds, written $(Q)_{\sqrt{}}$. To traverse edges in a state s, I define function *transfer* to update the state accordingly to the edge kind, and function *pred* to check that the respective edge kind predicate holds:

$$\text{transfer} \Uparrow f\, s \;\equiv\; f\, s, \qquad \text{transfer}\, (Q)_{\sqrt{}}\, s \;\equiv\; s$$
$$\text{pred} \Uparrow f\, s \;\equiv\; \text{True}, \qquad \text{pred}\, (Q)_{\sqrt{}}\, s \;\equiv\; Q\, s$$

I assume an (*-Entry-*) node, which must not have incoming edges. Multi-edges are not allowed in the framework, i.e., if the source and target nodes of two valid edges coincide, so do the two edges.

Edges can also be combined to paths: $n -as \rightarrow* n'$ denotes that node n can reach n' via edges $as :: 'edge\ list$. Paths are inductively defined by:

$$\frac{\text{valid-node } n}{n -[] \rightarrow* n}$$

$$\frac{n'' -as \rightarrow* n' \qquad \text{valid-edge } a \qquad src\ a = n \qquad trg\ a = n''}{n -a \cdot as \rightarrow* n'}$$

srcs, *trgs* and *kinds* map the respective functions to edge lists using standard function *map*. *transfer* and *pred* are lifted to lists of edge kinds via

$$\text{transfers}\ []\ s \;\equiv\; s, \qquad \text{transfers}\ (e \cdot es)\ s \;\equiv\; \text{transfers}\ es\ (\text{transfer}\ e\ s)$$
$$\text{preds}\ []\ s \;\equiv\; \text{True} \qquad \text{preds}\ (e \cdot es)\ s \;\equiv\; \text{pred}\ e\ s \wedge \text{preds}\ es\ (\text{transfer}\ e\ s)$$

If a unique end node is required, I assume its existence in locale *CFGExit*, call it (*-Exit-*) and allow only incoming edges. I also assume a special edge from (*-Entry-*) to (*-Exit-*) of kind $(\lambda s.\ False)_{\sqrt{}}$, a predicate that can never be fulfilled. It is needed for control dependences based on postdomination to behave correctly.

After having defined the structural properties of the CFG, we furthermore need:

(i) the *Def* and *Use* sets for the valid nodes, which collect the defined and used variables in this node, respectively,

(ii) some well-formedness properties, which guarantee that the *Def* and *Use* sets in source nodes agree with the semantic information in the respective edges, and

(iii) a function *state-val s V* returning the value currently stored in variable V in state s.

locale *CFG-wf* = *CFG* +
fixes *Def* :: *'node* $\Rightarrow$ *'var set*
fixes *Use* :: *'node* $\Rightarrow$ *'var set*
fixes *state-val* :: *'state* $\Rightarrow$ *'var* $\Rightarrow$ *'val*
assumes *Entry-empty*: *Def* (*-Entry-*) = {} $\wedge$ *Use* (*-Entry-*) = {}
and *no-Def-equal*: $[\![$*valid-edge a*; $V \notin Def$ (*src a*)$]\!]$
$\quad\Longrightarrow$ *state-val* (*transfer* (*kind a*) *s*) V = *state-val s V*
and *transfer-only-Use*:
$\quad[\![$*valid-edge a*; $\forall V \in Use$ (*src a*). *state-val s V* = *state-val s' V*$]\!]$
$\quad\Longrightarrow \forall V \in Def$ (*src a*). *state-val* (*transfer* (*kind a*) *s*) V =
$\qquad\qquad\qquad$ *state-val* (*transfer* (*kind a*) *s'*) V
and *Uses-pred-equal*: $[\![$*valid-edge a*; *pred* (*kind a*) *s*;
$\quad\forall V \in Use$ (*src a*). *state-val s V* = *state-val s' V*$]\!] \Longrightarrow$ *pred* (*kind a*) *s'*
and *deterministic*: $[\![$*valid-edge a*; *valid-edge a'*; *src a* = *src a'*; *trg a* $\neq$ *trg a'*$]\!]$
$\quad\Longrightarrow \exists Q\,Q'.$ *kind a* = $(Q)_\surd \wedge$ *kind a'* = $(Q')_\surd \wedge$
$\qquad\qquad (\forall s.\,(Q\,s \longrightarrow \neg\,Q'\,s) \wedge (Q'\,s \longrightarrow \neg\,Q\,s))$

locale *CFGExit-wf* = *CFGExit* + *CFG-wf* +
assumes *Exit-empty*: *Def* (*-Exit-*) = {} $\wedge$ *Use* (*-Exit-*) = {}

Figure 3.7.: Well-formedness properties of the abstract CFG

Variables (or more generally said: locations) are of type *'var*, values of type *'val*. The locales that define the well-formedness assumptions are shown in Fig. 3.7, in words:

- *Def* and *Use* sets of (*-Entry-*) (and (*-Exit-*), if defined) are empty;
- traversing an edge leaves all variables which are not defined in its source node unchanged;
- if two states agree on all variables in the *Use* set of the source node of an edge, then after traversing this edge the two states agree on all variables in the *Def* set of this node; i.e., different values in the variables not in the *Use* set cannot influence the values of the variables in the *Def* set after the semantic action;
- if two states agree on all variables in the *Use* set of the source node of a predicate edge and this predicate is valid in one state, it is also valid in the other one;
- any two valid edges with the same source, but differing target nodes, are predicate edges, such that for any state, one of these predicates holds, the other one does not; thus, there is no non-deterministic choice.

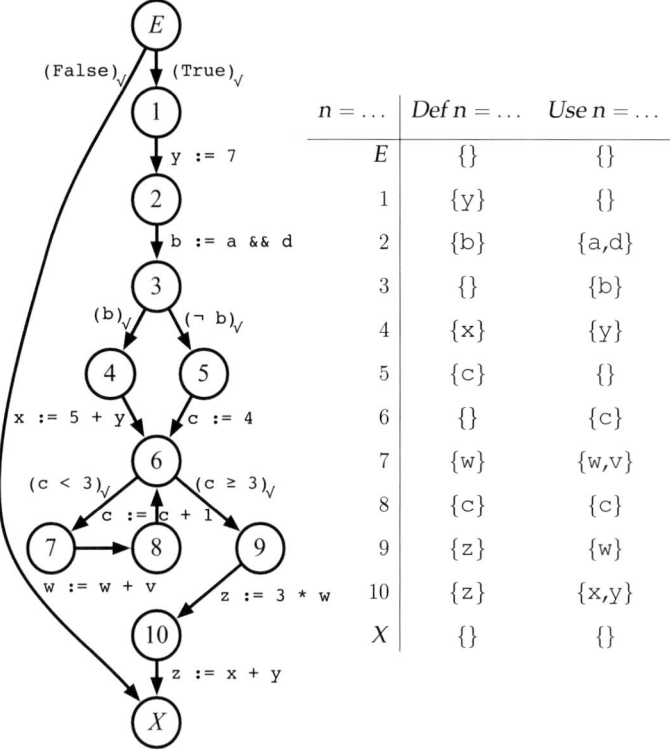

$n = \ldots$	$Def\ n = \ldots$	$Use\ n = \ldots$
E	{}	{}
1	{y}	{}
2	{b}	{a,d}
3	{}	{b}
4	{x}	{y}
5	{c}	{}
6	{}	{c}
7	{w}	{w,v}
8	{c}	{c}
9	{z}	{w}
10	{z}	{x,y}
X	{}	{}

Figure 3.8.: The edge kinds and Def and Use sets in the example CFG

Suppose we also have an operational semantics of the language, where $\langle c,s \rangle \Rightarrow \langle c',s' \rangle$ means that evaluating statement c in state s results in a residual statement c' and state s'. Mapping nodes to their corresponding statements using $\triangleq$, we then obtain another well-formedness property (called *semantically well-formed*):

$$\frac{n \triangleq c \qquad \langle c,s \rangle \Rightarrow \langle c',s' \rangle}{\exists n'\ as.\ n -as \rightarrow * n' \wedge n' \triangleq c' \wedge transfers\ (kinds\ as)\ s = s' \wedge preds\ (kinds\ as)\ s}$$

This property states that if the evaluation of statement c in state s results in a state s' and node n corresponds to statement c, then there is a path in the CFG beginning at n to a node n' that corresponds to the residual statement c', on which, taking s as initial state, all predicates in predicate edges hold and the traversal of the path edge kinds also yields state s'.

69

locale *Postdomination* = *CFGExit* +
assumes *Entry-path*: *valid-node n* $\Longrightarrow \exists\, as.$ (*-Entry-*) $-as \rightarrow * n$
and *Exit-path*: *valid-node n* $\Longrightarrow \exists\, as.\ n\ -as \rightarrow *$ (*-Exit-*)

Figure 3.9.: Locale with the constraints for postdomination

The left hand side of Fig. 3.8 shows the CFG from the running example in Fig. 3.3, annotated with its edge kinds. I use a simplified syntax for presentation, e.g. the assignment z := x + y in correct edge syntax would look like this: $\Uparrow(\lambda s.\ s(z \mapsto s(x) + s(y)))$. The table on the right hand side shows for every CFG node its *Def* and *Use* set. This CFG conforms to all the structural and well-formedness properties proposed in this section.

3.2.2. Formalizing Dependences

This section formalizes data dependence and the three control dependence relations from Sec. 3.1.1, based on the abstract control flow graph defined in the previous section.

Data Dependence

Formalizing data dependence is a straightforward translation of the informal definition given in Sec. 3.1.1:

$$n\ influences\ V\ in\ n' \equiv \exists\, a'\ as'.\ V \in Def\ n \wedge V \in Use\ n' \wedge n\ -a'\cdot as' \rightarrow * n' \wedge$$
$$(\forall\, n'' \in set\ (srcs\ as').\ V \notin Def\ n'')$$

Standard Control Dependence

Standard control dependence (SCD) employs the notion of postdomination. A node n' postdominates a node n, if n' occurs on every path from n to the exit node. Thus, postdomination only makes sense if we have such a (unique) exit node and can reach that node from every node in the program. Hence, locale *Postdomination* as shown in Fig. 3.9 extends locale *CFGExit* (thus inheriting the notion of a unique exit node) and fixes the assumption *Exit-path* which states the latter requirement. Furthermore, *Entry-path* formalizes the fact that every node can be reached from the entry node (i.e., there is no dead code). In this locale, postdomination is then defined via:

n' postdominates $n \equiv$ valid-node $n \wedge$ valid-node $n' \wedge$
$$(\forall \, as. \; n \, -as \rightarrow * \, (\text{-Exit-}) \longrightarrow n' \in set \, (srcs \, as))$$

postdominates is a partial order, as it is

reflexive for every valid node except (-Exit-):
   If valid-node n and $n \neq$ (-Exit-) then n postdominates n

transitive: If n' postdominates n'' and n'' postdominates n
   then n' postdominates n

antisymmetric: If n' postdominates n and n postdominates n' then $n = n'$.

Now, I define standard control dependence as in Sec. 3.1.1 and prove that this definition is equivalent to the widely used definition from [44]:

$$scd \; n \; n' \equiv \exists \, a \; a' \; as. \; n \, -a \cdot as \rightarrow * \, n' \wedge n' \notin set(srcs \, (a \cdot as)) \wedge \textit{valid-edge} \, a' \wedge$$
$$src \; a = n \wedge n' \; postdominates \; (trg \; a) \wedge src \; a' = n \wedge$$
$$\neg \, n' \; postdominates \; (trg \; a')$$

Lemma 3.1 *SCD Definition Variant (Ferrante et al.):*

$$scd \; n \; n' = (\exists \, as. \; n \, -as \rightarrow * \, n' \wedge n \neq n' \wedge \neg \, n' \; postdominates \; n \wedge$$
$$n' \notin set \, (srcs \, as) \wedge (\forall \, n'' \in set \, (trgs \, as). \; n' \; postdominates \; n''))$$

Proof. Left to right: Choose as to be the path $a \cdot as$ from the definition of scd. n' cannot postdominate n, otherwise the latter could not have the successor $trg \; a'$ not postdominated by n'. n' does postdominate every node on path $trgs \, (a \cdot as)$, because if it did not, then it could not postdominate $trg \; a$ either.

   Right to left: We choose $a \cdot as$ to be as from the right hand side, which has to be nonempty because of $n \neq n'$. n' has to postdominate the successor of n on path as from the right hand side, as it postdominates all nodes on this path except n. To get a second successor of n which n' does not postdominate, we obtain a path from n to (-Exit-) which does not contain n' by assumption *Exit-path* from locale *Postdomination* and because $\neg \, n'$ postdominates n. $\qquad \square$

locale *StrongPostdomination* = *Postdomination* +
assumes *successor-set-finite*:
  valid-node n $\Longrightarrow$ *finite* $\{n'. \exists a'.$ *valid-edge* $a' \wedge$ *src* $a' = n \wedge$ *trg* $a' = n'\}$

Figure 3.10.: Locale with the constraints for strong postdomination

Weak Control Dependence

Weak control dependence (WCD) is termination sensitive, thus we need a stronger postdomination notion which disallows postdomination along infinite paths (e.g. the path always running through a nonterminating loop). For strong postdomination to behave similarly to postdomination, we have to also disallow infinite branching, i.e., for every valid node, the number of target nodes of edges leaving this node must be finite. Fixing this in the assumption *successor-set-finite*, locale *StrongPostdomination* (see Fig. 3.10) extends locale *Postdomination* and defines strong postdomination as:

$$n'\ strongly\text{-}postdominates\ n \equiv n'\ postdominates\ n \wedge$$
$$(\exists k \geq 1.\ \forall\ as\ nx.\ n\ -as\rightarrow* nx \wedge length\ as \geq k \longrightarrow n' \in set\ (srcs\ as))$$

Note that as we assume finite branching, an infinite path exists only if there is a finite path longer than k for any fixed k (cf. König's lemma); if n' lies on any path longer than a certain k, this means that there is no infinite path between the two nodes. If there was a loop between the two nodes, there would however be an infinite path always traversing the loop. Hence this definition disallows nodes after a loop to strongly postdominate nodes before or in the loop.

Also *strongly-postdominates* constitutes a partial order, as it is provably reflexive (for all valid nodes except (*-Exit-*)), transitive and antisymmetric.

The definition of WCD is analogous to standard control dependence:

$$wcd\ n\ n' \equiv \exists a\ a'\ as.\ n\ -a\cdot as\rightarrow* n' \wedge n' \notin set\ (srcs\ a\cdot as) \wedge valid\text{-}edge\ a' \wedge$$
$$src\ a = n \wedge n'\ strongly\text{-}postdominates\ (trg\ a) \wedge$$
$$src\ a' = n \wedge \neg\ n'\ strongly\text{-}postdominates\ (trg\ a')$$

Weak Order Dependence

To define weak order dependence (WOD), we neither need a notion of an exit node nor any further assumptions on the CFG, only paths.

locale $PDG = CFGExit\text{-}wf +$
fixes $- \; controls - :: \; 'node \Rightarrow \; 'node \Rightarrow bool$
assumes $Exit\text{-}not\text{-}cdep$: $n \; controls \; n' \Longrightarrow n' \neq (\text{-}Exit\text{-})$
and $control\text{-}dependence\text{-}path$: $n \; controls \; n' \Longrightarrow \exists \, as. \; n \; -as \rightarrow * \; n' \wedge as \neq []$

Figure 3.11.: Locale describing a PDG

Thus, we can include it in the *CFG* locale:

$wod \; n \; n_1 \; n_2 \equiv$
$n_1 \neq n_2 \wedge (\exists \, as_1. \; n \; -as_1 \rightarrow * \; n_1 \wedge n_2 \notin set \; (srcs \; as_1)) \wedge$
$(\exists \, as_2. \; n \; -as_2 \rightarrow * \; n_2 \wedge n_1 \notin set \; (srcs \; as_2)) \wedge$
$(\exists \, a. \; valid\text{-}edge \; a \wedge n = src \; a \wedge$
$\quad ((\exists \, as_1'. \; trg \; a \; -as_1' \rightarrow * \; n_1 \wedge (\forall \, as'. \; trg \; a \; -as' \rightarrow * \; n_2 \longrightarrow n_1 \in set \; (srcs \; as'))) \vee$
$\quad ((\exists \, as_2'. \; trg \; a \; -as_2' \rightarrow * \; n_2 \wedge (\forall \, as'. \; trg \; a \; -as' \rightarrow * \; n_1 \longrightarrow n_2 \in set \; (srcs \; as')))))$

As weak order dependence is not a binary relation, the PDG is no help in defining the backward slice, it has to be done from scratch:

$$\frac{valid\text{-}node \; n_c}{n_c \in WOD\text{-}BS \; n_c} \qquad \frac{n \; influences \; V \; in \; n' \qquad n' \in WOD\text{-}BS \; n_c}{n \in WOD\text{-}BS \; n_c}$$

$$\frac{wod \; n \; n_1 \; n_2 \qquad n_1 \in WOD\text{-}BS \; n_c \qquad n_2 \in WOD\text{-}BS \; n_c}{n \in WOD\text{-}BS \; n_c}$$

3.2.3. Program Dependence Graph

For binary control dependences, the backward slice is defined using a program dependence graph. Thus, we use a locale to define a PDG (see Fig. 3.11) as "middle layer" between backward slice and control dependence definition. We extend the CFG well-formedness locale stipulating (*-Exit-*), fix a binary control dependence relation *controls* and assume that (*-Exit-*) is not control dependent on anything and that there exists a nonempty CFG path between control dependent nodes. Then we define the PDG's control and data flow edges via:

If $n \; controls \; n'$ then $n \longrightarrow_{cd} n'$

If $n \; influences \; V \; in \; n'$ then $n \; -V \rightarrow_{dd} n'$

PDG paths are the reflexive transitive closure of PDG edges and denoted $n \longrightarrow_{d*} n'$. The backward slice of node n_c is then defined straightforward via $PDG\text{-}BS \; n_c \equiv if \; valid\text{-}node \; n_c \; then \; \{n' \mid n' \longrightarrow_{d*} n_c\} \; else \; \emptyset$.

Now it remains to show that standard and weak control dependence are valid instantiations of the *PDG* locale. To this end, we define locales *StandardControlDependencePDG* and *WeakControlDependence-PDG*, respectively, the former extending *Postdomination* and *CFG-wf*, the latter *StrongPostdomination* and *CFG-wf*. In their proof contexts, we instantiate locale *PDG* with the respective control dependence definition by proving that it fulfils the assumptions for *controls*. This is easily done by unfolding their definitions and the fact that (*-Exit-*) is no source node of a non-empty path.

3.3 The Proof

Following Amtoft [3], I state correctness as a weak simulation property between nodes and states in the original and sliced control flow graph. The proof is based on the abstract control flow graph as shown above, not restricted to a specific language. It is also independent of a specific control dependence definition, but requires it to have one particular property.

Adapting the proof to any particular language just requires to show that the control flow graph of this language can be embedded into the abstract one by fulfilling all necessary conditions. In Sec. 3.4, I sketch this technique for two different languages. Likewise, changing the control dependence definition reduces to showing that the one required property holds; I have done so for the three dependence relations from Sec. 3.2.2, see Sec. 3.3.3. Hence, future verifications of algorithms basing on this correctness proof immediately gain a high level of robustness.

3.3.1. Weak Simulation

This section sketches the idea of the correctness proof of using a weak simulation to prove the correctness of static intraprocedural slicing, following an idea proposed by Amtoft's group [3, 90]. I define correctness as a *weak simulation property* of the observable behavior of the original and the sliced program, regarding the CFG as a labelled transition system (LTS); for details see the next section. As I regard nodes which are part of the slice as observable, an observable move traverses its outgoing edges.

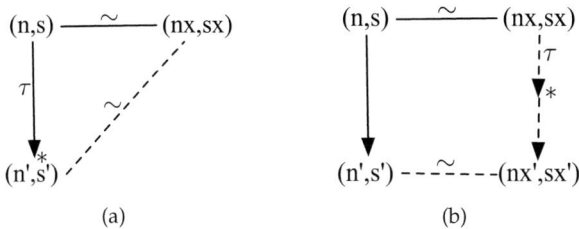

Figure 3.12.: Simulation diagrams

Correctness Property:
If we have two weakly similar LTS states and, starting in the first, an observable move is possible in the original CFG, then an observable move is also possible in the sliced CFG starting in the second, and the resulting LTS states are again weakly similar.

Moves that are not observable are called silent or τ-moves. Fig. 3.12 shows two simulation diagrams for a relation between LTS states with infix operator $\sim$. Solid lines denote hypotheses, dashed lines conclusions. If we can prove that these diagrams hold, $\sim$ is guaranteed to be a weak simulation; more accurately, it is the weak simulation equivalent of the *delay bisimulation* as presented in e.g. [120].

The sliced CFG consists of the same nodes and edges as the original CFG, but all edges whose source node is not in the slice get assigned no-op edge kinds.

3.3.2. Correctness Proof

To state correctness for static slicing we need:

(i) a formalization of observable sets,

(ii) a formalization of a statically sliced CFG,

(iii) a formalization of moves in the original and sliced graph and

(iv) a weak simulation between start and end points of these moves.

locale *BackwardSlice* = *CFG-wf* +
  fixes *backward-slice* :: *'node* ⇒ *'node set*
  assumes *refl*: *valid-node* n_c ⟹ n_c ∈ *backward-slice* n_c
  and *dd-closed*: ⟦n' ∈ *backward-slice* n_c; *n influences V in* n'⟧
  ⟹ *n* ∈ *backward-slice* n_c
  and *obs-finite*: *valid-node n* ⟹ *finite* (*obs n* (*backward-slice* n_c))
  and *obs-singleton*: *valid-node n* ⟹ *card* (*obs n* (*backward-slice* n_c)) ≤ 1

Figure 3.13.: Locale abstracting from a specific backward slice

Observable Sets

The observable set of node *n* in set *S* comprises all nodes *n'* in *S* reachable via a CFG path from *n* such that no other node on this path is in *S*:

$$\frac{n -as\!\rightarrow\!* \, n' \qquad \forall \, nx \in set \, (srcs \, as). \, nx \notin S \qquad n' \in S}{n' \in obs \, n \, S}$$

So every node being itself in set *S* has the singleton observable set only containing itself. Instantiating *S* with a backward slice, this set contains all possible next sources of labelled transitions.

The Statically Sliced Graph

A static (backward) slice for a node n_c (the slicing node) determines which nodes are in the sliced graph. Basically, every node that potentially influences control or data flow to n_c is in the backward slice of n_c, so the slice is defined in terms of data and control dependence.

To abstract from a concrete control dependence definition in the slice, we use a locale named *BackwardSlice* (see Fig. 3.13) to fix a function from a node to a set of nodes called *backward-slice* with properties that guarantee that the resulting node sets are indeed backward slices of the parameter node. Hence we formulate four assumptions:

(i) every node is in its own *backward-slice*,

(ii) if a node *n'* is in *backward-slice* n_c and this node is data dependent on node *n*, then *n* must also be in *backward-slice* n_c (i.e., *backward-slice* n_c is closed under data dependence),

(iii) the set of observable nodes of any valid node in *backward-slice* n_c is finite, and

(iv) the cardinality of this set is at most 1.[3]

---

[3]Note that in Isabelle/HOL, infinite sets have a cardinality of 0.

Only the last two assumptions *obs-finite* and *obs-singleton*, which guarantee that the set of observable nodes in the slice is for every valid node at most a singleton, are influenced by the control dependence used in the slice.

By this definition, we regard all nodes having the same set of observable nodes in set *backward-slice* n_c – being at most a singleton by assumption from locale *BackwardSlice* – as "equal" from the point of view of the slicing.

As mentioned above, the sliced CFG contains the same edges and nodes as the original CFG, but the kinds of edges whose source node is not in the slice are replaced by no-ops via the function *slice-kind* n_c (n_c denotes the slicing node). Analogously to *kind*, *slice-kind* n_c maps edges to the effect this edge has on the state, i.e., its edge kind. The rules can be found in Fig. 3.14 and will be explained in the following: if the source node of the considered edge is in *backward-slice* n_c, *slice-kind* n_c behaves just like *kind* (see rule SK1); if it is not and the edge is an update edge, *slice-kind* n_c returns the update no-op, which is $\Uparrow id$, see rule SK2.

For predicate edges whose source node is not in the slice, things are more complicated. There are two different no-ops for predicates, namely the predicate that always holds $(\lambda s.\ True)_{\sqrt{}}$, and the predicate that never holds $(\lambda s.\ False)_{\sqrt{}}$. Just picking one and returning this as *slice-kind* can make the graph either non-deterministic or its traversal impossible; e.g. think of an `if` whose predicate node is not in the slice and thus both branches are labelled either $(\lambda s.\ True)_{\sqrt{}}$ or $(\lambda s.\ False)_{\sqrt{}}$.

To determine which of the predicate no-ops *slice-kind* returns, we need more information; the *obs* information of the source node is a good starting point. If the *obs* set is not empty, we make only that edge traversable, whose target node is *closest* to the node in *obs* (remember that it is guaranteed that *obs* is at most a singleton). Distance is defined via

$$\frac{n -as\rightarrow* n' \qquad |as| = x \qquad \forall as'.\ n -as'\rightarrow* n' \longrightarrow x \leq |as'|}{distance\ n\ n'\ x}$$

Then, *trg a* is the successor of *src a closest* to *m*, iff *distance* (*trg a*) *m x* and *distance* (*src a*) *m* $(x + 1)$ for some *x*. To show that this choice is indeed sensible, consider Fig. 3.15. It shows the sliced CFGs for node 10 for the running example, the left graph is the result of slicing its CFG with standard control dependence, the right one with weak control dependence, according to their respective PDGs from Fig. 3.4. Node 6

$$\frac{src\ a \in backward\text{-}slice\ n_c}{slice\text{-}kind\ n_c\ a = kind\ a}\ \text{SK1} \qquad \frac{src\ a \notin backward\text{-}slice\ n_c \quad kind\ a = \Uparrow f}{slice\text{-}kind\ n_c\ a = \Uparrow id}\ \text{SK2}$$

$$\frac{\begin{array}{c} src\ a \notin backward\text{-}slice\ n_c \quad m \in obs\ (src\ a)\ (backward\text{-}slice\ n_c) \\ kind\ a = (Q)_{\surd} \quad distance\ (trg\ a)\ m\ x \quad distance\ (src\ a)\ m\ (x+1) \\ trg\ a = (SOME\ n.\ \exists a'.\ src\ a = src\ a' \wedge distance\ (trg\ a')\ m\ x\ \wedge \\ valid\text{-}edge\ a' \wedge trg\ a' = n) \end{array}}{slice\text{-}kind\ n_c\ a = (\lambda s.\ True)_{\surd}}\ \text{SK3}$$

$$\frac{\begin{array}{c} src\ a \notin backward\text{-}slice\ n_c \quad m \in obs\ (src\ a)\ (backward\text{-}slice\ n_c) \\ kind\ a = (Q)_{\surd} \quad distance\ (trg\ a)\ m\ x \quad distance\ (src\ a)\ m\ (x+1) \\ trg\ a \neq (SOME\ n.\ \exists a'.\ src\ a = src\ a' \wedge distance\ (trg\ a')\ m\ x\ \wedge \\ valid\text{-}edge\ a' \wedge trg\ a' = n) \end{array}}{slice\text{-}kind\ n_c\ a = (\lambda s.\ False)_{\surd}}\ \text{SK4}$$

$$\frac{\begin{array}{c} src\ a \notin backward\text{-}slice\ n_c \quad m \in obs\ (src\ a)\ (backward\text{-}slice\ n_c) \\ kind\ a = (Q)_{\surd} \quad \neg\, distance\ (trg\ a)\ m\ x \quad distance\ (src\ a)\ m\ (x+1) \end{array}}{slice\text{-}kind\ n_c\ a = (\lambda s.\ False)_{\surd}}\ \text{SK5}$$

$$\frac{\begin{array}{c} src\ a \notin backward\text{-}slice\ n_c \quad obs\ (src\ a)\ (backward\text{-}slice\ n_c) = \emptyset \\ trg\ a = (SOME\ n.\ \exists a'.\ src\ a = src\ a' \wedge valid\text{-}edge\ a' \wedge trg\ a' = n) \end{array}}{slice\text{-}kind\ n_c\ a = (\lambda s.\ True)_{\surd}}\ \text{SK6}$$

$$\frac{\begin{array}{c} src\ a \notin backward\text{-}slice\ n_c \quad obs\ (src\ a)\ (backward\text{-}slice\ n_c) = \emptyset \\ trg\ a \neq (SOME\ n.\ \exists a'.\ src\ a = src\ a' \wedge valid\text{-}edge\ a' \wedge trg\ a' = n) \end{array}}{slice\text{-}kind\ n_c\ a = (\lambda s.\ False)_{\surd}}\ \text{SK7}$$

Figure 3.14.: Rules for *slice-kind* n_c

is not part of the standard control dependence slice, so we assign no-ops to its ougoing edges. From its two successors 7 and 9, the latter is closer to the next observable node, which is 10. Hence, the edge to 9 is labelled $(\lambda s.\ True)_{\surd}$, the one to 7 $(\lambda s.\ False)_{\surd}$. Thus, we can never enter the loop body, which is the desirable behaviour.

However, again this does not suffice. Reconsider the left sliced CFG in Fig. 3.15, but assume that node 4 does not assign x, but z. Then, neither 4 would be in the slice for 10, nor its control dependence predecessor 3. The next observable node from 3 would then be 10, which is equidistant for both successors of 3, namely 4 and 5. Thus, both outgoing edges from 3 would have $(\lambda s.\ True)_{\surd}$ as *slice-kind*, rendering the sliced CFG non-deterministic. To avoid this, rule SK3 always chooses one *closest* target node via the *SOME* operator, Isabelle's anal-

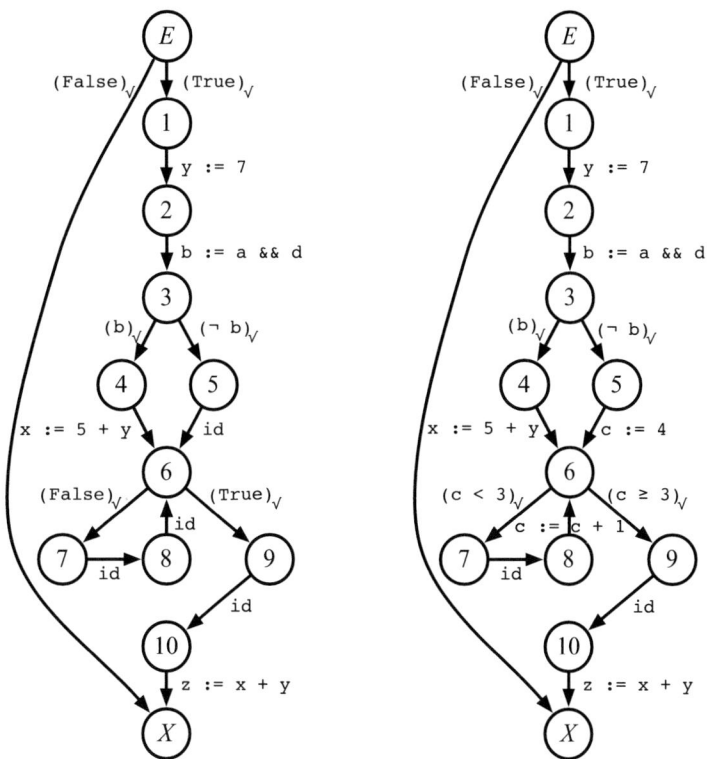

Figure 3.15.: Sliced CFGs for the example from Sec. 3.1.2

ogon for Hilbert's ε-operator, and assigns $(\lambda s.\ True)_{\sqrt{}}$ only to the edge that reaches this selected target node. Note that *SOME x. P x* always returns the same *x* that fulfils *P*. All other edges whose target nodes are nevertheless *closest*, but not selected via *SOME*, are labelled $(\lambda s.\ False)_{\sqrt{}}$, see rule SK4. In [3], Amtoft seems not to be aware of this problem, he assigns all edges with a closest successor with $(\lambda s.\ True)_{\sqrt{}}$. Following rule SK5, $(\lambda s.\ False)_{\sqrt{}}$ is also assigned to all edges whose target node is not closest to the next observable node.

If the source node's *obs* set is empty, we only have to take care that the sliced graph does not get non-deterministic; again, *SOME* takes care of this, see rules SK6 and SK7. Amtoft allows to assign either $(\lambda s.\ True)_{\sqrt{}}$ or $(\lambda s.\ False)_{\sqrt{}}$ to any edge whose source node's observable set is empty, ignoring the non-determinism problem.

By defining *slice-kind* this way, I could prove that the sliced graph is still deterministic (see the last rule in locale *CFG-wf* in Fig. 3.7); i.e., it is valid to replace *kind* with *slice-kind* n_c in rule *deterministic*, it would still hold. Amtoft's approach to allow more than one $(\lambda s.\ True)_{\sqrt{}}$ edge does not break the proof in the weak simulation sense. Yet, at the end of this section I will also provide correctness lemmas arguing about executions, i.e., control flow paths; in this case, the fact that only one path in the sliced graph can be executed is of great value.

To obtain a sliced CFG in the usual understanding, one would eliminate all no-op edges and the respective nodes, taking care of reachability issues. Since the paths in this graph have the same behaviour w.r.t. *preds* and *transfers* as the sliced CFG annotated with *slice-kind*s, all the following correctness properties also hold for this reduced graph.

Moves in the Graphs

As mentioned before, I consider the original and the sliced CFG as labelled transition systems (LTS); however, it is not yet clear what its states, transitions and labels are. I define an LTS state to be a (node, state) pair and call the LTS transitions *moves*. Moves capture the effect of traversing an edge a in one of the graphs, a τ-move $-a\rightarrow_\tau$ starting in a node not in the slice, whereas the source node of a non-τ-move $-a\rightarrow$ is part of the slice. Hence, the LTS labels are the edges whose source node is in the slice, i.e., whose semantic information is still present in the sliced CFG.

$$
\frac{\begin{array}{c} src\ a \notin backward\text{-}slice\ n_c \\ valid\text{-}edge\ a \\ pred\ (f\,a)\ s \qquad transfer\ (f\,a)\ s = s' \end{array}}{n_c,f \vdash (src\ a,s)\ -a\rightarrow_\tau (trg\ a,s')}
\qquad
\frac{\begin{array}{c} src\ a \in backward\text{-}slice\ n_c \\ valid\text{-}edge\ a \\ pred\ (f\,a)\ s \qquad transfer\ (f\,a)\ s = s' \end{array}}{n_c,f \vdash (src\ a,s)\ -a\rightarrow (trg\ a,s')}
$$

The parameter f is replaced with *kind* if we traverse the original, with *slice-kind* n_c if we traverse the sliced graph of n_c. An observable move $=\Rightarrow$ then consists of arbitrary many τ-moves $(=\Rightarrow_\tau$ is the reflexive transitive closure of $- \rightarrow_\tau$), followed by a non-τ-move:

$$
\frac{n_c,f \vdash (n,s) = as \Rightarrow_\tau (n',s') \qquad n_c,f \vdash (n',s') -a\rightarrow (n'',s'')}{n_c,f \vdash (n,s) = as@[a] \Rightarrow (n'',s'')}
$$

Note that the edge kind of a τ-move in the sliced graph is always a no-op; this is due to the fact that the source node of the respective edge is not in the slice. Analogously, *as* edges kinds in $=as \Rightarrow_\tau$ are no-ops.

The Weak Simulation

I define two (node, state) pairs to be weakly similar (i.e., in relation $WS\ n_c$), if both nodes are valid, the observable sets of both nodes w.r.t. *backward-slice* n_c are equal, and the values of all relevant variables are equal in both states:

$$\frac{\textit{valid-node } n \qquad \textit{valid-node } n' \\ \textit{obs } n \ (\textit{backward-slice } n_c) = \textit{obs } n' \ (\textit{backward-slice } n_c) \\ \forall V \in \textit{rv } n_c \ n. \ \textit{state-val } s \ V = \textit{state-val } s' \ V}{((n,s),(n',s')) \in WS\ n_c}$$

Relevant variables $\textit{rv } n_c \ n$ are all those variables which are used in some node being in the backward slice of n_c, reachable from n via a CFG path and not redefined on this path:

$$\frac{n \ -as \rightarrow* \ n' \\ n' \in \textit{backward-slice } n_c \qquad V \in \textit{Use } n' \qquad \forall nx \in \textit{set } (\textit{srcs } as). \ V \notin \textit{Def } nx}{V \in \textit{rv } n_c \ n}$$

To put it simply, only the values of the relevant variables of a node can influence other nodes in the slice. Thus, at some node n, states that have equal values in the relevant variables of n are observably equivalent for the slice; in combination with the observable sets being equal, two (node, state) configuration tuples are in the weak simulation if they are not distinguishable by the slice.

Via this weak simulation, I prove the correctness of static intraprocedural slicing by showing that the correctness property from Sec. 3.3.1 holds for $WS\ n_c$. The conclusion uses *transfer* (*slice-kind* n_c (*last as*)) s_2 instead of *transfers* (*map* (*slice-kind* n_c) (*as'*@(*last as*))) s_2, to highlight that only traversing *last as* has any semantic effect; the *slice-kind*s of the edges in *as'* are all no-ops, so both executions yield the same result.

Theorem 3.2 *Correctness of Static Intraprocedural Slicing:*

$$\frac{((n_1,s_1),(n_2,s_2)) \in WS\ n_c \qquad n_c, \textit{kind} \vdash (n_1,s_1) =as\Rightarrow (n_1',s_1')}{\exists s_2' \ as'. \ s_2' = \textit{transfer } (\textit{slice-kind } n_c \ (\textit{last as})) \ s_2 \wedge ((n_1',s_1'),(n_1',s_2')) \in WS\ n_c \wedge \\ n_c, \textit{slice-kind } n_c \vdash (n_2,s_2) =as'@(\textit{last as})\Rightarrow (n_1',s_2')}$$

Proof. The proof of this theorem uses two lemmas, which guarantee that both simulation diagrams from Fig. 3.12 hold:

(a) The weak simulation is invariant under τ-moves in the original graph, if the target node of the moves has a non-empty observable set:

$$\frac{((n_1,s_1),(n_2,s_2)) \in WS\ n_c \qquad n_c,kind \vdash (n_1,s_1) =as\Rightarrow_\tau (n_1',s_1') \qquad obs\ n_1'\ (backward\text{-}slice\ n_c) \neq \emptyset}{((n_1',s_1'),(n_2,s_2)) \in WS\ n_c}$$

I prove this first by an induction on the number of τ-moves, and second by guaranteeing that the values of the relevant variables in the target state are again equal to those in the initial state.

(b) To traverse an observable edge a in the original graph yields an observable move in the sliced graph via a path ending with a, whose initial similar state is updated as if it had also traversed just a:

$$\frac{((n_1,s_1),(n_2,s_2)) \in WS\ n_c \qquad n_c,kind \vdash (n_1,s_1) -a\rightarrow (n_1',s_1')}{\exists\ as\ s_2'.\ s_2' = transfer\ (slice\text{-}kind\ n_c\ a)\ s_2 \wedge ((n_1',s_1'),(n_1',s_2')) \in WS\ n_c\ \wedge \\ n_c,slice\text{-}kind\ n_c \vdash (n_2,s_2) =as@[a]\Rightarrow (n_1',s_2') \in WS\ n_c}$$

The crucial part in this proof is to make sure that the values of the relevant variables in the states after traversing edge a, both in the original and the sliced graph, remain equal.

$\square$

Fundamental Property of Slicing

Whereas the above proof guarantees that the intraprocedural slicing is indeed correct, its conclusion differs from the usual understanding of correctness of slicing. Intuitively, the wide-spread informal correctness requirement for slicing can be sketched like this: *"After performing the slicing algorithm, the observable effects at the slicing node are preserved."* These effects include which path was taken to reach the slicing node and which values the variables that are used in this node contain. Hence, I show another correctness theorem called *fundamental property of slicing*, which is stated along the lines of the intuitive description. To this end, we need a function *slice-edges*, which filters all edges from a given path whose source node is in the slice:

$$slice\text{-}edges\ n_c\ as \equiv [a \leftarrow as.\ src\ a \in backward\text{-}slice\ n_c]$$

The next two facts show that *slice-edges* on moves behaves as expected:

$$\frac{n_c,f \vdash (n,s) =as\Rightarrow_\tau (n',s')}{slice\text{-}edges\ n_c\ as = []} \qquad \frac{n_c,f \vdash (n,s) =as\Rightarrow (n',s')}{slice\text{-}edges\ n_c\ as = [last\ as]}$$

Now, we can define the alternative correctness property: assume a path *as* in the original graph from *n* to slicing node *n'*, whose predicates hold starting from initial state *s*. Then there exists a path *as'* in the sliced graph of *n'* between those nodes, whose predicates also hold when starting in *s*, and who has the same *slice-edges*, hence visits the same nodes in the slice in the same order as the original path. Moreover, the values of the variables used in *n'* are the same, no matter if we traverse *as* in the original or *as'* in the sliced graph starting in initial state *s*. Equality of both paths cannot be guaranteed: consider an `if` whose predicate and branches are not in the slice. Then the sliced path can traverse another branch as the original path, if the no-op predicates in the slice have been chosen unluckily.

Theorem 3.3 *Fundamental Property of Slicing:*

$$\frac{n -as\rightarrow* n' \qquad preds\ (kinds\ as)\ s}{\begin{array}{l} \exists\, as'.\ n -as'\rightarrow* n' \wedge preds\ (slice\text{-}kinds\ n'\ as')\ s\ \wedge \\ \quad slice\text{-}edges\ n'\ as = slice\text{-}edges\ n'\ as' \wedge \\ \quad (V \in Use\ n'.\ state\text{-}val\ (transfers\ (slice\text{-}kinds\ n'\ as')\ s)\ V = \\ \qquad state\text{-}val\ (transfers\ (kinds\ as)\ s)\ V) \end{array}}$$

Proof. To show the above property, we need the fact that traversing a path can always be split into several observable moves (one for every edge in its *slice-edges*), followed by τ-moves. Then, a case distinction determines if *slice-edges n' as* is empty, applying the weak simulation correctness property – lifted to arbitrary sequences of observable moves – if it is not. □

For semantically well-formed CFGs, we can lift this theorem from graphs to the semantics. Instead of a path in the original graph, we assume a semantic evaluation $\langle c,s \rangle \Rightarrow \langle c',s' \rangle$ and identify the nodes *n* and *n'* with *c* and *c'*, respectively. The conclusion now states equivalence of the behaviour of the path traversal in the slice with the result of the semantic evaluation:

Theorem 3.4 *Fundamental Property of Semantics and Slicing:*

$$\frac{n \triangleq c \qquad \langle c,s \rangle \Rightarrow \langle c',s' \rangle}{\begin{array}{l} \exists\, n'\ as.\ n -as\rightarrow* n' \wedge preds\ (slice\text{-}kinds\ n'\ as)\ s \wedge n' \triangleq c' \wedge \\ \quad (\forall\, V \in Use\ n'.\ state\text{-}val\ (transfers\ (slice\text{-}kinds\ n'\ as)\ s)\ V = state\text{-}val\ s'\ V) \end{array}}$$

83

3.3.3. Applying Control Dependences

The correctness proof in the previous section was parameterized by a function from nodes to node sets called *backward-slice* and certain constraints. In this section, I show how one can use the three different control dependences presented in Sec. 3.1.1 to formalize the respective backward slice and that each of these slices is a valid parameter of the *BackwardSlice* locale, i.e, it fulfils its assumption. Showing the correctness property for any further control dependences is analogously done by proving these assumptions, so no insight into the concrete correctness proof formalization is needed.

Standard and weak control dependence uses the *PDG* locale introduced in Sec. 3.2.3 to define the backward slice *PDG-BS*. To this end, all assumptions for *controls* from this locale have to hold for *scd* and *wcd* as defined in Sec. 3.2.2: *(-Exit-)* may not be control dependent on anything and a node must have a nonempty path to all the nodes it controls. This is easily proven by unfolding the definition of *scd* and *wcd* and the fact that *(-Exit-)* is no postdominator for any valid node.

Finally, it remains to show that *PDG-BS* meets the constraints of locale *BackwardSlice* from the previous section, regardless if it employs *scd* or *wcd*. Auxiliary lemmas guarantee that the backward slice is closed under the respective control dependence and that every node in the observable set of a node is a (strong) postdominator. I prove by contradiction, that the observable set of every valid node is either the empty set or a singleton: if a node had two distinct nodes in its observable set, then only one of them could (strongly) postdominate this node; yet, the auxiliary lemma states that every node in *obs* has to be a (strong) postdominator, contradiction. Together with the fact that the backward slice of a PDG is closed under data dependence, this suffices to fulfil the assumptions of *BackwardSlice*.

Weak order dependence does not use the *PDG* locale, but defines its own backward slice *WOD-BS*, see Sec. 3.2.2. The proof that the observable set w.r.t. *WOD-BS* is at most a singleton is surprisingly similar to the proofs above. Instead of arguing over (strong) postdomination a corresponding argument holds: if a node had two distinct nodes in its observable set, then the node itself, being a control dependence predecessor, has to be in the slice; however, in this case, the observable set of this node contains only itself.

3.4 Instantiations

Exploiting the above results, proving slicing correct for any language just boils down to providing a technique to formalize a CFG for any program in this language and proving that this formalization fulfils all properties required in the different locales. Thus, instantiating the correctness proof of slicing with a language requires no insight into the slicing definitions or proof details; anyone familiar with formalizing languages can reprove it for a wide variety of languages (imperative and object-oriented).

In the following, I show how to instantiate the framework with two different programming languages, a simple While language without procedures (Winskel [138] calls it **IMP**) and Jinja VM byte code [61]. Static slicing with weak order dependence is correct for both languages, as it does not need assumptions additional to those in locale *CFG*. However, for the correctness of slicing using standard and weak control dependence their respective prerequisites from locales *Postdomination* and *StrongPostdomination* (as described in Sec. 3.2.2) are shown to be valid.

There are also cases in which such an instantiation does not work, even if a formalized language semantics exist. For example, I considered instantiating the framework with Simpl [100], a very expressive sequential imperative programming language, formalized in Isabelle/HOL. Unfortunately, this language is inherently non-deterministic, e.g. the statement *Spec r* evaluates in some state *s* to an arbitrary state *t*, such that $(s,t) \in r$. However, my framework allows only deterministic update edges, so this behaviour cannot be simulated. Also, the formalization of the *Def* and *Use* sets of a node representing *Spec* is far from trivial, as statically you have to consider all possible executions at run-time. Hence, I dropped the thought of using Simpl.

3.4.1. A Simple Imperative Language: WHILE

WHILE features two value types *Intg::val* and *Bool::val*, which represent integer and boolean (i.e., *true* and *false*) values. Expressions consist of constant values, variables and binary operators. The language supports five different statements of type *cmd*: the no-op statement *Skip*, assignment of expression *e* to a variable *V*, written $V:=e$, sequential composition of statements ;;, conditionals *if* (*b*) c_1 *else* c_2 and while loops *while* (*b*) *c'*. Defining the state is easy: it is just a simple mapping

Basic: $c \vdash (\text{-Entry-}) - (\lambda s.\ \textit{False})_{\sqrt{}} \rightarrow (\text{-Exit-})$
$c \vdash (\text{-Entry-}) - (\lambda s.\ \textit{True})_{\sqrt{}} \rightarrow (\text{-}0\text{-})$

Skip: $\textit{Skip} \vdash (\text{-}0\text{-}) - \Uparrow id \rightarrow (\text{-Exit-})$

Ass: $V{:=}e \vdash (\text{-}0\text{-}) - \Uparrow \lambda s.\ s(V := [\![e]\!]s) \rightarrow (\text{-}1\text{-})$
$V{:=}e \vdash (\text{-}1\text{-}) - \Uparrow id \rightarrow (\text{-Exit-})$

Seq:
$$\frac{c_1 \vdash n -et\rightarrow (\text{-Exit-}) \qquad n \neq (\text{-Entry-})}{c_1{;;}\ c_2 \vdash n -et\rightarrow (\text{-}0\text{-}) \oplus \#{:}c_1}$$

$$\frac{c_1 \vdash n -et\rightarrow n' \quad n' \neq (\text{-Exit-})}{c_1{;;}\ c_2 \vdash n -et\rightarrow n'} \qquad \frac{c_2 \vdash n -et\rightarrow n' \quad n \neq (\text{-Entry-})}{c_1{;;}\ c_2 \vdash n \oplus \#{:}c_1 -et\rightarrow n' \oplus \#{:}c_1}$$

If: $if\ (b)\ c_1\ else\ c_2 \vdash (\text{-}0\text{-}) - (\lambda s.\ [\![b]\!]s = \lfloor true \rfloor)_{\sqrt{}} \rightarrow (\text{-}0\text{-}) \oplus 1$
$if\ (b)\ c_1\ else\ c_2 \vdash (\text{-}0\text{-}) - (\lambda s.\ [\![b]\!]s = \lfloor false \rfloor)_{\sqrt{}} \rightarrow (\text{-}0\text{-}) \oplus (\#{:}c_1 + 1)$

$$\frac{c_1 \vdash n -et\rightarrow n' \qquad n \neq (\text{-Entry-})}{if\ (b)\ c_1\ else\ c_2 \vdash n \oplus 1 -et\rightarrow n' \oplus 1}$$

$$\frac{c_2 \vdash n -et\rightarrow n' \qquad n \neq (\text{-Entry-})}{if\ (b)\ c_1\ else\ c_2 \vdash n \oplus (\#{:}c_1 + 1) -et\rightarrow n' \oplus (\#{:}c_1 + 1)}$$

While: $while\ (b)\ c' \vdash (\text{-}0\text{-}) - (\lambda s.\ [\![b]\!]s = \lfloor true \rfloor)_{\sqrt{}} \rightarrow (\text{-}0\text{-}) \oplus 2$
$while\ (b)\ c' \vdash (\text{-}0\text{-}) - (\lambda s.\ [\![b]\!]s = \lfloor false \rfloor)_{\sqrt{}} \rightarrow (\text{-}1\text{-})$
$while\ (b)\ c' \vdash (\text{-}1\text{-}) - \Uparrow id \rightarrow (\text{-Exit-})$

$$\frac{c' \vdash n -et\rightarrow (\text{-Exit-}) \qquad n \neq (\text{-Entry-})}{while\ (b)\ c' \vdash n \oplus 2 -et\rightarrow (\text{-}0\text{-})}$$

$$\frac{c' \vdash n -et\rightarrow n' \qquad n \neq (\text{-Entry-}) \qquad n' \neq (\text{-Exit-})}{while\ (b)\ c' \vdash n \oplus 2 -et\rightarrow n' \oplus 2}$$

Figure 3.16.: Rules for WHILE CFG edges

from variables to values $var \rightharpoonup val$. The partial function $[\![e]\!]s$ returns $\lfloor v \rfloor$, if expression e evaluates to value v in state s, and $None$, if e cannot be evaluated in state s (e.g. in the case of mal-formed programs).

As any graph, the CFG for an arbitrary WHILE program is defined via its nodes and edges. Nodes are of type $w\text{-}node$, which incorporates inner nodes $(\text{-}l\text{-})$ bearing a label l of type nat, and the special nodes (-Entry-) and (-Exit-). $n \oplus i$ adds i to the label number of n and returns a new node bearing this number as label, if n is an inner node, (-Entry-) and (-Exit-) are unchanged. $\#{:}c$ denotes the number of inner nodes we need for a CFG of statement c.

WHILE CFG edges have type *w-edge* = *w-node* × *state edge-kind* × *w-node*. A CFG edge valid for program *prog* is written $prog \vdash n -et\rightarrow n'$ and consists of a description of the program *prog* of type *cmd* for which this CFG is generated, a source node n, an edge kind *et* of type *state edge-kind* and a target node n'. Fig. 3.16 shows the formal rules: basically, the CFG is constructed via first constructing recursively the CFGs for the sub-statements, then combining these graphs into a single one, eventually adjusting the labels so that they remain unique. Also, we add one additional node after every variable assignment node and every *while* node (reachable via the edge where the loop predicate is false). These nodes are inserted for semantic well-formedness: as the semantic reduction of a variable assignment or while loop with invalid predicate leads to a *Skip* statement, we also need a CFG edge from the respective nodes to a node corresponding to a *Skip* statement. As the outgoing edge of this node is by construction of the CFG a no-op edge (function *id* is applied to the state, see the second rule for *V*:=*e* and the third rule for *while* (*b*) *c'* in Fig. 3.16), this adjustment is valid.

Next, I prove that these definitions fulfil the assumptions made in locale *CFG*. Hence, I define *src*, *trg* and *kind* as projections from *w-edge* and that *a* is a valid edge for a program *prog* iff $prog \vdash src\, a -kind\, a\rightarrow trg\, a$ holds. The *Use* set is the set of all variables in the expression on the right hand side of a variable assignment and of those occurring in a condition or loop predicate. The *Def* set contains only the variable that eventually gets assigned. The structural and well-formedness properties of the WHILE CFG are then easily shown via rule induction on the CFG edge rules.

To show that the CFG behaviour corresponds to the intended semantics (i.e., the CFG is semantically well-formed, see Sec. 3.2.1), I formalize a standard semantics for WHILE and a mapping from nodes bearing a label to the statement they represent. The latter is used to define a *label semantics*, a relation between (*cmd*,*state*,*nat*) tuples, which bridges the gap between the evaluation of the semantics and the transition system behaviour of the traversal of CFG edges. Using this label semantics, the proof for semantic well-formedness is quite straightforward, for details see [131, Sec. 3].

By construction, (i) every CFG node is reachable from the entry node, (ii) can reach the unique exit node, and (iii) has a finite number of successors. Together with the proof of the locale assumptions above, this guarantees the correctness of static intraprocedural using

$$\frac{\begin{array}{c}(\textit{instrs-of } P\ C\ M)_{[pc]} \in \{\text{LOAD } idx, \text{STORE } idx, \text{PUSH } val, \text{POP}, \text{IADD}, \text{CMPEQ}\} \\ f = (\lambda s.\ \textit{exec-instr } (\textit{instrs-of } P\ C\ M)_{[pc]}\ P\ s\ (\textit{length } cs)\ (\textit{stkLength } P\ C\ M\ pc)) \\ \textit{valid-callstack } (P, C_0, \textit{Main})\ ((C, M, pc)\cdot cs)\end{array}}{(P, C_0, \textit{Main}) \vdash (\text{-}(C, M, pc)\cdot cs, \textit{None} \text{ -}) - \Uparrow f \rightarrow (\text{-}(C, M, \textit{Suc } pc)\cdot cs, \textit{None} \text{ -})}$$

Figure 3.17.: Example of Jinja CFG edges for simple instructions

standard and weak control dependence as well as weak order dependence for any WHILE program.

3.4.2. A Sophisticated Object Oriented Byte Code Language: Jinja VM Byte Code

This instantiation was accomplished by my colleague, Denis Lohner, thus is no contribution of this theses; yet it is included, as it is an impressive demonstration of the applicability of the slicing framework.

Jinja [61] models a large subset of the Java language, including operational semantics for the source code and the virtual machine byte code, both with type safety proofs, a compiler from the former to the latter and a byte code verifier (BCV), both verified. Jinja is fully object-oriented and features exception throwing and catching. Slicing such languages is far from trivial. Even though the framework is for intraprocedural slicing, it can still be instantiated with a large subset of Jinja, as non-recursive methods can be sliced by inlining method calls; for programs without method calls the intraprocedural slice is well-defined anyway.

Proving slicing correct with the framework requires instantiations of the locales *CFG-wf* and (if standard or weak control dependence shall be used) *CFGExit-wf*, *Postdomination* and *StrongPostdomination*, which all extend the *CFG* locale. Hence, again, the first step is to formalize an appropriate CFG for Jinja byte code.

The Jinja byte code language is, to put it simply, a goto-language using a stack machine with a program counter identifying the current statement in an instruction list. A program P consists of a list of class declarations, each with its method declarations where the method bodies are the aforementioned instruction lists. Each CFG node is labelled with a call stack cs storing the call frames that consist of class name C, method name M and instruction pointer pc; its top element determines the instruction to execute. Although a call stack is not necessary when methods are inlined, we use them in our formalization, as it makes the adaption to the interprocedural case (see Sec. 5.4.2) much easier; basically, when we say method inlining, we mean that we include the method's CFG edges at all its respective call sites.

The edges are labelled with appropriate predicates, e.g. for method dispatch and exception handler delegation, or with updates via the *exec-instr* function, which simulates Jinja's *exec* function appropriately for our state representation; the latter executes one step of the byte code semantics in Jinja. Simple instructions like LOAD, IADD, etc., have one outgoing edge to a node where the instruction pointer is increased by one, see Fig. 3.17 (*valid-callstack* ensures some required well-formedness properties of the current program point, the use of *None* will be explained later). GOTO increases the instruction pointer with the provided parameter. IFFALSE has two successors, INVOKE outgoing edges for every statically determinable dispatch target.[4] All instructions that could trigger exceptions, like NEW, PUTFIELD, CHECKCAST, THROW, have additional edges for exceptional control flow to exception handlers or, if not provided, to the exit node.

Many instructions (e.g. INVOKE or THROW) can only be modeled with multiple edges, first predicate ones to determine the target, each followed by one edge updating the state accordingly; hence we need additional CFG nodes in between. Such intermediate nodes cannot be identified by a call frame, as they do not match a concrete instruction. Hence, they carry in addition to the call frame of their predecessor node also a continuation, stating the next node to execute; for non-intermediate nodes, this continuation is obviously *None*.

Next, the locale *CFG-wf* has to be instantiated. The problem here is that Jinja byte code uses a stack machine, thus keeping track of the variables is a bit tricky. For example, a program could LOAD a value onto the stack, then do some stack-involving computation where this variable is not used, and thereafter STORE the value again; then the STORE must be data dependent on the corresponding LOAD, which means the same variable must be in the LOAD's *Def* set and in the STORE's *Use* set. Therefore, we say every stack position corresponds to a variable (counted from bottom up); also the local variables are identified through their index positions. Additionally, to distinguish variables of different methods, stack and local variables are labelled with the appropriate call depth available from the CFG node. The heap is treated as a whole and thus instructions are regarded either to define or use the complete heap or to not define and use it at all. This

---

[4]Using points-to analysis one could narrow this set, hence gaining precision.

is a conservative approximation, but the properties of *CFG-wf* are not violated. One could gain precision here by using a points-to analysis.

The tricky part is to determine the index position of the stack variables that are defined or used at a given node. However, fixing the *Def* and *Use* set is no problem, if the index of the stack's top element is known. Jinja's BCV, which guarantees the stack length to be the same at any fixed program point, no matter how one gets there, provides this index. The state is then defined as a pair of a mapping from the set of variables to appropriate values and a heap.

By means of these formalizations we are finally able to instantiate the *CFG-wf* locale and to show that the assumed properties hold. Except for *Entry-empty* (we simply define the *Def* and *Use* set of the entry node to be empty), these properties are shown by case analysis. Having the locale instantiated, we have done all to show slicing correct for Jinja byte code using weak order dependence. We define a CFG as valid, if every node reaches the exit node and is reached by the entry node. Together with a proof that the CFG is finitely branching, we were able to instantiate the locales *Postdomination* and *StrongPostdomination*; hence we proved slicing correct for standard and weak control dependence.

We also proved our formalization of the Jinja byte code CFG to be semantically equivalent to Jinja's *exec* function, which defines the operational semantics of Jinja byte code. Furthermore, we have explicitly proven state conformance as stated by Jinja's BCV to be invariant under the *transfer* function from Sec. 3.2.1 for the CFG.

4

Correctness of Dynamic Slicing

Some slicing algorithms assume that run-time information, e.g. input values or concrete execution traces, is available. Then, slicing is applied only in this concrete situation. These approaches can be subsumed under *dynamic slicing*, and are applied in e.g. debugging [142].

A question that now naturally arises is: is the framework presented in the previous chapter also applicable for dynamic slicing? As it turns out, most of the framework can be reused for this task, with only some minor changes in connotation such as dynamic dependences and dynamic dependence graphs, see the next section. Dynamic slicing itself only considers a specific trace in an initial state instead of the whole CFG, but again replaces semantic information of non-slice edges with no-ops, via a bit vector as shown in Sec. 4.2. I prove in Sec. 4.3 the correctness of dynamic slicing, along the lines of the "Fundamental Property of Slicing" as introduced in Sec. 3.3.2. As no graph is sliced, but only a specific trace, i.e., a certain path in the program, I use the notion *path slicing* for this special kind of dynamic slicing.

4.1 Framework Adaptions

A path in the abstract CFG of the framework in the previous section is equivalent to an *execution trace*. However, as the framework is purely intraprocedural, we assume that in the respective CFG the bodies of all procedure calls are *inlined*; this is exactly what you can see when examining a trace. In the presence of unrestricted recursion this may lead to infinite paths in the CFG and thus, to an infinite CFG. However, this poses no problem for the framework, as we claim nowhere that the set of nodes or edges has to be finite. Yet, for programs with recursion, this approach of dynamic slicing is of course questionable.

We call a CFG where all method calls are inlined and whose paths are considered traces *trace control flow graph* (short: TCFG). Apart from that, we reuse all the locales and definitions presented in Sec. 3.2.1, they are also valid for TCFGs.

As we only want to slice given traces, we are no longer interested in arbitrary dependences in the CFG, but focus on those which occur along the path under consideration. To capture this in the dependence definitions, we need an additional parameter for the path, see the following definition of dynamic data dependence:

$$n \text{ influences } V \text{ in } n' \text{ via } as \equiv V \in Def\ n \land V \in Use\ n' \land n -as \to* n' \land$$
$$(\exists a'\ as'.\ as = a' \cdot as' \land (\forall n'' \in set\ (srcs\ as').\ V \notin Def\ n''))$$

It holds that n *influences* V *in* $n' = (\exists as.\ n$ *influences* V *in* n' *via* $as)$.

It is not clear how to define weak order dependence on traces. A naive lifting of a ternary relation to two binary relations may introduce spurious dependences. Consider again the weak order triples in the example in Sec. 3.1.2. If we assume a control dependence between a node and any node that occurs in one of its successor pairs, we could come up with a huge amount of dependences; e.g. node 3 would have control dependences leading to every node except 1, 2 and E, of which many are spurious. Hence, dynamic slicing in this framework restricts to binary control dependences and a (dynamic) program dependence graph can be used, parameterized with a dynamic binary control dependence n *controls* n' *via* as. To this end, I defined a locale *DynPDG* analogous to locale *PDG* (see Fig. 3.11), all occurrences of the static dependences (*influences in* and *controls*) replaced with their dynamic counterparts (*influences in via* and *controls via*). Therefore, the edges of the dynamic PDG as well as their reflexive transitive closure $(n -as \to_{d*} n')$ now carry the respective path information:

$$\text{If } n \text{ controls } n' \text{ via } as \text{ then } n -as \to_{cd} n'$$
$$\text{If } n \text{ influences } V \text{ in } n' \text{ via } as \text{ then } n -\{V\}as \to_{dd} n'$$

The dynamic PDG can be instantiated with the dynamic variants of standard and weak control dependence; their definitions are straightforward. Yet, in dynamic slicing, control dependences are often omitted: as we only consider one trace in a certain initial state, the information which node controls which is sometimes unnecessary. In fact, the dynamic PDG can be instantiated with the empty control dependence relation, so that we only perform a data slice, and still the correctness property shown in Sec. 4.3 holds. Moreover, because of this, it can be instantiated with *any* control dependence, as a nonempty control dependence yields a slice containing more nodes, i.e., more edges keep their original semantics.

4.2 Dynamic Backward Slicing

The only relevant information the slice of a path has to provide is if a certain edge gets included in it or not; this determines if the semantic information of the edge is kept or replaced with a no-op. Thus, I modeled a path slice via a bit vector, i.e., a *bool list*, of the same length as the edge list *as* of the path, being *True* at position i iff the edge at position i of edge list *as* is part of the slice. An edge is in the path slice if its source node has a PDG path to the slicing node n' with an edge list corresponding to the appropriate suffix of *as*. The function *slice-path as* computes this bit vector by traversing the edge list *as*. Note that the last node of the reduced path being the slicing node n' is invariant throughout this computation:

$$\begin{aligned}
\textit{slice-path } [] \quad &\equiv [] \\
\textit{slice-path } (a{\cdot}as) &\equiv \textit{let } n' = \textit{last } (\textit{trgs } (a{\cdot}as)) \textit{ in} \\
&\quad (\textit{src } a\ -a{\cdot}as{\rightarrow}_d* \ n'){\cdot}\textit{slice-path as}
\end{aligned}$$

The relation $\preceq_b$ compares bit vectors: $bs \preceq_b bs'$ holds if they agree in length and bs' is *True* at least at those elements where bs is *True*. The maximal element w.r.t. $\preceq_b$ is *True* in every entry.

Combining the bit vector and the initial path yields the edge kind list of the sliced path. To do so, we need some machinery. The function *no-op et* returns for every edge kind *et* the respective no-op:

$$\textit{no-op } {\Uparrow}f \equiv {\Uparrow}id \qquad \textit{no-op } (Q)_{\sqrt{}} \equiv (\lambda s.\ \textit{True})_{\sqrt{}}$$

The function *select-edge-kinds* filters from an edge list *as* all its edge kinds as indicated via the bit vector *bs*; the edge kinds that are not kept are replaced with no-ops:

$$\begin{aligned}
\textit{select-edge-kinds } [] \ [] \ &\equiv \ [] \\
\textit{select-edge-kinds } (a{\cdot}as) \ (b{\cdot}bs) \ &\equiv \ (\textit{if } b \textit{ then kind } a \textit{ else no-op } (\textit{kind } a))
\end{aligned}$$

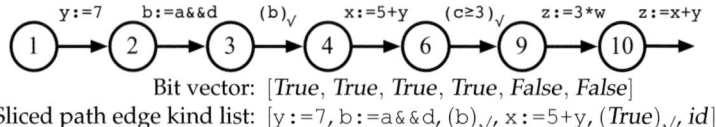

Bit vector: [*True*, *True*, *True*, *True*, *False*, *False*]
Sliced path edge kind list: [y:=7, b:=a&&d, (b)$_\sqrt{}$, x:=5+y, (*True*)$_\sqrt{}$, *id*]

Figure 4.1.: A trace, its bit vector and sliced path for node 10

I define *slice-kinds as* as a shortcut for *select-edge-kinds as* (*slice-path as*).

See Fig. 4.1 for an example of a trace – a path in simplified syntax, again taken from the running example from Sec. 3.1.2 –, the bit vector representing its sliced path (using dynamic standard control dependence) and the edge kind list of the respective sliced path.

4.3 Correctness Proof

Analogous to the "Fundamental Property of Slicing" (see Sec. 3.3.2), I call the correctness property of dynamic slicing "Fundamental Property of Dynamic Path Slicing". It states that traversing the edge kinds in the sliced path yields in the final state the same values for the variables used in the slicing node as traversing those on the original path, both starting in the same initial state, and that if all predicates on the original path are satisfiable, so are they in the sliced path.

A property about paths is naturally proved by induction, however, dynamic dependences begin and end in discrete points in the path; of course, induction cannot preserve such properties. Hence, we need an induction invariant that captures the effect of dependences, but also holds in intermediate points on the path. The function *dep-live-vars n as* collects all variables that can affect the value of a variable used in node n, the slicing node. Intuitively, *dep-live-vars* computes a kind of *Live Variables Analysis* as described in [80], restricted to only one path and ignoring those nodes, on which the parameter node is not (transitively) dependent.

Basically, dependent live variables serve the same purpose as the relevant variables as introduced in Sec. 3.3.2. However, in the dynamic case, just collecting the variables does not suffice. The analysis also has to provide information via which TCFG path we reach the node where this variable was used, such that no other node in the path redefines the variable; remember that this node must have a transitive dependence path to the slicing node. As a variable can be used multi-

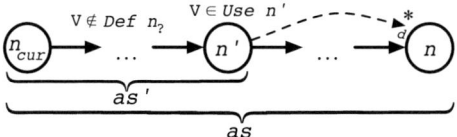

Figure 4.2.: Visualization of $(V, as') \in$ *dep-live-vars n as*

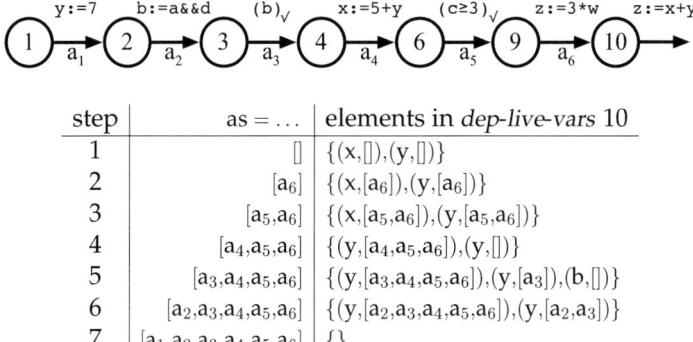

step	$as = \ldots$	elements in *dep-live-vars* 10
1	$[]$	$\{(x,[]),(y,[])\}$
2	$[a_6]$	$\{(x,[a_6]),(y,[a_6])\}$
3	$[a_5,a_6]$	$\{(x,[a_5,a_6]),(y,[a_5,a_6])\}$
4	$[a_4,a_5,a_6]$	$\{(y,[a_4,a_5,a_6]),(y,[])\}$
5	$[a_3,a_4,a_5,a_6]$	$\{(y,[a_3,a_4,a_5,a_6]),(y,[a_3]),(b,[])\}$
6	$[a_2,a_3,a_4,a_5,a_6]$	$\{(y,[a_2,a_3,a_4,a_5,a_6]),(y,[a_2,a_3])\}$
7	$[a_1,a_2,a_3,a_4,a_5,a_6]$	$\{\}$

Figure 4.3.: Calculation of dep-live-vars for node 10

ple times without being redefined in between, more than one path can satisfy this condition. Hence, *dep-live-vars* returns a (variable, edge list) pair set; i.e., a variable can be in this set multiple times if its reaching path component differs. *dep-live-vars* carries two parameters, first the node n for which this calculation is made, and second the edge list *as*, which denotes the executed sub-path from the current node to n (note that *dep-live-vars* traverses the path from right to left). An example: $(V, as') \in$ *dep-live-vars n as* states that our current position is the node that reaches n via path *as* and that a node where V is used can be reached via edges *as'*, on which no node redefines V; this node has dependences leading to n. Fig. 4.2 visualizes this construction. By definition, *as'* is always a prefix of *as*.

Instead of discussing its concrete rules, Fig. 4.3 shows an example computation on a trace of the running example. The path edges carry a label a_i, where $i \in 1 \ldots 6$, and its edge kind in the simplified syntax as introduced in Fig. 3.8. We assume dependences as depicted in the PDG in Fig. 3.3 (b), which uses standard control dependence. The

$$\frac{V \in \textit{Use } n'}{(V, [\,]) \in \textit{dep-live-vars } n' \,[\,]}$$

$$\frac{V \in \textit{Use } (\textit{src } a) \qquad \textit{src } a - a{\cdot}\textit{as}' \rightarrow_{cd} n'' \qquad n'' - \textit{as}'' \rightarrow_{d*} n'}{(V, [\,]) \in \textit{dep-live-vars } n' \, (a{\cdot}(\textit{as}' \,@\, \textit{as}''))}$$

$$\frac{(V, \textit{as}') \in \textit{dep-live-vars } n' \, \textit{as} \qquad V' \in \textit{Use } (\textit{src } a)}{n' = \textit{last } (\textit{trgs } (a{\cdot}\textit{as})) \qquad \textit{src } a - \{V\}a{\cdot}\textit{as}' \rightarrow_{dd} \textit{last}(\textit{trgs } (a{\cdot}\textit{as}'))}{(V', [\,]) \in \textit{dep-live-vars } n' \, (a{\cdot}\textit{as})}$$

$$\frac{(V, \textit{as}') \in \textit{dep-live-vars } n' \, \textit{as}}{n' = \textit{last } (\textit{trgs } (a{\cdot}\textit{as})) \qquad \neg \; \textit{src } a - \{V\}a{\cdot}\textit{as}' \rightarrow_{dd} \textit{last}(\textit{trgs } (a{\cdot}\textit{as}'))}{(V, a{\cdot}\textit{as}') \in \textit{dep-live-vars } n' \, (a{\cdot}\textit{as})}$$

Figure 4.4.: Formal rules for *dep-live-vars*

table at the bottom shows the computation step-by-step, traversing the path right to left. In the first step, we include both variables in the *Use* set of node 10, x and y, in the set, each with an empty path component. This component is prolonged in the next steps 2 and 3, no new pair is added to the set, as neither node 9 not 6 has a dependence path leading to 10. Step 4 eliminates all pairs with variable x from the set but adds a new pair (y,[]), as x is defined and y used in node 4, which has a data dependence to node 10. Node 3 adds b to the set in step 5, as this node controls node 4 – hence, due to node 4's outgoing data dependence edge there is a dependence path to node 10 – and uses b. Step 6 eliminates b again, since it is defined in node 2 , which has a data dependence to node 3. In steps 4 to 6, we kept the y-pairs, only adjusted the path components, because y was not defined in any of the visited nodes. Eventually, y is defined in the last step in node 1, eliminating the last pairs and thus returning the empty set. If you are interested in the concrete realization, the formal rules for *dep-live-vars* can be found in Fig. 4.4.

The induction of the correctness proof needs a relation between dependent live variables and dynamic dependences: as the sliced path only keeps those edges whose source node has a dynamic dependence path to the slicing node, the induction invariant *dep-live-vars* must be able to determine if such a path exists or not at the current position in the path. Or short: when do dependent live variables give rise to dependence paths? Suppose we have a pair $(V, \textit{as}')$ in *dep-live-vars* n *as* and a TCFG path from the target node of a valid edge a leading to n via edges as. If now V gets defined at the source node of edge a, there is a dynamic PDG path from $src\ a$ via edges $a \cdot as$ to n with a leading data dependence edge for variable V:

Lemma 4.1 *Relating Dependent Live Variables and Dependences:*

$$\frac{(V, as') \in dep\text{-}live\text{-}vars\ n\ as \qquad valid\text{-}edge\ a \qquad V \in Def\ (src\ a) \qquad trg\ a\ -as\!\rightarrow\!*\ n}{\exists\, nx\ as''.\ as = as'@as'' \land src\ a\ -\{V\}a\cdot as' \!\rightarrow_{dd}\ nx \land nx\ -as''\!\rightarrow_{d}*\ n}$$

I omit the proof of this lemma, the interested reader can find a proof sketch in [131], all the details can be found in [128].

This lemma is the key to prove a generalized version of the desired correctness result: assume a TCFG path $n\ -as\!\rightarrow\!*\ n'$ and two bit vectors $bs \preceq_b bs'$ the first one the result of *slice-path as*. Applying *slice-path as* to both of them yields edge kind lists es and es', respectively. Furthermore we have two states s and s' which agree on all variables in the *dep-live-vars* set of the slicing node n' on edge list as. If while traversing es' from initial state s' all predicates hold, so do all predicates on traversing es in initial state s and the values of all used variables in n' agree in the final states yielded by both traversals.

Lemma 4.2 *Generalized Correctness:*

$$\frac{\begin{array}{c} n\ -as\!\rightarrow\!*\ n' \\ bs \preceq_b bs' \qquad slice\text{-}path\ as = bs \qquad select\text{-}edge\text{-}kinds\ as\ bs = es \\ select\text{-}edge\text{-}kinds\ as\ bs' = es' \qquad preds\ es'\ s' \\ \forall\, V\ as'.\ (V, as') \in dep\text{-}live\text{-}vars\ n'\ as\ \longrightarrow\ state\text{-}val\ s\ V = state\text{-}val\ s'\ V \end{array}}{\begin{array}{c} preds\ es\ s\ \land \\ (\forall\, V \in Use\ n'.\ state\text{-}val\ (transfers\ es\ s)\ V = state\text{-}val\ (transfers\ es'\ s')\ V) \end{array}}$$

Proof. We prove this lemma by induction on bs, where the base case ($bs = []$ and thus $bs' = []$) is trivial. In the induction step we know that since bs is nonempty, path as consists of a (valid) leading edge a' and the tail list as'. The proof then does the following case analysis: if traversing edge list as changes one of the values in the *Use* set of n' w.r.t. traversing just the tail edge list as', the source node n of the leading edge a' has to define a variable in the dependent live variables set of n', which is reached via as' – otherwise no such influence would be possible. This implies – by Lem. 4.1 above – that there is a PDG path from n to n', hence edge a' must be part of the slice, i.e., the first element of bs (and thus bs', by definition of $\preceq_b$) must be *True*. If however traversing edge list as yields the same values in the *Use* set of n' w.r.t.

traversing just the tail edge list *as'*, the semantic effect of traversing the leading edge *a'* is irrelevant for the variables used in slicing node *n'*. This proposition, combined with the induction hypothesis and the well-formedness properties of the TCFG, concludes the proof of this lemma. □

Replacing *bs'* with the maximal bit vector w.r.t. $\preceq_b$ of the matching size, using the definition of *slice-kinds* and instantiating *s* and *s'* with the same state *s*, the fundamental property is now an easy consequence:

Theorem 4.3 *Fundamental Property of Dynamic Path Slicing:*

$$\frac{n -as\rightarrow* n' \qquad preds\ (kinds\ as)\ s}{(\forall\ V \in Use\ n'.\ state\text{-}val\ (transfers\ (slice\text{-}kinds\ as)\ s)\ V = \\ state\text{-}val\ (transfers\ (kinds\ as)\ s)\ V) \land preds\ (slice\text{-}kinds\ as)\ s}$$

In contrast to the Fundamental Property of Static Slicing (Thm. 3.3), the original and the sliced path are equal in dynamic slicing – this comes as no surprise, as we only consider one trace –, whereas in static slicing, we cannot guarantee both paths being equal.

Provided that the TCFG is also semantically well-formed, Thm. 4.3 can be carried over to the semantics: a statement *c* evaluated in state *s* returns statement *c'* and state *s'*. Then there exists a path between the corresponding nodes of the statements, such that, after traversing the sliced version of this path, all variables used in the target node have the same values as in the final state of the semantic evaluation.

Theorem 4.4 *Fundamental Property of Semantics and Dynamic Slicing:*

$$\frac{n \triangleq c \qquad \langle c,s \rangle \Rightarrow \langle c',s' \rangle}{\exists n'\ as.\ n -as\rightarrow* n' \land preds\ (slice\text{-}kinds\ as)\ s \land n' \triangleq c' \land \\ (\forall\ V \in Use\ n'.\ state\text{-}val\ (transfers\ (slice\text{-}kinds\ as)\ s)\ V = state\text{-}val\ s'\ V)}$$

5

Correctness of Static Interprocedural Slicing

In static interprocedural slicing, procedure calls introduce a large number of new dependences for passing control flow and parameters. These new kinds of dependences make interprocedural slicing much more sophisticated than intraprocedural slicing. Two factors are crucial for an interprocedural slice: (i) it should again be as small as possible, but still correct, and (ii) its computation should be as fast as possible. Today, the slicing algorithm by Horwitz, Reps, and Binkley [57] using dependence graphs is the quasi standard for interprocedural slicing, as (i) it is context-sensitive, i.e., eliminates many spurious nodes, and (ii) summary edges keep its runtime acceptable. The latter can be computed efficiently via an improvement by Reps et al. [91]. Evaluation [62, 23, 65, 22] shows that a context-sensitive slice collapses to half its size, and, thanks to summary edges, computation takes less than half of the time.

Though the Horwitz-Reps-Binkley algorithm for slicing is widely used and its correctness was never questioned, there is no formal correctness proof, neither on paper nor in a proof assistant. Surprisingly, the literature lacks correctness results for any kind of interprocedural slicing algorithm which is based on dependence graphs; I remedy this shortcoming with the work described in the following.

In this chapter, I augment the slicing framework from the previous chapters with a formalization of system dependence graphs (SDGs) with summary edges and the slicing algorithm by Horwitz, Reps, and Binkley (HRB). I show that this slice definition is precise, i.e., every node in the slice lies on a context-sensitive SDG path from the program entry to the slicing node. Furthermore, I provide the first formal proof that HRB slicing is indeed correct. To this end, I lift the weak simulation property as introduced in Sec. 3.3.2 to the interprocedural case and show that this new weak simulation property agrees with the usual understanding of the correctness of interprocedural slicing. All proofs are again machine-checked, the proof scripts are available online [129].

5.1 The Slicer of Horwitz, Reps, and Binkley

The algorithm by Horwitz, Reps, and Binkley is based on the interprocedural analogue of the PDG, the *system dependence graph* (SDG). The SDG adds the following elements to the PDG:

(i) parameter nodes, which represent the formal and actual in- and out-parameters of method calls,

(ii) call edges, and

(iii) parameter-in and parameter-out edges, which take care of the parameter passing.

Parameter-in edges connect the actual parameter nodes of a call site with the respective formal-in parameter nodes of the called procedure, parameter-out edges the formal-out parameter nodes of the called procedure with the actual-out parameter nodes of the call site.

In the intraprocedural case, backward slicing is merely a reachability analysis on the PDG. One could easily carry this idea over to SDGs; however, the resulting slice would contain many spurious nodes, i.e., nodes that cannot influence the slicing node. Consider the example SDG in Fig. 5.1(a): the nodes in the main procedure carry numbers, the entry node is labelled E. In the called procedure, the nodes carry Roman numbers, the entry node is labelled e. The small nodes on the left and the right of nodes 2 and 6 denote the actual-in and -out parameters of the procedure call, respectively. Analogously, the ones next to e denote the procedure's formal parameters; hence, the procedure has exactly one in- and one out-parameter. Solid arrows denote control, dashed ones data dependences. The dotted arrows identify call and parameter edges. If we regard node 7 as slicing node and just perform a reachability analysis, the resulting set would contain all the nodes that are not greyed out in the SDG in Fig. 5.1(b). This would mean that we consider that nodes 1 and 2 can possibly influence node

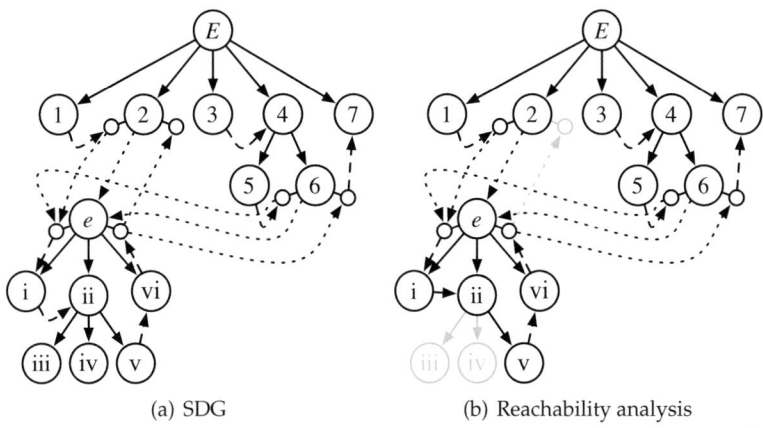

(a) SDG   (b) Reachability analysis

Figure 5.1.: Example SDG and nodes that reach node 7

7. However, the computations in these nodes are irrelevant for the slicing node, as no information from the procedure call in 2 can propagate to any node after the call. As a mere reachability analysis does not distinguish between different call contexts, we get these spurious nodes in the slice.

The slicing algorithm of Horwitz, Reps, and Binkley (HRB algorithm) [57] is context sensitive, i.e., it eliminates such nodes. It makes sure that the backward traversal in the SDG uses only *realizable* paths; on such paths, each called procedure must be left via edges that return to the previously visited call site. Consider again Fig. 5.1(a) and let *fip* be an abbreviation for formal-in, *fop* for formal-out, *aip* for actual-in and *aop* for actual-out parameter nodes in the following: the path [3, 4, 6, e, ii, v, vi, fop e, aop 6, 7] is realizable, whereas [1, aip 2, fip e, i, ii, v, vi, fop e, aop 6, 7] is not; in the latter case, the path enters the procedure at the call site of 2, but leaves it at the call site of 6.

Summary edges are the key to efficiently compute an interprocedural, context-sensitive slice. Such an edge connects an actual-in parameter node to an actual-out, if there is a realizable dependence path between the corresponding formal-in and formal-out parameter node in the called procedure. A summary edge can therefore be seen as a "shortcut" of the dependence path without descending in the called procedure.

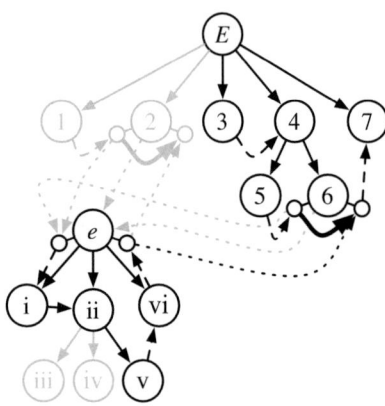

Figure 5.2.: Example of a Horwitz-Reps-Binkley slice

The HRB algorithm computes the slice in two phases:

Phase 1: all nodes that reach the slicing node via data and control dependences, summary, call and parameter-in edges (not parameter-out edges) are added to the slice;

Phase 2: all nodes that reach an actual-out parameter node, which has been included in the slice in the first phase, via data and control dependences, summary and parameter-out edges (not call or parameter-in edges) are inserted in the slice.

This slice is called Horwitz-Reps-Binkley slice, or HRB slice for short. Since we never descend to a caller in Phase 1 (as we may not follow parameter-out edges) nor ascend to a callee in Phase 2 (as we may not follow call or parameter-in edges), we cannot return to a wrong call site. Summary edges make sure that nodes prior to a call are inserted in the slice, if necessary.

See Fig. 5.2 for the HRB slice of node 7 in our example SDG. The bold edge between the aip and aop of node 6 is the necessary summary edge, as the fip and fop of e in the called procedure are connected via the dependence path [fip e, i, ii, v, vi, fop e]. Note that a summary edge also connects the actual parameter nodes of 2 for the same reason; however, as this edge is not traversed in the algorithm, it is greyed out. The summary edge at 6 takes care that node 5 is correctly inserted in the slice. As desired, nodes 1 and 2 are no longer part of the slice.

5.2 The Formalization

This section shows the formalization of the required graph structures for HRB slicing as well as the formalization of HRB slicing itself. As in the static intraprocedural and dynamic case, the interprocedural framework again builds on the formalization of an abstract CFG. It extends the framework from the previous chapters, thus, I only mark explicit changes and addenda.

5.2.1. The Abstract Interprocedural Control Flow Graph

In the interprocedural framework, it is not possible to leave the type of the state completely arbitrary as in the intraprocedural case (where it was of type *'state*). Instead, it has to reflect the fact that called procedures have their own call frame, which stores the value of local variables and remembers where to return. Thus, in a call frame, a mapping from variables (or locations) to values should suffice for the local variables, whereas the type of the return information is left arbitrary via type variable *'ret*. Hence, I define the state as a *call stack*, i.e., as a list of call frames:

$$('var, 'val) \; local\text{-}vars = 'var \rightharpoonup 'val$$
$$('var, 'val, 'ret) \; call\text{-}frame = ('var, 'val) \; local\text{-}vars \times 'ret$$
$$('var, 'val, 'ret) \; state = ('var, 'val, 'ret) \; call\text{-}frame \; list$$

Rather than just two, we now have four different edge kinds:

⇑**f:** updating the current local variables in the call frame with a function *f*,

$(\boldsymbol{Q})_{\sqrt{}}$**:** assuring that a predicate *Q* holds in the call frame,

Q:*r*↪$_p$**fs:** calling procedure *p* if *Q* holds in the current call frame, thereby remembering return information *r* and generating the new call frame via a list of functions *fs* (one for each parameter), and

Q↩$_p$**f:** returning from procedure *p* if *Q* holds in the current call frame, with *f* taking care of the call stack and assigning return values.

The first two denote intraprocedural edges, written *intra-kind* (*kind a*). Note that their functions and predicates no longer take states but call

locale *CFG* =

  . . .

fixes *kind* :: *'edge* ⇒ (*'var*, *'val*, *'ret*, *'pname*) *edge-kind*
fixes *get-proc* :: *'node* ⇒ *'pname*
fixes *get-return-edges* :: *'edge* ⇒ *'edge set*
fixes *procs* :: (*'pname* × *'var list* × *'var list*) *list*
fixes *Main* :: *'pname*

  . . .

Figure 5.3.: Changes in the locale for the interprocedural abstract CFG

frames as parameters. The predicate of the call edge can model e.g. dynamic dispatch, the one of the return edge takes care that the edge returns to the correct call site – usually with the help of the return information in the call frame.

Fig. 5.3 and 5.4 depicts the changes from the intra- to the interprocedural *CFG* locale, keeping all the **fixes** and **assumes** from before. The type of *kind* has changed due to the new *state* type. The locale introduces four new elements:

- a function *get-proc*, which returns for a given node the procedure of type *'pname* lies in;

- a function *get-return-edges*, which returns for a call edge the set of return edges that return to its call site;

- an associative list of triples *procs*, where each triple identifies a procedure with its name and its in- and out-parameters;

- a special procedure *Main*, in which program execution starts.

I adopt a standard trick and introduce an additional return node for every call in the CFG. Hence, each call site consists of a call and corresponding return node; e.g. the source of a call edge *a* and the targets of all edges contained in *get-return-edges a* constitute such a call site node pair.

As you can see in Fig. 5.4, we need a good deal of structural properties to achieve what we intuitively consider a standard interprocedural CFG. In the following, we will look at these rules one by one:

- *get-proc-Entry* and *Entry-no-call* state that the program entry is in the *Main* method and not the source of a procedure call;

- the *Main* procedure may neither be called nor returned from, see *Main-no-call-target* and *Main-no-return-source*;

. . .

assumes *get-proc-Entry*: *get-proc* (*-Entry-*) = *Main*

and *Entry-no-call*: ⟦*valid-edge a*; *kind a* = $Q{:}r{\hookrightarrow}_p fs$; *src a* = (*-Entry-*)⟧
  $\Longrightarrow$ *False*

and *Main-no-call-target*: ⟦*valid-edge a*; *kind a* = $Q{:}r{\hookrightarrow}_{Main} fs$⟧ $\Longrightarrow$ *False*

and *Main-no-return-source*: ⟦*valid-edge a*; *kind a* = $Q{\hookleftarrow}_{Main} f$⟧ $\Longrightarrow$ *False*

and *callee-in-procs*:
  ⟦*valid-edge a*; *kind a* = $Q{:}r{\hookrightarrow}_p fs$⟧ $\Longrightarrow \exists$ *ins outs*. (*p*, *ins*, *outs*) $\in$ *set procs*

and *get-proc-intra*:
  ⟦*valid-edge a*; *intra-kind* (*kind a*)⟧ $\Longrightarrow$ *get-proc* (*src a*) = *get-proc* (*trg a*)

and *get-proc-call*: ⟦*valid-edge a*; *kind a* = $Q{:}r{\hookrightarrow}_p fs$⟧ $\Longrightarrow$ *get-proc* (*trg a*) = *p*

and *get-proc-return*: ⟦*valid-edge a*; *kind a* = $Q{\hookleftarrow}_p f$⟧ $\Longrightarrow$ *get-proc* (*src a*) = *p*

and *call-edges-only*: ⟦*valid-edge a*; *kind a* = $Q{:}r{\hookrightarrow}_p fs$⟧ $\Longrightarrow$
  $\forall a'$. *valid-edge* $a' \land$ *trg* a' = *trg a* $\longrightarrow$ ($\exists Q'$ *r'* *fs'*. *kind* a' = $Q'{:}r'{\hookrightarrow}_p fs'$)

and *return-edges-only*: ⟦*valid-edge a*; *kind a* = $Q{\hookleftarrow}_p f$⟧ $\Longrightarrow$
  $\forall a'$. *valid-edge* $a' \land$ *src* a' = *src a* $\longrightarrow$ ($\exists Q'$ *f'*. *kind* a' = $Q'{\hookleftarrow}_p f'$)

and *gre-call*: ⟦*valid-edge a*; *kind a* = $Q{:}r{\hookrightarrow}_p fs$⟧ $\Longrightarrow$ *get-return-edges a* $\neq \emptyset$

and *only-call-gre*:
  ⟦*valid-edge a*; $a' \in$ *get-return-edges a*⟧ $\Longrightarrow \exists Q$ *r p fs*. *kind a* = $Q{:}r{\hookrightarrow}_p fs$

and *gre-valid*: ⟦*valid-edge a*; $a' \in$ *get-return-edges a*⟧ $\Longrightarrow$ *valid-edge* a'

and *call-return-edges*: ⟦*valid-edge a*; *kind a* = $Q{:}r{\hookrightarrow}_p fs$;
  $a' \in$ *get-return-edges a*⟧ $\Longrightarrow \exists Q'$ *f*. *kind* a' = $Q'{\hookleftarrow}_p f$

and *return-needs-call*: ⟦*valid-edge a*; *kind a* = $Q{\hookleftarrow}_p f$⟧ $\Longrightarrow$
  $\exists ! a'$. *valid-edge* $a' \land$ ($\exists Q'$ *r fs*. *kind* a' = $Q'{:}r{\hookrightarrow}_p fs$) $\land a \in$ *get-return-edges* a'

and *intra-proc-additional-edge*: ⟦*valid-edge a*; $a' \in$ *get-return-edges a*⟧
  $\Longrightarrow \exists a''$. *valid-edge* $a'' \land$ *src* a'' = *trg a* $\land$ *trg* a'' = *src* $a' \land$
      kind a'' = (λcf. *False*)$_{\surd}$

and *call-return-node-edge*: ⟦*valid-edge a*; $a' \in$ *get-return-edges a*⟧
  $\Longrightarrow \exists a''$. *valid-edge* $a'' \land$ *src* a'' = *src a* $\land$ *trg* a'' = *trg* $a' \land$
      kind a'' = (λcf. *False*)$_{\surd}$

and *call-only-one-intra-edge*: ⟦*valid-edge a*; *kind a* = $Q{\hookrightarrow}_p fs$⟧
  $\Longrightarrow \exists ! a'$. *valid-edge* $a' \land$ *src* a' = *src a* $\land$ *intra-kind* (*kind* a')

 and *return-only-one-intra-edge*: ⟦*valid-edge a*; *kind a* = $Q{\hookleftarrow}_p f$⟧
  $\Longrightarrow \exists ! a'$. *valid-edge* $a' \land$ *trg* a' = *trg a* $\land$ *intra-kind* (*kind* a')

and *call-unique-target*: ⟦*valid-edge a*; *valid-edge* a'; *kind a* = $Q_1{\hookrightarrow}_p fs_1$;
  kind a' = $Q_2{\hookrightarrow}_p fs_2$⟧ $\Longrightarrow$ *trg a* = *trg* a'

and *unique-callers*: *distinct* (*map fst procs*)

and *distinct-formal-ins*: (*p*,*ins*,*outs*) $\in$ *set procs* $\Longrightarrow$ *distinct ins*

and *distinct-formal-outs*: (*p*,*ins*,*outs*) $\in$ *set procs* $\Longrightarrow$ *distinct outs*

Figure 5.4.: Changes in the locale for the interprocedural abstract CFG

- *callee-in-procs* guarantees that every call edge calls a procedure that is present in the procedure list *procs*;

- *get-proc-intra* states that source and target node of an intraprocedural edge are in the same procedure. Conversely the target node of a call edge as well as the source node of a return edge lie in the respective called or left procedure, see *get-proc-call* and *get-proc-return*;

- rules *call-edges-only* and *return-edges-only* guarantee that the target of a call is reached only by call edges, and that the source of a return can only be left by other return edges;

- *gre-call* and *only-call-gre* state that call edges must and only call edges can have a nonempty *get-return-edges* set;

- according to *gre-valid* and *call-return-edges*, this set contains only valid return edges, whose procedure parameter agrees to the respective call;

- *return-needs-call* guarantees that every return edge matches exactly one valid call edge;

- according to *intra-proc-additional-edge* and *call-return-node-edge*, there exist edges with an unsatisfiable predicate between a procedure entry and exit as well as between a call and its matching return node; the former is necessary for control dependences, remember the required (-*Entry*-)–(-*Exit*-) edge from the intraprocedural *CFG* locale;

- rules *call*- and *return-only-one-intra-edge* guarantee that the above assumed ($\lambda cf.\ False$)$_{\sqrt{}}$-edge which connects call and return node is the only intraprocedural edge leaving a call node or entering a return node;

- according to *call-unique-target*, all calls to the same procedure reach the same target node;

- *unique-callers*, *distinct-formal-ins* and *distinct-formal-outs*, the remaining three rules, state that no procedure occurs twice in the procedure list, and that the formal-in and -out parameters of every procedure are *distinct*.

Whereas it is not explicit in the abstract CFG, these rules implicitly define a structure on it, i.e., they define the interplay of the procedures. *Main* is the special procedure in which program execution starts; the global entry as well as the global exit are in this method. Procedure entries and exits are implicitly defined as target nodes of call and source nodes of return edges, respectively. Every node is associated to a procedure via *get-proc*.

After defining the structure of the abstract CFG, we will now take a closer look on its semantics. Function *params* defined in locale *CFG* takes care of the parameter instantiation. It applies a list of functions *fs* of type $((\mathit{'var}, \mathit{'val})\ \mathit{local\text{-}vars} \rightharpoonup \mathit{'val})\ \mathit{list}$ as given in a call edge to the local variables of a call frame, which returns a list with the values of the instantiated parameters after the call:

$$\mathit{params\ fs\ lv} \equiv \mathit{map}\ (\lambda f.\ f\ lv)\ fs$$

Functions *transfer* and *pred* now work on the new call stack state. If it is empty, the rules are straightforward:

$$\mathit{transfer\ et}\ [] \equiv []\qquad \mathit{pred\ et}\ [] \equiv \mathit{False}$$

The rules for update and predicate edges are as in the intraprocedural case, except that they check and alter only the local variables of the top call frame instead of the whole state. Call and return edges are treated as follows:

$$
\begin{aligned}
&\mathit{transfer}\ (Q{\hookrightarrow}_p\mathit{fs})\ (\mathit{cf}{\cdot}\mathit{cfs}) \equiv (\mathit{empty}(\mathit{ins}\ [:=]\ \mathit{params\ fs\ cf}))\cdot\mathit{cf}\cdot\mathit{cfs},\\
&\hspace{6em}\text{if } (p,\mathit{ins},\mathit{outs}) \in \mathit{set\ procs}\\
&\mathit{transfer}\ (Q{\hookleftarrow}_p f)\ (\mathit{cf}{\cdot}\mathit{cfs}) \equiv \mathit{case\ cfs\ of}\ [] \Rightarrow []\ \mid \mathit{cf'}{\cdot}\mathit{cfs'} \Rightarrow (f\ \mathit{cf\ cf'})\cdot\mathit{cfs'}\\[1ex]
&\mathit{pred}\ (Q{\hookrightarrow}_p\mathit{fs})\ (\mathit{cf}{\cdot}\mathit{cfs}) \hspace{2em}\equiv Q\ \mathit{cf}\\
&\mathit{pred}\ (Q{\hookleftarrow}_p f)\ (\mathit{cf}{\cdot}\mathit{cfs}) \hspace{2.3em}\equiv Q\ \mathit{cf} \wedge \mathit{cfs} \neq []
\end{aligned}
$$

$\mathit{empty}(\mathit{ins}\ [:=]\ \mathit{params\ fs\ cf})$ creates a new call frame by assigning the formal-in parameters *ins* the values of the parameter instantiation. Note that the predicates of the call and return edge take the whole call frame as parameter – not only the local variables as do predicate edges –, since they also may take the return information into account. Note also that function *f* of the return edges is still unspecified; a well-formedness property will take care of this. The lifting to edge kind lists, i.e., *transfers* and *preds* is straightforward.

In locale *CFGExit* (see Fig. 5.5), only two rules have to be added, which mirror the (*-Entry-*) rules shown above for (*-Exit-*): *get-proc-Exit* and *Exit-no-return* state that the program exit is in the *Main* method and may not be the direct target of a return edge.

locale *CFGExit* =
assumes *get-proc-Exit*: *get-proc* (*-Exit-*) = *Main*
and *Exit-no-return*: [*valid-edge a*; *kind a* = $Q\hookleftarrow_p f$; *trg a* = (*-Exit-*)] $\Longrightarrow$ *False*

Figure 5.5.: Changes in locale *CFGExit*

We also need to extend the well-formedness properties of locale *CFG-wf*. We keep those from the intraprocedural case as shown in Fig. 3.7, but require that in rules *no-Def-equal* and *transfer-only-use*, the edge *a* under consideration is intraprocedural, i.e., *intra-kind* (*kind a*). Furthermore, instead of states, all rules are adapted to work on call frames.

Besides *Def* and *Use*, locale *CFG-wf* now also defines two more sets, *ParamDefs* and *ParamUses*, see Fig. 5.6. *ParamUses* collects all locations that are used in argument passing at call nodes; intuitively, think of it as a list of *Use* sets, one for each argument expression. *ParamDefs* consists of the actual-out parameters for return nodes, i.e., the locations in which the return values are to be stored. Most of the new well-formedness rules that are shown in Fig. 5.6 reason about these sets. Note that now *state-val s V* is instantiated with (*fst* (*hd s*)) *V*, i.e., it returns the value of a location *V* in the local variables in the top call frame of state *s*. These are the well-formedness rules:

- the length of the *ParamUses* of a call node agrees to the length of the formal-in parameters of the called procedure, see *PU-length*;

- the length of the *ParamDefs* of a return node agrees to the length of the formal-out parameters of the left procedure, see *PD-length*;

- *PD-in-Def* guarantees that every location in the *ParamDefs* set of a node is also in its *Def* set;

- *ins-in-Def* states that the formal-in parameters of a procedure are in the *Def* set of the target node of a call edge (i.e., the procedure entry), whereas the *Def* set of its source node is empty according to *call-Def-empty*;

- *PU-in-Use* requires all locations in any of the sets in *ParamUses* of a node to be in the node's *Use* set;

- all out-parameters of a procedure are in the *Use* set of its procedure exit nodes according to *outs-in-Use*;

- *call-length* states that the length of the function list of a call edge and the length of the procedure's in-parameters agree;

locale *CFG-wf* =

$\dots$

fixes *ParamDefs* :: $'node \Rightarrow 'var\ list$
fixes *ParamUses* :: $'node \Rightarrow 'var\ set\ list$
assumes *PU-length*: $[\![valid\text{-}edge\ a;\ kind\ a = Q\hookrightarrow_p fs;\ (p,ins,outs) \in set\ procs]\!]$
  $\Longrightarrow |ParamUses\ (src\ a)| = |ins|$
and *distinct-PD*: $valid\text{-}node\ n \Longrightarrow distinct\ (ParamDefs\ n)$
and *PD-length*: $[\![valid\text{-}edge\ a;\ kind\ a = Q\hookleftarrow_p f';\ (p,ins,outs) \in set\ procs]\!]$
  $\Longrightarrow |ParamDefs\ (trg\ a)| = |outs|$
and *PD-in-Def*: $valid\text{-}node\ n \Longrightarrow set\ (ParamDefs\ n) \subseteq Def\ n$
and *ins-in-Def*: $[\![valid\text{-}edge\ a;\ kind\ a = Q\hookrightarrow_p fs;\ (p,ins,outs) \in set\ procs]\!]$
  $\Longrightarrow set\ ins \subseteq Def\ (trg\ a)$
and *call-Def-empty*: $[\![valid\text{-}edge\ a;\ kind\ a = Q\hookrightarrow_p fs]\!] \Longrightarrow Def\ (src\ a) = \{\}$
and *PU-in-Use*: $valid\text{-}node\ n \Longrightarrow \bigcup set\ (ParamUses\ n) \subseteq Use\ n$
and *outs-in-Use*: $[\![valid\text{-}edge\ a;\ kind\ a = Q\hookleftarrow_p f;\ (p,ins,outs) \in set\ procs]\!]$
  $\Longrightarrow set\ outs \subseteq Use\ (src\ a)$
and *call-length*:
  $[\![valid\text{-}edge\ a;\ kind\ a = Q\hookrightarrow_p fs;\ (p,ins,outs) \in set\ procs]\!] \Longrightarrow |fs| = |ins|$
and *call-determ*: $[\![valid\text{-}edge\ a;\ valid\text{-}edge\ a';\ src\ a = src\ a';$
  $kind\ a = Q\hookrightarrow_p fs;\ kind\ a' = Q'\hookrightarrow_{p'} fs';\ pred\ (kind\ a)\ s;\ pred\ (kind\ a')\ s]\!]$
  $\Longrightarrow a = a'$
and *call-params*: $[\![valid\text{-}edge\ a;\ kind\ a = Q\hookrightarrow_p fs;\ i < |ins|;$
  $(p,ins,outs) \in set\ procs;\ pred\ (kind\ a)\ s;\ pred\ (kind\ a)\ s';$
  $\forall V \in (ParamUses\ (src\ a))_{[i]}.\ (hd\ s)\ V = (hd\ s')\ V]\!]$
  $\Longrightarrow (params\ fs\ (fst\ (hd\ s)))_{[i]} = (params\ fs\ (fst\ (hd\ s')))_{[i]}$
and *return-fun*: $[\![valid\text{-}edge\ a;\ kind\ a = Q\hookleftarrow f'_p;\ (p,ins,outs) \in set\ procs]\!]$
  $\Longrightarrow f'\ lv\ lv' = lv'(ParamDefs\ (trg\ a)\ [:=]\ map\ lv\ outs)$

Figure 5.6.: Changes in locale *CFG-wf*

- predicates of all call edges from the same call node do not overlap, see *equal-Use-equal-Call*;

- *call-params* guarantees that for two states which fulfil the predicate of a call edge and which agree on the values of all variables in the *ParamUses* of the call node for an index i, the value assigned to the ith parameter also agrees for both top call frame of those states;

- *return-fun* requires that the function of a return edge passes the return values to the call frame before the call, i.e., it updates the locations where these values are to be stored with the value of the respective out-parameter in the top call frame within the procedure. This construction avoids cyclic dependences: defining the effect of return function f directly in *transfer* in locale *CFG* would require the notion of *ParamDefs*, which is not introduced until in *CFG*'s sublocale *CFG-wf*, whose assumptions however require the definition of *transfer*.

5.2.2. Valid Control Flow Paths

Again, locale *CFG* defines the notion of paths in the CFG. In the intraprocedural case, paths were a mere concatenation of matching edges. The interprocedural CFG needs more specific definitions for:

(i) intraprocedural paths,

(ii) valid paths, i.e., paths that can actually be taken in a program run,

(iii) same level paths, i.e., valid paths that may only ascend in called procedures and return to the procedure in which they started.

Intraprocedural Paths

Defining intraprocedural paths, for which we write $-\rightarrow_i*$, is easy: every edge in the path must be intraprocedural.

$$n -as\rightarrow_i* n' \equiv n -as\rightarrow* n' \wedge (\forall a \in set\ as.\ intra\text{-}kind(kind\ a))$$

Every subpath of an intraprocedural path is again intraprocedural. Two lemmas guarantee that intraprocedural paths may be appended and that its source and target node reside in the same procedure:

$$\frac{n -as\rightarrow_i* n'' \qquad n'' -as'\rightarrow_i* n'}{n -as@as'\rightarrow_i* n'} \qquad \frac{n -as\rightarrow_i* n'}{get\text{-}proc\ n = get\text{-}proc\ n'}$$

Valid Paths

Valid paths capture the effect of context-sensitivity: called procedures must return to its previously visited call site. Therefore, if there is a return edge in a valid path, it must match the call edge taken to enter this procedure in the prefix of the path, if such a call edge is present (i.e., a valid path is allowed to return from procedures that have not been entered in the path before). Fig. 5.7 shows some examples of paths that are valid. As only valid paths correspond to actual program

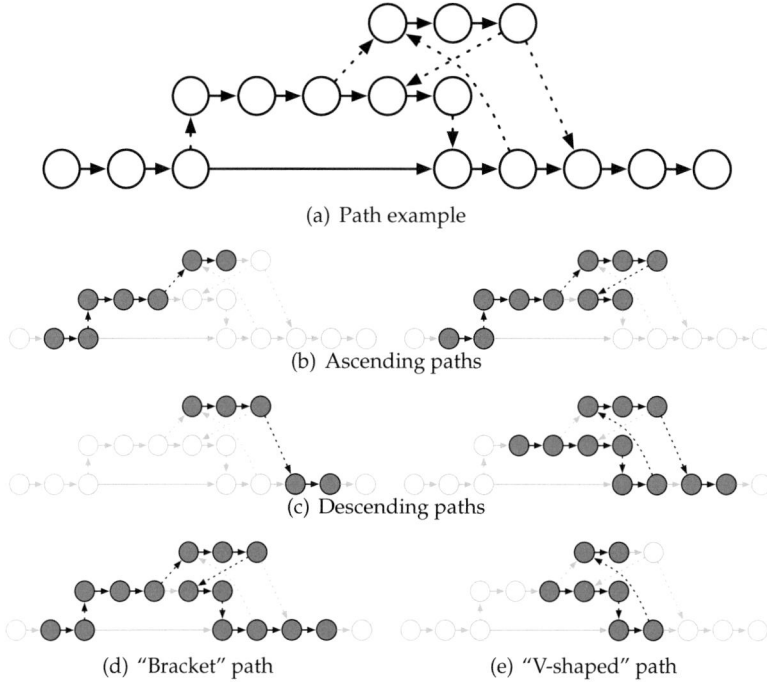

(a) Path example

(b) Ascending paths

(c) Descending paths

(d) "Bracket" path

(e) "V-shaped" path

Figure 5.7.: Examples of valid paths

executions, they will be of utmost importance in the interprocedural fundamental property of slicing.

While the structure of valid paths seems to be related to bracket grammars, I refrained from defining them in this manner. Instead, I use a predicate *valid-path* that identifies suffixes of valid paths using a stack of call edges. As this predicate is defined by primitive recursion on the edge list followed by a case distinction on the edge kind of the first edge, it works well with the usual list induction as commonly used in proofs.

valid-path cs as states that if the traversal of a path prefix resulted in a stack of call edges *cs*, i.e., calls to procedures that have not yet been left, and the path suffix is *as*, the whole path is valid. Basically, we push leading call edges onto the call edge stack and check for return edges if they match the top element of the call edge stack. The formal rules for *valid-path* can be found in Fig. 5.8.

$$\frac{}{\text{valid-path } cs \; []} \qquad \frac{\text{intra-kind } (\text{kind } a) \quad \text{valid-path } cs \; as}{\text{valid-path } cs \; (a \cdot as)}$$

$$\frac{\text{kind } a = Q \hookrightarrow_p fs \quad \text{valid-path } (a \cdot cs) \; as}{\text{valid-path } cs \; (a \cdot as)}$$

$$\frac{\text{kind } a = Q \hookleftarrow_p f}{\text{valid-path } [] \; as} \qquad \frac{\text{kind } a = Q \hookleftarrow_p f \quad a \in \text{get-return-edges } c' \quad \text{valid-path } cs' \; as}{\text{valid-path } (c' \cdot cs') \; (a \cdot as)}$$

Figure 5.8.: Recursive rules for valid paths

A path is a valid path, written $- \to_{\sqrt{}*}$, if the following holds:

$$n \; -as \to_{\sqrt{}*} n' \equiv n \; -as \to * \; n' \land \text{valid-path } [] \; as$$

Contrary to intraprocedural paths, valid paths may not be appended arbitrarily, as appending an ascending and a descending path could violate context-sensitivity; however, splitting a valid path results only in valid paths.

Same Level Paths

Same level paths are context-sensitive CFG paths that begin and end in the same initial procedure, which is never left in between. Hence, same level paths form a subset of valid paths; the only same level path in Fig. 5.7 is the "bracket" path in subfigure (d).

Again, a predicate *same-level-path* defines same level paths. Its rules agree to the ones of *valid-path* as shown above, without the return rule with an empty stack of call edges, since it is not allowed to return from the initial procedure. While *same-level-path* guarantees the latter and that the path is context-sensitive, it cannot make sure that the path returns again to the procedure in which it started, e.g. see Fig. 5.7 (b). This would be the case if the call edge stack has been processed completely. Hence, I define a function *upd-cs* which takes a call edge stack and a path as parameters and returns the final call edge stack which mirrors all the changes applied in the traversal of the path. So, if *upd-cs* $[] \; as = []$ holds, we know that traversing path as ended in the same procedure in which it began. Finally, we can define same level paths, for which we write $- \to_{sl}*$, as:

$$n \; -as \to_{sl}* n' \equiv n \; -as \to * \; n' \land \text{same-level-path } [] \; as \land \text{upd-cs } [] \; as = []$$

Appending same level paths leads again to same level paths; yet, splitting them does not result in same level paths. Source and target node of a same level path lie in the same procedure.

$$\frac{n -as \to_{sl}* n'' \qquad n'' -as' \to_{sl}* n'}{n -as@as' \to_{sl}* n'} \qquad\qquad \frac{n -as \to_{sl}* n'}{get\text{-}proc\ n = get\text{-}proc\ n'}$$

Relations between Paths

These three kinds of paths are related like this:

$$n -as \to_i* n' \implies n -as \to_{sl}* n' \implies n -as \to_{\sqrt{}}* n'$$

Naturally, the converse directions do not hold. However, as we can shortcut every procedure call with the intraprocedural edge required by rule *call-return-node-edge* in locale *CFG*, we can prove that for every same level path there is an intraprocedural path which connects the same nodes using a subset of the former's edges:

Lemma 5.1 *From Same Level Paths to Intraprocedural Paths:*

$$\frac{n -as \to_{sl}* n'}{\exists as'.\ n -as' \to_i* n' \land set\ (srcs\ as') \subseteq set\ (srcs\ as)}$$

While valid paths may not be appended, we may however append a same level path as a prefix or suffix to a valid path and receive again a valid path:

$$\frac{n -as \to_{sl}* n'' \qquad n'' -as' \to_{\sqrt{}}* n'}{n -as@as' \to_{\sqrt{}}* n'} \qquad \frac{n -as \to_{\sqrt{}}* n'' \qquad n'' -as' \to_{sl}* n'}{n -as@as' \to_{\sqrt{}}* n'}$$

Finally, using the above lemmas and several more, we can prove that every valid path beginning in (*-Entry-*) gives rise to an ascending path, i.e., a path which contains only intraprocedural and call edges, between the same nodes. Analogously, for every valid path which ends in (*-Exit-*) there exists a descending path with only intraprocedural and return edges:

$$\frac{(\text{-}Entry\text{-}) -as \to_{\sqrt{}}* n}{\begin{array}{c} \exists as'.\ (\text{-}Entry\text{-}) -as' \to_{\sqrt{}}* n \land set(srcs\ as') \subseteq set(srcs\ as) \land \\ (\forall a' \in set\ as'.\ intra\text{-}kind(kind\ a') \lor (\exists Q\ r\ fs\ p.\ kind\ a' = Q{:}r \hookrightarrow_p fs)) \end{array}}$$

$$\frac{n -as \to_{\sqrt{}}* (\text{-}Exit\text{-})}{\begin{array}{c} \exists as'.\ n -as' \to_{\sqrt{}}* (\text{-}Exit\text{-}) \land set(srcs\ as') \subseteq set(srcs\ as) \\ (\forall a' \in set\ as'.\ intra\text{-}kind(kind\ a') \lor (\exists Q\ f\ p.\ kind\ a' = Q \hookleftarrow_p f)) \end{array}}$$

5.2.3. System Dependence Graph

Instead of constructing a PDG for every procedure and connecting them with call and parameter edges to obtain the SDG, I construct the SDG itself immediately; since we have a CFG for the complete program, not one for each separate procedure, this is a natural approach.

The definitions in this section are all subsumed in locale *SDG*, which extends locales *CFGExit-wf* and *Postdomination*. *CFGExit-wf* is again the bottom locale of the CFG locales diamond as in the intraprocedural case, cf. Fig. 3.5. *Postdomination* agrees to the intraprocedural locale as shown in Fig. 3.9, except that now a postdominator for a node lies on all *intraprocedural* paths from this node to the *procedure* exit, not the global exit. *SDG* also provides the context in which the precision and correctness proofs (see Sec. 5.3) are carried out.

SDG nodes

The SDG reuses the nodes of the CFG, but also introduces new nodes for actual and formal in- and out-parameters. The former are prefixed with *CFG-node*, the latter carry a tuple parameter (m,x), where m denotes the corresponding CFG call or return node and x is a numerical index to distinguish between parameters for calls with multiple in- and/or out-parameters. *Actual-in* nodes belong to call, *Actual-out* to return nodes, *Formal-in* to procedure entry and *Formal-out* to procedure exit nodes.

For every SDG node n, $\lfloor n \rfloor_{CFG}$ returns the "parent" CFG node, i.e., for lifted CFG nodes just the "unlifted node", and for parameter nodes the CFG node which they carry as parameter.

Analogously to *valid-node*, there is a predicate *valid-SDG-node* that guarantees that the respective SDG node is indeed valid. Effectively, it checks for every parameter node that the numerical index is smaller than the number of the respective formal-in or -out parameters; moreover, for all nodes the parent node has to be a valid CFG node.

Dependences

The edges of the SDG can be divided in two subclasses: edges that occur only within procedures and edges between procedures. Control and data dependence edges fall into the former category; they will be the focus of this section. For the respective intraprocedural definitions see Sec. 3.2.2.

In the SDG, locations are also defined and used at call sites due to argument passing. Hence, we need analogous notions of *Def* and *Use* sets for SDG nodes; I call them Def_{SDG} and Use_{SDG}. For a *CFG-node*, these sets contain the same elements as the *Def* and *Use* sets of its parent node.

Parameter nodes have to take care that the parameters are defined and used where necessary. Each formal parameter is either defined in its respective formal-in or used in its formal-out parameter node. The ith actual-in parameter node uses all locations in its ith *ParamUses* entry, while every actual-out node defines the respective element of its *ParamDefs* list.

Data dependence is basically defined as in the intraprocedural case, but connects SDG instead of CFG nodes: a node n' is data dependent on node n, if location V is defined in n and used in n' and the parent nodes of n and n' are connected via an intraprocedural CFG path, such that no other valid node n'' whose parent node is on the path redefines V. As dependences between parameter nodes and their parent nodes are allowed, we drop the requirement that this path has to be nonempty; regrettably, along with the explicit conversion from SDG to CFG nodes, this makes the formal definition harder to read:

$$n \text{ influences } V \text{ in } n' \equiv$$
$$\exists\, as.\ V \in Def_{SDG}\, n \wedge V \in Use_{SDG}\, n' \wedge \lfloor n \rfloor_{CFG} - as \rightarrow_{i^*} \lfloor n' \rfloor_{CFG} \wedge$$
$$(\forall\, n''.\ valid\text{-}SDG\text{-}node\ n'' \wedge \lfloor n'' \rfloor_{CFG} \in set\ (srcs\ (tl\ as)) \longrightarrow V \notin Def_{SDG}\, n'')$$

Parameter nodes are not affected by control dependences. As they are not part of the CFG, their execution can neither influence the execution of other nodes nor are they directly influenced by the execution other nodes. In the latter case, they are only executed if their corresponding parent CFG node is executed. Hence, it suffices to define control dependence on CFG nodes. I define standard control dependence as in the intraprocedural case:

$$n \text{ controls } n' \equiv \exists a\, a'\, as.\ n - a \cdot as \rightarrow_{i^*} n' \wedge n' \notin set\ (srcs\ (a \cdot as)) \wedge$$
$$intra\text{-}kind\ (kind\ a) \wedge n'\ postdominates\ trg\ a \wedge valid\text{-}edge\ a' \wedge$$
$$intra\text{-}kind\ (kind\ a') \wedge \neg\, n'\ postdominates\ trg\ a' \wedge src\ a' = n$$

Contrary to the intraprocedural case, I had to pin down the control dependence definition in the SDG, as other control dependence definitions either lead to non-local additions of dependences, or their interprocedural meaning is not quite clear. Termination sensitive control dependences like *weak control dependence* by Podgurski and Clarke [88] would render all nodes after the return node of a possibly non-terminating procedure – due to endless recursion or loops – control dependent on the return node of this procedure. Thus, the framework cannot be modularized for control dependence as easily as in the intraprocedural case, so I refrained from integrating such control dependences; integration would be possible with some changes to the framework, yet yielding a different SDG formalization. Adapting the interprocedural framework for non-binary control dependences such as *weak order dependence* by Amtoft [3] requires more insight into what such dependences mean in the presence of procedures. Other works define interprocedural control dependences across procedure boundaries, e.g. see [106]; however, as this approach is not context-sensitive at all, it is not applicable for HRB slicing.

SDG edges

As the definition of summary edges requires dependence paths, I first define an SDG with just the usual dependence edges. Thereafter, the notions of matched and realizable paths in this SDG are introduced, which finally help in defining a complete SDG with summary edges.

Fig. 5.9 shows the formal rules for the SDG edges, they define the following edges:

- data dependence $n -V \to_{dd} n'$, if n influences V in n';
- control dependence $n \longrightarrow_{cd} n'$, if (i) n and n' are lifted CFG nodes and $\lfloor n \rfloor_{CFG}$ controls $\lfloor n' \rfloor_{CFG}$ holds, or (ii) n' is a parameter node attached to n, or (iii) n is the entry and n' the exit node of the same procedure;
- call $n -p \to_{call} n'$, if n is a call node and n' the corresponding entry node of procedure p;
- return $n -p \to_{ret} n'$, if n is the exit node of procedure p and n' the return node at a matching call site of p;
- parameter-in $n -p{:}V \to_{in} n'$, if V is the ith formal-in parameter, n the ith actual-in and n' the ith formal-in parameter node of the respective call of p;
- parameter-out $n -p{:}V \to_{out} n'$, if V is the ith formal-out parameter, n the ith formal-out and n' the ith actual-out parameter node of the respective return from p.

$$\frac{n \text{ influences } V \text{ in } n'}{n - V \to_{dd} n'} \; dd \qquad \frac{m \text{ controls } m'}{CFG\text{-}node \; m \longrightarrow_{cd} CFG\text{-}node \; m'} \; cd(\text{i})$$

$$\frac{valid\text{-}SDG\text{-}node \; n' \qquad n = CFG\text{-}node \; \lfloor n' \rfloor_{CFG} \qquad n \neq n'}{n \longrightarrow_{cd} n'} \; cd(\text{ii})$$

$$\frac{valid\text{-}edge \; a \qquad kind \; a = Q{:}r \hookrightarrow_p fs \qquad a' \in get\text{-}return\text{-}edges \; a}{CFG\text{-}node \; (trg \; a) \longrightarrow_{cd} CFG\text{-}node \; (src \; a')} \; cd(\text{iii})$$

$$\frac{valid\text{-}edge \; a \qquad kind \; a = Q{:}r \hookrightarrow_p fs}{CFG\text{-}node \; (src \; a) - p \to_{call} CFG\text{-}node \; (trg \; a)} \; call$$

$$\frac{valid\text{-}edge \; a \qquad kind \; a = Q \hookleftarrow_p f}{CFG\text{-}node \; (src \; a) - p \to_{ret} CFG\text{-}node \; (trg \; a)} \; ret$$

$$\frac{valid\text{-}edge \; a}{kind \; a = Q{:}r \hookrightarrow_p fs \quad (p, ins, outs) \in set \; procs \quad V = ins_{[x]}}{Actual\text{-}in \; (src \; a, x) - p{:}V \to_{in} Formal\text{-}in \; (trg \; a, x)} \; in$$

$$\frac{valid\text{-}edge \; a}{kind \; a = Q \hookleftarrow_p f \quad (p, ins, outs) \in set \; procs \quad V = outs_{[x]}}{Formal\text{-}out \; (src \; a, x) - p{:}V \to_{out} Actual\text{-}out \; (trg \; a, x)} \; out$$

Figure 5.9.: Formal rules for edges in the SDG

SDG paths

The dependence edges can now be assembled into various dependence paths. For example $n \; i - ns \to_{d*} n'$ denotes an intraprocedural dependence path, i.e., which uses only data and control dependences, or $n \; cc - ns \to_{d*} n'$ represents a dependence path which uses only (SDG) call and control dependence edges; ns in both paths collects all nodes[1] visited on these paths. One important lemma concerning these paths shows that $(\text{-}Entry\text{-})$ reaches every valid SDG node via a call-control-dependence path:

$$\frac{valid\text{-}SDG\text{-}node \; n \qquad parent\text{-}node \; n \neq (\text{-}Exit\text{-})}{\exists ns. \; CFG\text{-}node \; (\text{-}Entry\text{-}) \; cc - ns \to_{d*} n}$$

---

[1]In CFG paths, we collect edges as we are interested in their semantic effect. In SDG paths, we are merely interested in reachability properties, hence collecting nodes is sufficient.

$$\frac{valid\text{-}SDG\text{-}node\ n}{matched\ n\ []\ n}\ \text{M1} \qquad \frac{matched\ n\ ns\ n'' \qquad n''\ i - ns' \rightarrow_{d*} n'}{matched\ n\ (ns\ @\ ns')\ n'}\ \text{M2}$$

$$\frac{\begin{array}{c} matched\ n_0\ ns\ n_1 \qquad n_1 - p \rightarrow_{call} n_2 \qquad matched\ n_2\ ns'\ n_3 \\ n_3 - p \rightarrow_{ret} n_4 \vee n_3 - p{:}V \rightarrow_{out} n_4 \qquad call\text{-}of\text{-}return\text{-}node\ \lfloor n_4 \rfloor_{CFG}\ \lfloor n_1 \rfloor_{CFG} \end{array}}{matched\ n_0\ (ns\ @\ [n_1]\ @\ ns'\ @\ [n_3])\ n_4} \\ \text{M3}$$

$$\frac{\begin{array}{c} matched\ n_0\ ns\ n_1 \qquad n_1 - p{:}V \rightarrow_{in} n_2 \qquad matched\ n_2\ ns'\ n_3 \\ n_3 - p{:}V' \rightarrow_{out} n_4 \qquad call\text{-}of\text{-}return\text{-}node\ \lfloor n_4 \rfloor_{CFG}\ \lfloor n_1 \rfloor_{CFG} \end{array}}{matched\ n_0\ (ns\ @\ [n_1]\ @\ ns'\ @\ [n_3])\ n_4}\ \text{M4}$$

$$\frac{matched\ n\ ns\ n'}{realizable\ n\ ns\ n'}\ \text{R1} \qquad \frac{\begin{array}{c} realizable\ n_0\ ns\ n_1 \\ n_1 - p \rightarrow_{call} n_2 \vee n_1 - p{:}V \rightarrow_{in} n_2 \\ matched\ n_2\ ns'\ n_3 \end{array}}{realizable\ n_0\ (ns\ @\ n_1 \cdot ns')\ n_3}\ \text{R2}$$

Figure 5.10.: Formal rules for *matched* and *realizable*

To determine the summary edges, which are indispensable for efficient context-sensitive interprocedural slicing, we need to formalize *realizable* paths in the SDG, i.e., paths on which a finished procedure call always returns to the site of the most recently executed unmatched call. Analogously to [91], where this is done using a grammar, we define a predicate *matched* describing *same-level realizable* SDG paths. *matched n ns n'* states that there is a context-sensitive SDG path from node n to n', visiting nodes *ns* on its way; it can be viewed as the SDG analogue to same-level paths in the CFG. The formal rules for *matched* are shown in Fig. 5.10. Rules M3 and M4 are mostly identical, they describe a *matched* path via a call edge and a parameter-in edge, resp. Predicate *call-of-return-node n n'* determines for a return node n its matching call node n'; basically, it uses *get-return-edges* to determine this. The predicate *realizable* describes general *realizable* paths and is easily defined using *matched*, see rules R1 and R2 in Fig. 5.10.

Fig. 5.11 (a) depicts a variation of the example SDG from the beginning, but how it would be formalized in the framework: nodes 2 and 6 are split in a call and return node each, the latter are labeled with an additional $'$ and reached from return edges that originate in the newly introduced method exit node x of the called procedure. The actual-out parameter nodes are now attached to the new return nodes instead of

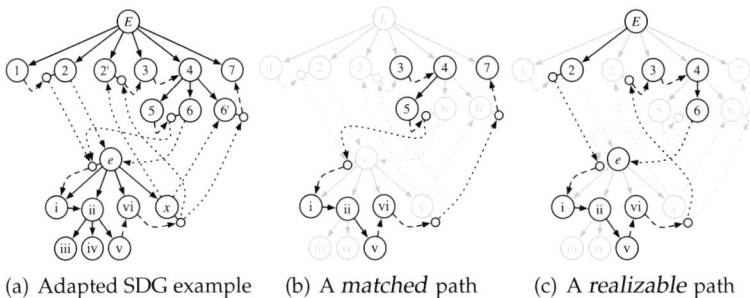

(a) Adapted SDG example   (b) A *matched* path   (c) A *realizable* path

Figure 5.11.: Examples for a *matched* and a *realizable* path

the call nodes. The only semantic change is an additional data dependence edge between the actual-out parameter node at return node $2'$ and node 3. Subfigures (b) and (c) now show a *matched* and a *realizable* path example in this graph. Both include a complete traversal of the called procedure, but whereas the former starts and ends in the Main method, the latter calls the procedure again.

Summary edges

Now, we have the means to define the SDG with summary edges $-p\rightarrow_{sum}$. They are drawn in two cases at a call site of procedure p: (i) connecting the call node and its respective return node, and (ii) connecting an *Actual-in* with an *Actual-out* parameter node, if the matching *Formal-in* and *Formal-out* parameter nodes in procedure p are connected via a *matched* path. The formal rules can be found in Fig. 5.12.

$$\frac{valid\text{-}edge\ a \qquad kind\ a = Q\hookrightarrow_p fs \qquad a' \in get\text{-}return\text{-}edges\ a}{CFG\text{-}node\ (src\ a)\ -p\rightarrow_{sum} CFG\text{-}node\ (trg\ a')}\ sum(i)$$

$$\frac{\begin{array}{c} valid\text{-}edge\ a \qquad kind\ a = Q\hookrightarrow_p fs \qquad a' \in get\text{-}return\text{-}edges\ a \\ matched\ (Formal\text{-}in\ (trg\ a,x))\ ns\ (Formal\text{-}out\ (src\ a',x')) \\ (p,ins,outs) \in set\ procs \qquad x < |ins| \qquad x' < |outs| \end{array}}{Actual\text{-}in\ (src\ a,x)\ -p\rightarrow_{sum} Actual\text{-}out\ (trg\ a',x')}\ sum(ii)$$

Figure 5.12.: Formal rules for summary edges in the SDG

5.2.4. Formalizing the Horwitz-Reps-Binkley Slicer

As already mentioned in Sec. 5.1, the slicing algorithm by Horwitz, Reps, and Binkley works in two phases: First, beginning at the slicing node n, we traverse backwards all intraprocedural dependence, call, parameter-in and summary edges, but no return or parameter-out edges, and insert all visited nodes into the slice. Second, beginning at all actual-out and return nodes visited in Phase 1, we traverse all intraprocedural dependence, return, parameter-out and summary edges, but no call or parameter-in edges, and again include all visited nodes in the slice. This approach guarantees a context-sensitive slice; for more details see [57, 91].

In Isabelle, I use two sets *sum-SDG-slice1 n* and *sum-SDG-slice2 n* to formalize this. They collect the nodes of the transitive hull of the edges traversed in Phase 1 and 2, respectively, beginning at node n. The following definitions are not pure Isabelle, but simpler and more intuitive:

$$sum\text{-}SDG\text{-}slice1\ n = \{n'.\ n' \longrightarrow_{\{cd,dd,call,in,sum\}} *\ n\}$$
$$sum\text{-}SDG\text{-}slice2\ n = \{n'.\ n' \longrightarrow_{\{cd,dd,ret,out,sum\}} *\ n\}$$

The slice of node n is the set *HRB-slice n*, defined via the following rules:

$$\frac{n' \in sum\text{-}SDG\text{-}slice1\ n}{n' \in HRB\text{-}slice\ n}$$

$$\frac{n'' \in sum\text{-}SDG\text{-}slice1\ n \qquad n''' - p\rightarrow_{ret} CFG\text{-}node\ \lfloor n'' \rfloor_{CFG} \qquad n' \in sum\text{-}SDG\text{-}slice2\ n''}{n' \in HRB\text{-}slice\ n}$$

Each of these rules takes care of one phase, i.e., that all of the nodes collected in this phase are actually included in the slice. Note that the premise $n''' - p\rightarrow_{ret} CFG\text{-}node\ \lfloor n'' \rfloor_{CFG}$ guarantees that $CFG\text{-}node\ \lfloor n'' \rfloor_{CFG}$ is an SDG return node, so n'' is either itself the return node or one of its *Actual-out* parameter nodes.

5.3 The Proofs

I verified the above formalization of the Horwitz-Reps-Binkley slicing algorithm in two respects: *precision* and *correctness*.

5.3.1. Precision

A slicing algorithm is precise, if the computed slice indeed contains exactly the nodes that should be included in it. Or, as Reps et al. put it in [91]: *"An interprocedural-slicing algorithm is precise up to realizable paths if, for a given vertex v, it determines the set of vertices that lie on some realizable path from the entry vertex of the main procedure to v."* Note that this does not consider possible influence; this will be looked at in the correctness proof. Formalizing this in Isabelle/HOL we get the following:

Theorem 5.2 *Precision of the Horwitz-Reps-Binkley Slicing Algorithm:*

$$\frac{\text{valid-SDG-node } n' \qquad n \neq n'}{(n \in \text{HRB-slice } n') = (\exists \, ns. \text{ realizable } (\text{CFG-node } (\text{-Entry-})) \, ns \, n' \wedge n \in \text{set } ns)}$$

Proof. I show the implication from left-to-right via a case distinction on the derivation of $n \in \text{HRB-slice } n'$. Each case identifies one algorithm phase and uses two auxiliary lemmas:

(i) $n \in \text{sum-SDG-slice1 } n'$ induces a path from *CFG-node* (*-Entry-*) to n', which only contains the edges traversed in Phase 1 (written $ics{-}ns{\rightarrow}_{d*}$) and visits n, and from this path a *realizable* path between the same nodes follows, which visits at least all the nodes in ns:

$$\frac{n \in \text{sum-SDG-slice1 } n' \qquad n \neq n'}{\exists \, ns. \text{ CFG-node } (\text{-Entry-}) \, ics{-}ns{\rightarrow}_{d*} \, n' \wedge n \in \text{set } ns}$$

$$\frac{n \, ics{-}ns{\rightarrow}_{d*} \, n'}{\exists \, ns'. \text{ realizable } n \, ns' \, n' \wedge \text{set } ns \subseteq \text{set } ns'}$$

(ii) *sum-SDG-slice2* n' is indeed the transitive closure of the edges traversed in Phase 2, and the respective path (written $irs{-}ns{\rightarrow}_{d*}$) from a node n in this set induces a *realizable* path from *CFG-node* (*-Entry-*) to n', on which n lies:

$$\frac{n \in \text{sum-SDG-slice2 } n' \qquad \text{valid-SDG-node } n'}{\exists \, ns. \, n \, irs{-}ns{\rightarrow}_{d*} \, n'}$$

$$\frac{n \, irs{-}ns{\rightarrow}_{d*} \, n' \qquad n \neq n'}{\exists \, ns'. \text{ realizable } (\text{CFG-node } (\text{-Entry-})) \, ns' \, n' \wedge n \in \text{set } ns'}$$

```
1 int main() {     7 int f(int v) {    11 int g(int x) {
2    a := 13;       8    int w := g(v);  12    int y := x + 7;
3    b := f(5);      9    return 2*w;    13    return y;
4    c := g(a);     10 }                 14 }
5    print c;
6 }
```

Figure 5.13.: Example exhibiting problems when determining silent moves

In contrast, the implication from right-to-left is merely an easy induction on the rules of *realizable*:

$$\frac{realizable\ n\ ns\ n' \qquad n'' \in set\ ns}{n'' \in HRB\text{-}slice\ n'}$$

Combining both directions concludes the proof of the precision theorem. □

5.3.2. Correctness

Amtoft's approach to showing slicing correct via a simulation property of two labelled transition systems (LTS, cf. Sec. 3.3.1) seems not to be restricted to the intraprocedural case; yet, I am not aware of prior approaches that use it for interprocedural evidence. In the remainder of this section, I will show how I lifted the weak simulation so that correctness can again be proved, and which adaptions to the definitions from Sec. 3.3.2 are necessary for that.

Naively, we could consider to again use a (node, state) pair for the LTS states as in the intraprocedural case and use edges, whose source nodes are in the slice, as labels. But, in the interprocedural case, just determining if the source node of an edge is in the slice is not sufficient to distinguish between a silent and observable move. We rather have to take the whole call history into account, the example in Fig. 5.13 shows why. At the top, we see the source code of a simple program, below its CFG. The nodes that are greyed out are not part of the slice for the `print c;` statement in the `main` procedure, whose corresponding node 5 is shown in black. The question is now: Is traversing the outgoing edge of the grey node 12 – i.e., statement `int y := x + 7;` in procedure g – a silent move or not? According to the intraprocedural definitions, this traversal would be observable. This means that the sliced graph has to traverse this edge whenever the original graph does. However, look at the bold arrow depicting a valid path in the original CFG: it reaches procedure g via procedure f, whose call node 3 is not part of the slice, though. Hence, the corresponding path in the sliced graph would never descend in procedure f, but remain in `main`, so the sliced graph can not simulate traversing the outgoing edge of node 12 in this case. However, when visiting the grey node the second time, after `main` having directly called g, this call in node 4 is part of the slice, hence both traversals in the original and the sliced CFG have to include the edge after the grey node – this time, this move has to be observable.

Hence, the moves as well as the weak simulation itself use a node list instead of just one node. Analogously to a call stack, every node in this *node stack* identifies the call site visited at that point. We will return to this topic in the next subsection.

Observable Sets

Recall that an observable set collects all elements which can be the source of the next observable transition. Interprocedurally, the parameter as well as the elements in the set are now node stacks. We first define *obs-intra* analogously to *obs* in the intraprocedural case (see Sec. 3.3.2): *obs-intra n S* collects for a node n all nodes n' reachable from n via an intraprocedural path, such that n' is in a set S, but no other node on this path.

The observable set of a node stack $n·ns$, i.e., *obs* $(n·ns)$ S, is then determined recursively on this list: if *obs-intra* of n is empty or there is at least one node in ns, such that the respective node of the call site is not in S, we calculate *obs* recursively on the remainder of the list. Otherwise, the observable sets consists of all call stacks $n'·ns$ where n' is in *obs-intra n S*.

In the previous subsection, I introduced node stacks which collect call sites, but did not give a complete definition. As a call site in the CFG can be identified by either the call or the return node, we

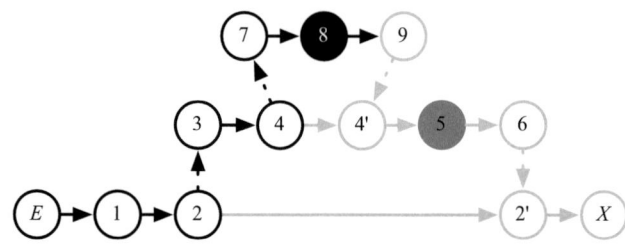

Figure 5.14.: A CFG example for observable set computation

have to decide which of the two suits best to be collected in the node stack. Intuitively, the call node seems a good choice. However, this would result in observable sets that are not only counter-intuitive, but will be obstructive in the definition of the weak simulation. Consider Fig. 5.14: all nodes that are not greyed out are in the slice S of the black node 8; this includes both call nodes 2 and 4, but not the return nodes 2' and 4'. The observable set of the grey node 5 in the slice in this call context would then be determined via *obs* (5·[2]) S, which yields {2}. As 5 cannot even reach node 2, this seems strange; moreover, as 5 lies behind slicing node 8, we would expect an empty observable set. Thus, collecting call nodes in the node stack is not the right choice.

However, if we determine that the return nodes of a call site identify the call site, we do not run into these problems. In the above example, the observable set of 5 in this calling context is *obs* (5·[2']) S, which yields the empty set as desired, as 2' is not in slice S.

Whenever a return node is in a slice, its matching call node is also included; the converse does not hold, as we have just seen in the example. Hence, choosing return nodes is the right option, thus a node stack consists – except for the top node – of the return nodes of the call sites just visited. Predicate *return-node* identifies return nodes; recall that predicate *call-of-return-node n n'* determines for a return node n its call node n'.

As the interprocedural framework features only standard control dependence, I do not assume that the observable set in the slice for every node is at most a singleton, but prove it directly. Lifting $\lfloor\ \rfloor_{CFG}$ to node sets such that it returns for every SDG node set the set of its CFG "parent" nodes, the first lemma concerns observable nodes within a procedure (the proof is along the lines of the proof for standard control dependence as sketched in Sec. 3.3.3):

$$\frac{valid\text{-}node\ n}{(\exists n'.\ obs\text{-}intra\ n\ \lfloor HRB\text{-}slice\ n_c \rfloor_{CFG} = \{n'\}) \vee obs\text{-}intra\ n\ \lfloor HRB\text{-}slice\ n_c \rfloor_{CFG} = \emptyset}$$

Then, proving an equivalent lemma for *obs* is easy: we just have to make sure that the node stack – without the top node – consists of return nodes as illustrated above:

$$\frac{ns' \in obs\ ns\ \lfloor HRB\text{-}slice\ n_c \rfloor_{CFG} \qquad \forall n \in set\ (tl\ ns).\ return\text{-}node\ n}{obs\ ns\ \lfloor HRB\text{-}slice\ n_c \rfloor_{CFG} = \{ns'\}}$$

The Statically Sliced Graph

Analogously to the intraprocedural case, the sliced CFG consists of the same nodes and edges as the original CFG, but a new mapping from edges to their semantic effect via *slice-kind* is introduced.

As in rule SK1 in Fig. 3.14 in Sec. 3.3.2, I keep both intraprocedural edge kinds in the sliced CFG if their respective source node is in the slice. Moreover, I still replace update edges with $\Uparrow id$ if it is not, as it is done in rule SK2. The rules for replacing predicate edges with a no-op, however, need to be adjusted: if the source node of the edge has no observable node in this procedure, it is no longer sufficient to arbitrarily determine one of its outgoing edges to hold in the sliced CFG, whereas all other edges do not hold. We now have to make sure that, even in such cases, there is a path to the procedure exit in the sliced CFG, which can be traversed in any state. To this end, I keep rules SK3-5, just replacing *obs* with *obs-intra*, but replace rules SK6 and SK7 from Fig. 3.14 by new rules SK6-8 as shown in Fig. 5.15: they mirror the effect of rules SK3-5, but instead of the shortest distance to the next node in the observable set – which is now empty –, they take the distance to the procedure exit of the current procedure into account. Procedure exits and the global exit are identified by predicate *method-exit*.

For call and return edges, we need new rules altogether. If the source node of an edge is not in the slice, we replace the edge kind with a no-op effect. The no-op for call looks as follows: $(\lambda cf.\ False){:}r \hookrightarrow_p fs$, we just replace the predicate with one that is never satisfiable. For return edges, the sliced edge kind is equally simple: $(\lambda cf.\ True) \hookleftarrow_p (\lambda cf\ cf'.\ cf')$, with a predicate that is always satisfiable (making the proofs much easier than the unsatisfiable $\lambda cf.\ False$) and a function that discards the call frame of the procedure, hence restores the state before the call.

$$\frac{\begin{array}{c} src\ a \notin \lfloor HRB\text{-}slice\ n_c \rfloor_{CFG} \qquad obs\text{-}intra\ (src\ a)\ \lfloor HRB\text{-}slice\ n_c \rfloor_{CFG} = \emptyset \\ kind\ a = (Q)_{\sqrt{}} \qquad method\text{-}exit\ mex \qquad get\text{-}proc\ (src\ a) = get\text{-}proc\ mex \\ distance\ (trg\ a)\ mex\ x \qquad distance\ (src\ a)\ mex\ (x+1) \\ trg\ a = (SOME\ n.\ \exists a'.\ src\ a = src\ a' \wedge distance\ (trg\ a')\ mex\ x\ \wedge \\ valid\text{-}edge\ a' \wedge intra\text{-}kind\ (kind\ a') \wedge trg\ a' = n) \end{array}}{slice\text{-}kind\ n_c\ a = (\lambda s.\ True)_{\sqrt{}}}\ \text{SK6}$$

$$\frac{\begin{array}{c} src\ a \notin \lfloor HRB\text{-}slice\ n_c \rfloor_{CFG} \qquad obs\text{-}intra\ (src\ a)\ \lfloor HRB\text{-}slice\ n_c \rfloor_{CFG} = \emptyset \\ kind\ a = (Q)_{\sqrt{}} \qquad method\text{-}exit\ mex \qquad get\text{-}proc\ (src\ a) = get\text{-}proc\ mex \\ distance\ (trg\ a)\ mex\ x \qquad distance\ (src\ a)\ mex\ (x+1) \\ trg\ a \neq (SOME\ n.\ \exists a'.\ src\ a = src\ a' \wedge distance\ (trg\ a')\ mex\ x\ \wedge \\ valid\text{-}edge\ a' \wedge intra\text{-}kind\ (kind\ a') \wedge trg\ a' = n) \end{array}}{slice\text{-}kind\ n_c\ a = (\lambda s.\ False)_{\sqrt{}}}\ \text{SK7}$$

$$\frac{\begin{array}{c} src\ a \notin \lfloor HRB\text{-}slice\ n_c \rfloor_{CFG} \qquad obs\text{-}intra\ (src\ a)\ \lfloor HRB\text{-}slice\ n_c \rfloor_{CFG} = \emptyset \\ kind\ a = (Q)_{\sqrt{}} \qquad method\text{-}exit\ mex \qquad get\text{-}proc\ (src\ a) = get\text{-}proc\ mex \\ \neg\ distance\ (trg\ a)\ mex\ x \qquad distance\ (src\ a)\ mex\ (x+1) \end{array}}{slice\text{-}kind\ n_c\ a = (\lambda s.\ False)_{\sqrt{}}}\ \text{SK8}$$

Figure 5.15.: New rules for the *slice-kind* n_c of predicate edges with empty *obs-intra*

If the source node of a call or return edge is in the slice, it may nonetheless be necessary to adapt its edge kind, if one or more of its corresponding parameter nodes are not in the slice. With call edges, only those formal parameters whose *Formal-in* is in the slice get assigned the passed argument value in the new call frame; otherwise, the parameter is not initialized. Similarly with return edges, only those return variables whose *Actual-out* is in the slice get assigned the return value, the other variables keep the value from before the call. The auxiliary functions *cspp* (for "call slice parameter passing") and *rspp* (for "return slice parameter passing") modify the parameter passing functions of call and return edges to take care of this.

Fig. 5.16 shows the formal rules for the *slice-kind* of call and return edges. Instead of the concrete definitions for *cspp* and *rspp*, I present some lemmas that clarify their behaviour at the top. Together with the new rules for predicate edges, these rules guarantee that "slicing out" a call node makes the intraprocedural "shortcut" to the return node traversable in any state:

$$\frac{x < |fs| \qquad \textit{Formal-in } (m,x) \notin S}{(\textit{cspp } m \ S \ fs)_{[x]} = \textit{empty}} \qquad \frac{x < |fs| \qquad \textit{Formal-in } (m,x) \in S}{(\textit{cspp } m \ S \ fs)_{[x]} = fs_{[x]}}$$

$$\frac{x < |\textit{Param-Defs } (\textit{trg } a)|}{\textit{valid-edge } a \qquad |\textit{Param-Defs } (\textit{trg } a)| = |xs| \qquad \textit{Actual-out } (\textit{trg } a,x) \in S}{(\textit{rspp } (\textit{trg } a) \ S \ xs \ f \ g) \ ((\textit{Param-Defs } (\textit{trg } a))_{[x]}) = g(xs_{[x]})}$$

$$\frac{x < |\textit{Param-Defs } (\textit{trg } a)|}{\textit{valid-edge } a \qquad |\textit{Param-Defs } (\textit{trg } a)| = |xs| \qquad \textit{Actual-out } (\textit{trg } a,x) \notin S}{(\textit{rspp } (\textit{trg } a) \ S \ xs \ f \ g) \ ((\textit{Param-Defs } (\textit{trg } a))_{[x]}) = f((\textit{Param-Defs } (\textit{trg } a))_{[x]})}$$

$$\frac{\textit{src } a \notin \lfloor \textit{HRB-slice } n_c \rfloor_{CFG} \qquad \textit{kind } a = Q{:}r{\hookrightarrow}_p fs}{\textit{slice-kind } a = (\lambda cf. \ \textit{False}){:}r{\hookrightarrow}_p fs}$$

$$\frac{\textit{src } a \in \lfloor \textit{HRB-slice } n_c \rfloor_{CFG} \qquad \textit{kind } a = Q{:}r{\hookrightarrow}_p fs}{\textit{slice-kind } a = Q{:}r{\hookrightarrow}_p(\textit{cspp } (\textit{trg } a) \ (\textit{HRB-slice } n_c) \ fs)}$$

$$\frac{\textit{src } a \notin \lfloor \textit{HRB-slice } n_c \rfloor_{CFG} \qquad \textit{kind } a = Q{\hookleftarrow}_p f}{(\lambda cf. \ \textit{True}) \hookleftarrow_p (\lambda cf \ cf'. \ cf')}$$

$$\frac{\textit{src } a \in \lfloor \textit{HRB-slice } n_c \rfloor_{CFG}}{\textit{kind } a = Q{\hookleftarrow}_p f \qquad \textit{valid-edge } a \qquad (p,\textit{ins},\textit{outs}) \in \textit{set procs}}{Q \hookleftarrow_p (\lambda cf \ cf'. \ \textit{rspp } (\textit{trg } a) \ (\textit{HRB-slice } n_c) \ \textit{outs } cf' \ cf)}$$

Figure 5.16.: Formal rules for the *slice-kind*s of call and return edges

$$\frac{\textit{src } a \notin \lfloor \textit{HRB-slice } n_c \rfloor_{CFG} \qquad \textit{valid-edge } a \qquad \textit{intra-kind } (\textit{kind } a)}{\textit{valid-edge } a' \qquad \textit{kind } a' = Q{:}r{\hookrightarrow}_p fs \qquad \textit{src } a = \textit{src } a'}{\textit{slice-kind } n_c \ a = (\lambda s. \ \textit{True})_{\sqrt{}}}$$

The rules above also guarantee that the sliced CFG is still deterministic.

Moves in the Graphs

Moves in the interprocedural case are relations between (node stack, state) tuples, which traverse either an edge or an edge list. Traversing some edge kinds (i.e., call and return) alters the node stack, while other (intraprocedural ones) only change its top element, if any.

Generally, a move is a non-τ-move iff the top node as well as the corresponding call nodes of the remaining nodes in the node stack (which are all return nodes) are in the slice. However, for return edges, it suffices that the corresponding call nodes of the nodes in the tail stack are in the slice, regardless of the top node being in the slice. Why do we need this special treatment of return edges? Revisit Fig. 5.14, where the slicing node is not in the *Main* procedure. If we consider traversals across the slicing node, e.g. complete program runs to the program exit X, we have to descend to the *Main* procedure in both the original and the sliced graph. To this end, both traverse the same return edges (in Fig. 5.14 edges 9-4′ and 6-2′), hence it is valid to make them non-τ-moves. This scenario can only be the case if the top node of the stack is not in the slice whereas the corresponding call nodes of the remaining nodes are; e.g. the node stack for traversing return edge 9-4′ is [9, 4′, 2′], where 9 is not in the slice, but 4 and 2 are. Remember that the top node of the node stack when traversing a return edge is a procedure exit. If this node is not in the slice, as is node 9 in the example, the return node of its call site, i.e., node 4′, cannot be part of it either. If its matching call node is not in the slice, above rule for return edges does not apply; hence we have a silent τ-move. If, however, the call node is in the slice, as is node 4 in the example, while the return node is not, we know that the slicing node must lie either in the procedure which is called at this site or in a procedure called recursively in it. Hence, in this case, the procedure exit of the called procedure has to occur after the slicing node, just as node 9 in the example in Fig. 5.14 occurs after slicing node 8.

Fig. 5.17 shows the formal rules for the non-τ-moves. Apart from the requirement discussed above, which guarantees that the move is indeed a non-τ-move, the rules need some more assumptions:

- the traversed edge is valid, its predicate has to hold in the initial state and its traversal in the initial state yields the final state,

- the top node of the initial node stack is the source node of the traversed edge, the top node of the final call stack its target node,

- all nodes in the node stack except the top node are return nodes,

- node stack and state – remember that a state is a stack of call frames – have the same length in the initial tuple,

- an intraprocedural edge leaves the tails of node and call stack unchanged,

$$\frac{\begin{array}{c} \textit{valid-edge } a \\ \textit{pred } (f\,a)\,s \qquad \textit{transfer } (f\,a)\,s = s' \qquad \textit{intra-kind } (\textit{kind } a) \\ \forall\,nx \in \textit{set ns}.\ \exists\,nx'.\ \textit{call-of-return-node } nx\ nx' \wedge nx' \in \lfloor \textit{HRB-slice } n_c \rfloor_{CFG} \\ \textit{src } a \in \lfloor \textit{HRB-slice } n_c \rfloor_{CFG} \qquad \forall\,nx \in \textit{set ns}.\ \textit{return-node } nx \\ |s| = |ns| + 1 \qquad |s'| = |s| \end{array}}{n_c,f \vdash ((\textit{src } a)\cdot ns, s) \ -a\to ((\textit{trg } a)\cdot ns, s')}$$

$$\frac{\begin{array}{c} \textit{valid-edge } a \qquad \textit{pred } (f\,a)\,s \\ \textit{transfer } (f\,a)\,s = s' \qquad \textit{kind } a = Q{:}r\hookrightarrow_p fs \qquad a' \in \textit{get-return-edges } a \\ \forall\,nx \in \textit{set ns}.\ \exists\,nx'.\ \textit{call-of-return-node } nx\ nx' \wedge nx' \in \lfloor \textit{HRB-slice } n_c \rfloor_{CFG} \\ \textit{src } a \in \lfloor \textit{HRB-slice } n_c \rfloor_{CFG} \qquad \forall\,nx \in \textit{set ns}.\ \textit{return-node } nx \\ |s| = |ns| + 1 \qquad |s'| = |s| + 1 \end{array}}{n_c,f \vdash ((\textit{src } a)\cdot ns, s) \ -a\to ((\textit{trg } a)\cdot(\textit{trg } a')\cdot ns, s')}$$

$$\frac{\begin{array}{c} \textit{valid-edge } a \qquad \textit{pred } (f\,a)\,s \qquad \textit{transfer } (f\,a)\,s = s' \qquad \textit{kind } a = Q\hookleftarrow_p f \\ \forall\,nx \in \textit{set ns}.\ \exists\,nx'.\ \textit{call-of-return-node } nx\ nx' \wedge nx' \in \lfloor \textit{HRB-slice } n_c \rfloor_{CFG} \\ \forall\,nx \in \textit{set ns}.\ \textit{return-node } nx \qquad \textit{hd } ns = \textit{trg } a \\ |s| = |ns| + 1 \qquad |s'| + 1 = |s| \qquad s' \neq [] \end{array}}{n_c,f \vdash ((\textit{src } a)\cdot ns, s) \ -a\to (ns, s')}$$

Figure 5.17.: Formal rules for the non-τ-moves

- a call edge pushes its matching return node and the procedure entry on the node stack, and the final state extends the initial by one call frame, and

- a return edge removes the top elements from the node and call stacks, but only if this does not result in empty stacks.

As in the intraprocedural case, the rules carry a parameter f, which is replaced with *kind* when traversing the original CFG, with *slice-kind* n_c when traversing the sliced CFG of n_c.

The rules for τ-moves, see Fig. 5.18, require that the matching call node of one node in the tail of the node stack is not in the slice; for intraprocedural and call edges, it is also sufficient that the top node of the node stack is not in the slice. This is just the negation of the respective assumptions in the τ-move rules, as we know that every return node has exactly one matching call node. All other assumptions are kept.

$=\Rightarrow_\tau$ again denotes the reflexive transitive closure of τ-moves, an observable move $=\Rightarrow$ consists of such an arbitrary sequence of silent moves, followed by a non-τ-move.

$$\frac{\begin{array}{c} \textit{valid-edge } a \\ \textit{pred } (f\,a)\,s \qquad \textit{transfer } (f\,a)\,s = s' \qquad \textit{intra-kind } (\textit{kind } a) \\ (\exists\,nx \in \textit{set } ns.\ \exists\,nx'.\ \textit{call-of-return-node } nx\ nx' \wedge nx' \notin \lfloor \textit{HRB-slice } n_c \rfloor_{CFG}) \vee \\ \textit{src } a \notin \lfloor \textit{HRB-slice } n_c \rfloor_{CFG} \qquad \forall\,nx \in \textit{set } ns.\ \textit{return-node } nx \\ |s| = |ns| + 1 \qquad |s'| = |s| \end{array}}{n_c,f \vdash ((\textit{src } a)\cdot ns,s)\ -a\!\rightarrow_\tau\ ((\textit{trg } a)\cdot ns,s')}$$

$$\frac{\begin{array}{c} \textit{valid-edge } a \qquad \textit{pred } (f\,a)\,s \\ \textit{transfer } (f\,a)\,s = s' \qquad \textit{kind } a = Q{:}r\hookrightarrow_p fs \qquad a' \in \textit{get-return-edges } a \\ (\exists\,nx \in \textit{set } ns.\ \exists\,nx'.\ \textit{call-of-return-node } nx\ nx' \wedge nx' \notin \lfloor \textit{HRB-slice } n_c \rfloor_{CFG}) \vee \\ \textit{src } a \notin \lfloor \textit{HRB-slice } n_c \rfloor_{CFG} \qquad \forall\,nx \in \textit{set } ns.\ \textit{return-node } nx \\ |s| = |ns| + 1 \qquad |s'| = |s| + 1 \end{array}}{n_c,f \vdash ((\textit{src } a)\cdot ns,s)\ -a\!\rightarrow_\tau\ ((\textit{trg } a)\cdot(\textit{trg } a')\cdot ns,s')}$$

$$\frac{\begin{array}{c} \textit{valid-edge } a \qquad \textit{pred } (f\,a)\,s \qquad \textit{transfer } (f\,a)\,s = s' \qquad \textit{kind } a = Q\hookleftarrow_p f \\ \exists\,nx \in \textit{set } ns.\ \exists\,nx'.\ \textit{call-of-return-node } nx\ nx' \wedge nx' \notin \lfloor \textit{HRB-slice } n_c \rfloor_{CFG} \\ \forall\,nx \in \textit{set } ns.\ \textit{return-node } nx \qquad \textit{hd } ns = \textit{trg } a \\ |s| = |ns| + 1 \qquad |s'| + 1 = |s| \qquad s' \neq [] \end{array}}{n_c,f \vdash ((\textit{src } a)\cdot ns,s)\ -a\!\rightarrow_\tau\ (ns,s')}$$

Figure 5.18.: Formal rules for the τ-moves

The following results show that silent moves preserve observable sets:

Lemma 5.3 *Silent Moves Preserve Observable Sets:*

$$\frac{\begin{array}{c} n_c,\textit{kind} \vdash (ns,s) =as\Rightarrow_\tau (ns',s') \\ nsx \in \textit{obs } ns' \lfloor \textit{HRB-slice } n_c \rfloor_{CFG} \qquad \forall\,n \in \textit{set } (tl\ ns').\ \textit{return-node } n \end{array}}{nsx \in \textit{obs } ns \lfloor \textit{HRB-slice } n_c \rfloor_{CFG} \wedge (\forall\,n \in \textit{set } (tl\ ns).\ \textit{return-node } n)}$$

$$\frac{\begin{array}{c} n_c,f \vdash (ns,s) =as\Rightarrow_\tau (ns',s') \\ \textit{obs } ns' \lfloor \textit{HRB-slice } n_c \rfloor_{CFG} = sasymemptyset \end{array}}{\textit{obs } ns \lfloor \textit{HRB-slice } n_c \rfloor_{CFG} = sasymemptyset}$$

If the intraprocedural observable set of node n contains a node n', then there exist silent moves in the sliced CFG from a node stack with n at the top to one with n' at the top, its tails equal, where the initial and final state agree. If the intraprocedural observable set is empty, the same holds with n' being the procedure exit of n's procedure:

$$\frac{\begin{array}{c} \forall\, n \in set\ ns.\ valid\text{-}node\ n \qquad \forall\, n' \in set\ ns'.\ valid\text{-}node\ n' \\ \forall\, n \in set\ (tl\ ns).\ return\text{-}node\ n \qquad |ns| = |s| \qquad |ns'| = |s'| \qquad s \neq [] \\ s' \neq [] \qquad ns = nsx\ @\ nx{\cdot}tl\ ns' \qquad get\text{-}proc\ nx = get\text{-}proc\ (hd\ ns') \\ \forall\, n \in (tl\ ns').\ \exists\, n'.\ call\text{-}of\text{-}return\text{-}node\ n\ n' \wedge n' \in \lfloor HRB\text{-}slice\ n_c \rfloor_{CFG} \\ nsx \neq [] \longrightarrow (\exists\, nx'.\ call\text{-}of\text{-}return\text{-}node\ nx\ nx' \wedge nx' \notin \lfloor HRB\text{-}slice\ n_c \rfloor_{CFG}) \\ obs\ ns\ \lfloor HRB\text{-}slice\ n_c \rfloor_{CFG} = obs\ ns'\ \lfloor HRB\text{-}slice\ n_c \rfloor_{CFG} \\ \forall\, i < |ns'|.\ snd\ s_{[|nsx| + i]} = snd\ s'_{[i]} \\ \forall\, i < |ns'|.\ \forall\, V \in rv\ n_c\ (CFG\text{-}node\ (nx{\cdot}tl\ ns')_{[i]}).\ (fst\ s_{[|nsx| + i]})\ V = (fst\ s'_{[i]})\ V \end{array}}{((ns,s),(ns',s')) \in WS\ n_c}$$

Figure 5.19.: The formal definition of the interprocedural $WS\ n_c$

Lemma 5.4 *Observable Sets and Silent Moves in the Sliced CFG:*

$$\frac{\begin{array}{c} m' \in obs\text{-}intra\ n\ \lfloor HRB\text{-}slice\ n_c \rfloor_{CFG} \\ |s| = |n{\cdot}nsx'| \qquad \forall\, n \in set\ nsx'.\ return\text{-}node\ n \end{array}}{\exists\, as.\ n_c, slice\text{-}kind\ n_c \vdash (n{\cdot}nsx',s) = as \Rightarrow_{\tau} (n'{\cdot}nsx',s)}$$

$$\frac{\begin{array}{c} obs\text{-}intra\ n\ \lfloor HRB\text{-}slice\ n_c \rfloor_{CFG} = \emptyset \\ method\text{-}exit\ n' \qquad get\text{-}proc\ n = get\text{-}proc\ n' \\ valid\text{-}node\ n \qquad |s| = |n{\cdot}nsx'| \qquad \forall\, n \in set\ nsx'.\ return\text{-}node\ n \end{array}}{\exists\, as.\ n_c, slice\text{-}kind\ n_c \vdash (n{\cdot}nsx',s) = as \Rightarrow_{\tau} (n'{\cdot}nsx',s)}$$

The Weak Simulation

The relevant variables rv are defined analogously to the intraprocedural case. $V \in rv\ n_c\ n$ holds if in the HRB slice of n_c there is a SDG node n' which uses V and whose parent CFG node is reachable from the parent CFG node of n via an intraprocedural path, such that no other SDG node, whose parent node is on this path, redefines V:

$$\frac{\lfloor n \rfloor_{CFG} - as \to_{i*} \lfloor n' \rfloor_{CFG} \qquad n' \in HRB\text{-}slice\ n_c \qquad V \in Use_{SDG}\ n' \\ \forall\, n''.\ valid\text{-}SDG\text{-}node\ n'' \wedge \lfloor n'' \rfloor_{CFG} \in set\ (srcs\ as) \longrightarrow V \notin Def_{SDG}\ n''}{V \in rv\ n_c\ n}$$

Yet, the definition of the weak simulation $WS\ n_c$ is considerably more complex than in the intraprocedural case, see Fig. 5.19. It is a relation between (node stack, state) pairs (ns,s) and (ns',s'), denoting the positions in the original and sliced graph, respectively, such that

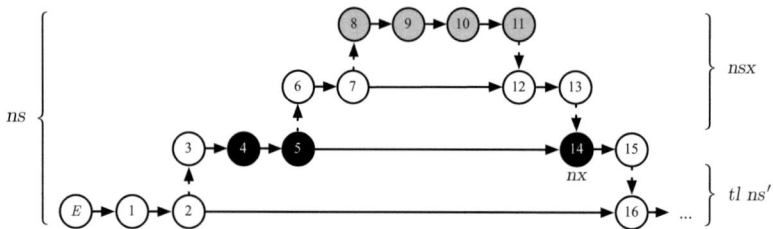

Figure 5.20.: Example of weak similar node stacks

- all nodes in *ns* and *ns'* are valid,

- all nodes in *ns* except its top node are return nodes,

- the lengths of *ns* and *s* as well as those of *ns'* and *s'* (all nonempty) agree,

- *ns* is of the form *nsx* @ *nx·tl ns'*, i.e., it has the second node stack, without its top node, as suffix,

- both nodes *nx* and *hd ns'* lie in the same procedure,

- the matching call nodes to all return nodes in the common suffix *tl ns'* of both node stacks are in the slice,

- if *nsx* is not empty, *nx*'s matching call node is not in the slice,

- the observable sets of *ns* and *ns'* are equal,

- the return information (the *snd* part of every call frame) is equal in the bottom |*ns'*|-many call frames of *s* and *s'*, and

- the local variables (the *fst* part) of these call frames agree in the values of the relevant variables, calculated w.r.t. the nodes in the *ns* node stack which conform to these call frames.

For an example, see Fig. 5.20. It depicts a CFG, where all the black nodes are not in the slice. Hence, a traversal in the original CFG may descend in the procedure in which the grey nodes lie, whereas in the sliced CFG it must remain in the procedure of the black nodes. So e.g. the node stacks *ns* = [9,12] @ 14·[16] in the original and *ns'* = [5,16] in the sliced CFG are (tupled with adequate states) weakly similar; all node stacks of the grey nodes are related this way to the node stacks of the black nodes. Note that the observable set of all these node stacks is {[15,16]}.

The correctness theorem then looks as in the intraprocedural case (see Thm. 3.2), except that instead of nodes, we now argue about node stacks:

Theorem 5.5 *Correctness of Horwitz-Reps-Binkley Slicing:*

$$\frac{((ns_1,s_1),(ns_2,s_2)) \in WS\ n_c \qquad n_c,kind \vdash (ns_1,s_1) =as\Rightarrow (ns_1',s_1')}{\exists s_2'\ as'.\ s_2' = transfer\ (slice\text{-}kind\ n_c\ (last\ as))\ s_2) \wedge ((ns_1',s_1'),(ns_1',s_2')) \in WS\ n_c\ \wedge \\ n_c,slice\text{-}kind\ n_c \vdash (ns_2,s_2) =as'@(last\ as)\Rightarrow (ns_1',s_2')}$$

Proof. Again, the key to prove this theorem is to show that the simulation diagrams from Fig. 3.12 hold.

(a) To prove the lemma that the first diagram holds does not require the observable set to be empty any more; basically, this is due to the new rules for determining the no-op for "sliced-out" predicate edges.

$$\frac{((ns_1,s_1),(ns_2,s_2)) \in WS\ n_c \qquad n_c,kind \vdash (ns_1,s_1) =as\Rightarrow_\tau (ns_1',s_1')}{((ns_1',s_1'),(ns_2,s_2)) \in WS\ n_c}$$

The proof of the one-step variant of this lemma – by case distinction on the τ-move – is tedious, as all the assumptions of the weak simulation have to hold again after the move. In each case there is another case distinction if the weakly similar node stacks are in the same procedure, i.e., if nsx is empty. If it is, we have to prove that the values of the relevant variables after the step are as required, which is quite trivial if it is not. The lemma above is just a simple lifting of this result.

(b) The lemma for the second diagram is exactly the same as in the intraprocedural case, except for node stacks instead of nodes:

$$\frac{((ns_1,s_1),(ns_2,s_2)) \in WS\ n_c \qquad n_c,kind \vdash (ns_1,s_1) -a\rightarrow (ns_1',s_1')}{\exists as\ s_2'.\ s_2' = transfer\ (slice\text{-}kind\ n_c\ a)\ s_2 \wedge ((ns_1',s_1'),(ns_1',s_2')) \in WS\ n_c\ \wedge \\ n_c,slice\text{-}kind\ n_c \vdash (ns_2,s_2) =as@[a]\Rightarrow (ns_1',s_2') \in WS\ n_c}$$

I prove this by case distinction on the non-τ-move. In each case, I show that the weakly similar node stacks identify nodes in the same procedure, i.e., nsx is empty. Hence, the tails of the node stacks ns_1 and ns_2 are equal. As also

$hd\ ns_1 \in obs\text{-}intra\ (hd\ ns_2)\ \lfloor HRB\text{-}slice\ n_c \rfloor_{CFG}$ can be derived, we can apply Lem. 5.4, which gives rise to silent moves in the sliced CFG between these node stacks. Together with the non-τ-move in the sliced graph, which simulates the assumed non-τ-move of the original graph, we obtain an observable move in the sliced graph. To guarantee that the weak simulation still holds after this move, we need to show all its conditions; again, the one concerning the relevant variables is the most tedious.

$\square$

Fundamental Property of Horwitz-Reps-Binkley Slicing

As before, I use Thm. 5.5 to derive the fundamental property for the slicing algorithm of Horwitz, Reps, and Binkley, namely that the observable effects at the slicing node are preserved. However, contrary to the intraprocedural case, program executions do not match arbitrary CFG paths, but only valid ones. Hence, we need lemmas which relate moves with the latter:

Lemma 5.6 *Moves and Valid Paths:*

$$
\frac{n_c,f \vdash (n\cdot ns,s) =as\Rightarrow_\tau (n'\cdot ns',s') \quad valid\text{-}node\ n \quad ns = trgs\ rs \quad \forall i < |rs|.\ rs_{[i]} \in get\text{-}return\text{-}edges\ cs_{[i]} \quad valid\text{-}return\text{-}list\ rs\ n \quad |rs| = |cs|}{n -as\rightarrow* n' \wedge valid\text{-}path\ cs\ as}
$$

$$
\frac{n_c,f \vdash (n\cdot ns,s) -a\rightarrow (n'\cdot ns',s') \quad valid\text{-}node\ n \quad ns = trgs\ rs \quad \forall i < |rs|.\ rs_{[i]} \in get\text{-}return\text{-}edges\ cs_{[i]} \quad valid\text{-}return\text{-}list\ rs\ n \quad |rs| = |cs|}{n -[a]\rightarrow* n' \wedge valid\text{-}path\ cs\ [a]}
$$

The key issue in both lemmas is how to relate the call edge stack cs of the *valid-path* predicate with the node stack ns of the moves. To this end, we determine a stack of return edges rs, which (i) match the call edges in the stack one-by-one, and (ii) whose target nodes are the return nodes collected in the node stack ns. Predicate *valid-return-list* guarantees that its first parameter is indeed a list of return edges which descends from the procedure in which its second parameter, a node, lies, such that each return edge leaves the procedure which was the target of the return edges directly above it in the stack. Many auxiliary lemmas guarantee that these premises relating call and return edge stacks are preserved by the different moves.

The following lemmas relate silent moves and same level paths: (i) silent moves whose node stack tails – or more accurately, the call nodes matching them – are in the slice induce a same level path between their top nodes, and thus the node stack tails are in fact equal;

(ii) if we have silent moves and a same level path between the top nodes of its node stacks, we know that their tails are equal:

Lemma 5.7 *Silent Moves and Same Level Paths:*

$$n_c, f \vdash (n \cdot ns, s) = as \Rightarrow_\tau (n' \cdot ns', s') \qquad \text{valid-node } n$$
$$\forall nx \in set \; ns. \; \exists nx'. \; \text{call-of-return-node } nx \; nx' \land nx' \in \lfloor HRB\text{-slice } n_c \rfloor_{CFG}$$
$$\forall nx \in set \; ns'. \; \exists nx'. \; \text{call-of-return-node } nx \; nx' \land nx' \in \lfloor HRB\text{-slice } n_c \rfloor_{CFG}$$

$$\frac{n - as \rightarrow_{sl*} n' \land ns = ns'}{}$$

$$\frac{n_c, f \vdash (n \cdot ns, s) = as \Rightarrow_\tau (n' \cdot ns', s') \qquad n - as \rightarrow_{sl*} n'}{ns = ns'}$$

In the intraprocedural case, *slice-edges* is a simple filter which keeps only those edges of a list whose source node is in the slice. Hence, the edge list of silent moves was empty after applying this filter. For an observable move, only the last edge (which corresponds to the only non-τ-move) remained. In the interprocedural case, this filter approach does not work, as we again have to take the call context into account. So, I first define *slice-edge* which determines for a given call edge stack *cs* if an edge *a* – or more accurately its edge kind – affects the slice. This is the case if the source nodes of all call edges in *cs* as well as the source node of *a* are in the slice; the latter need not hold for return edges (cf. non-τ-*moves* Fig. 5.17):

$$slice\text{-edge } n_c \; cs \; a \equiv (\forall c \in set \; cs. \; src \; c \in \lfloor HRB\text{-slice } n_c \rfloor_{CFG}) \land$$
$$(case \; (kind \; a) \; of \; Q \hookleftarrow_p f \Rightarrow True \mid \text{-} \Rightarrow src \; a \in \lfloor HRB\text{-slice } n_c \rfloor_{CFG})$$

slice-edges lifts this to an edge lists by traversing it from left to right: it keeps an edge *a* if *slice-edge n_c (upd-cs cs as′) a* holds, where *as′* is the prefix on *as* before visiting *a*, otherwise the edge is discarded. This definition fulfills the desired properties (if the call and node stacks agree):

$$\frac{n_c, f \vdash (ns, s) = as \Rightarrow_\tau (ns', s') \qquad tl \; ns = trgs \; rs}{|rs| = |cs| \qquad \forall i < |cs|. \; \text{call-of-return-node } (tl \; ns)_{[i]} \; (src \; cs_{[i]})}$$
$$\overline{slice\text{-edges } n_c \; cs \; as = []}$$

$$\frac{n_c, f \vdash (ns, s) = as \Rightarrow (ns', s') \qquad tl \; ns = trgs \; rs}{|rs| = |cs| \qquad \forall i < |cs|. \; \text{call-of-return-node } (tl \; ns)_{[i]} \; (src \; cs_{[i]})}$$
$$\overline{slice\text{-edges } n_c \; cs \; as = [last \; as]}$$

The following key lemma guarantees that a valid path whose predicates hold in initial state *s* gives rise to another valid path connecting the same nodes, whose traversal can be split into a series of observable moves (= $\Rightarrow$* is the reflexive transitive closure of = $\Rightarrow$) followed by silent moves such that their *slice-edges* agree. As we argue "within" a valid path, the remaining conditions take care that the various edge and node stacks conform (*valid-call-list* ensures that *cs* is a call edge stack whose edges constitute a call chain to *n*):

Lemma 5.8 *Splitting Valid Paths into Moves:*

$$\frac{\begin{array}{lll} \textit{valid-path cs as} & n -\textit{as} \rightarrow * n' & \textit{preds (kinds as) s} \\ \textit{valid-call-list cs n} & \forall i < |rs|.\ rs_{[i]} \in \textit{get-return-edges cs}_{[i]} & \\ \textit{valid-return-list rs n} & |rs| = |cs| & |s| = |cs| + 1 \end{array}}{\begin{array}{l} \exists ns\ ns'\ ns''\ s''\ as'\ as''.\ \textit{valid-path cs }(as''\ @\ as') \wedge n -\textit{as}'' @\ as' \rightarrow * n' \wedge \\ \quad n_c, kind \vdash (n \cdot ns, s) = \textit{slice-edges } n_c\ cs\ as \Rightarrow * (ns'', s'') \wedge \\ \quad n_c, kind \vdash (ns'', s'') = as' \Rightarrow_\tau (n' \cdot ns', s') \wedge ns = \textit{trgs rs} \wedge \\ \quad |ns| = |cs| \wedge \textit{slice-edges } n_c\ cs\ as = \textit{slice-edges } n_c\ cs\ as'' \wedge \\ \quad \forall i < |cs|.\ \textit{call-of-return-node } ns_{[i]}\ (\textit{src cs}_{[i]}) \end{array}}$$

Proof. I prove this by induction on the rules which define *valid-path*, followed by a case distinction in each case, if all the call nodes which correspond to the return nodes in the initial node stack *ns* are in the slice. The lemmas relating moves and valid paths are applied where necessary. □

Now, we have all the means to tackle the proof of the fundamental property theorem. Note that this theorem only concerns valid paths starting in the *Main* procedure, as the initial state and node stack consist of only one element. This framework is not powerful enough to state a similar theorem where the valid path in the original graph may start in an arbitrary node. This would require to derive from the return information present in the initial call stack the necessary initial node stack for the moves. Hence, either the return information would have to be fixed to be a node (or the like) instead of the current arbitrary type *'ret*, or a new function need to be assumed in one of the locales, which is able to perform this derivation.

Theorem 5.9 *Fundamental Property of Horwitz-Reps-Binkley Slicing:*

$$\frac{n -\textit{as} \rightarrow_{\sqrt{}} * n' \qquad \textit{preds (kinds as) } [cf]}{\begin{array}{l} \exists as'.\ n -\textit{as}' \rightarrow_{\sqrt{}} * n' \wedge \textit{preds (slice-kinds (CFG-node } n')\ as')\ [cf] \wedge \\ \quad \textit{slice-edges (CFG-node } n')\ []\ as = \textit{slice-edges (CFG-node } n')\ []\ as' \wedge \\ \quad (V \in \textit{Use } n'.\ \textit{state-val (transfers (slice-kinds (CFG-node } n')\ as')\ [cf])\ V = \\ \quad\quad \textit{state-val (transfers (kinds as) } [cf])\ V) \end{array}}$$

Proof. First, using Lem. 5.8, we obtain from the valid path a series of observable moves, one for each slice edge, followed by silent moves, which traverse a valid path whose *slice-edges* agree to those of the assumed valid path in the original CFG. Then, we do a case distinction if these *slice-edges* are actually empty:

If *slice-edges* (*CFG-node n'*) [] *as* = [], the traversal consists only of silent moves with final node stack $n' \cdot ns'$. As n' is the slicing node, the call nodes corresponding to any node stack leading to it must always be in the slice. With Lem. 5.7, we know that ns' must then be empty and n and n' connected via a same level path. As showed in Lem. 5.1, such a path gives rise to an intraprocedural path between the same nodes; moreover, traversing the latter in the sliced CFG yields the same result as traversing the former. As the *slice-edges* are empty, and thus all edge kinds replaced with no-ops, this result is [*cf*]. With the help of a weak simulation we also know that the values of the relevant variables of n' are equal, regardless if we take their value in the initial state [*cf*] or of the final state after traversing the edges in the original graph. As the variables used in n' are also relevant variables, and due to the results for the sliced CFG, we obtain the conclusion.

If *slice-edges* (*CFG-node n'*) [] *as* $\neq$ [], we apply Thm. 5.5 lifted to arbitrary sequences of observable moves, taking ([n],[*cf*]) as initial similar configurations in both CFGs. With the result of this and the lemma which we proved for Thm. 5.5(a), we know from the weak simulation property that the values of the relevant variables for n' (and thus, its used variables) agree, regardless if we take the final state of traversing *as* in the original or its *slice-edges* in the sliced CFG. A lifted version of Lem. 5.6 guarantees that due to the observable moves, there exists a valid path between n and n'' – the top node of the final node stack of these moves – so that traversing this path in the sliced CFG yields the same result as just traversing its *slice-edges*. The silent moves are treated very similarly to the first case, hence obtaining a same level path between n'' and n', which is combined with the valid path between n and n'' into one valid path. It just remains to show that traversing the edges of this combined path in the sliced CFG yields the same as traversing just its sliced edges, and that the sliced edges of this combined path and the sliced edges of path *as* are equal; with the result above about the used variables in n', we obtain the result.

□

If we can prove that the CFG agrees to an operational semantics, i.e., the CFG is semantically well-formed, we get another fundamental property: analogous to the intraprocedural Thm. 3.4, it considers the effect of HRB-slicing to the semantics:

Theorem 5.10 *Fundamental Property of Semantics and HRB Slicing:*

$$\frac{n \triangleq c \qquad \langle c,s \rangle \Rightarrow \langle c',s' \rangle}{\exists\, n'\, as.\ n -as \rightarrow_{\sqrt{}*} n' \wedge preds\ (slice\text{-}kinds\ (CFG\text{-}node\ n'))\ as)\ s \wedge n' \triangleq c' \wedge}$$
$$(\forall\, V \in Use\ n'.\ state\text{-}val\ (transfers\ (slice\text{-}kinds\ (CFG\text{-}node\ n')\ as')\ s)\ V = state\text{-}val\ s'\ V)$$

Note that also in this fundamental property, evaluation has to start in the *Main* procedure, i.e., the initial state consists of only one call frame.

5.4 Instantiations

In Sec. 3.4, I showed how the intraprocedural framework can be instantiated with two different languages. This section presents the instantiation of the interprocedural framework with two different languages: a simple While language with procedures, and the object oriented byte code language of Jinja.

5.4.1. WHILE **with Procedures:** PROC

Basically, PROC describes the same language as WHILE does, but it features a new calling statement: *Call p es rets* dispatches to procedure *p* with argument expressions *es* and variables *rets* to store the return values. The procedures that exist in a program are collected in a list *procs*, it contains a quadruple for each procedure, which comprises its name, formal-in and -out parameters and method body.

The CFG of a program is built in two phases: first, construct the intraprocedural CFG of any procedure as if it was a WHILE program; i.e., the nodes except *Entry* and *Exit* bear a label which uniquely identifies them in the graph, the edges are written *IEdge et*, *et* being the respective edge kind. The subgraph of a *Call* statement connects a call and the subsequent return node (which is basically an additional node corresponding to a *Skip* statement) with a dummy intraprocedural edge, written *CEdge*, which just stores the procedure and parameter information of the call statement. The syntax for edges in a procedure CFG is *prog* ⊢ *n* −*x*→$_i$ *n'*, where *x* is either a *IEdge* or *CEdge*.

The second phase joins all these graphs together in one big interprocedural CFG (the "real" CFG). Its nodes consists of the intraprocedural nodes, tupled with the procedure name in which they lie. The edges, which now also carry the program's procedure list as a parameter, are written $prog,procs \vdash (p, n) -et \rightarrow (p', n')$. The formal rules to construct the edges shows Fig. 5.21, we will take a closer look on them in the following.

Rules I1, C1, R1 and F1 concern edges whose source and/or target node is in the *Main* procedure of the program. Rule I1 lifts an intraprocedural *IEdge* to the CFG by just taking its parameter as edge kind and tupling its nodes with procedure *Main*.

A *CEdge* gives rise to three CFG edges: a call edge (see rule C1), a return edge (see rule R1) and the $(\lambda s.\ False)_{\sqrt{}}$ between call and return node (see rule F1). Since PROC has no late binding or the like, the predicate of the call edge kind has to hold for any call frame. It also saves the return node of the *CEdge* (in procedure *Main*) as return information. Finally, the function list for argument passing is realized by mapping the expression evaluation function $[\,]$ on the list of arguments. The target node of a call to procedure p is its entry node $(p,(\text{-}Entry\text{-}))$.

The predicate of the return edge kind checks if the top call frame contains the target node of the *CEdge* (again in procedure *Main*) as return information, which is then the target node of the CFG edge. Its source node is the procedure exit. The function specified in the edge kind has to take care that the return values are stored in the respective values while popping the call stack. Hence, it restores the call frame from before the call, but updates all variables which are declared as return variables with the value of the respective out parameter in the call frame of the procedure. The remaining assumptions of rules C1, R1 and F1 are just simple checks that the length of certain lists agree and that the specified return variables are distinct.

Rules I2, C2, R2 and F2 match the rules above, but describe the respective situation within a called procedure. To this end, I use predicate *containsCall procs prog ps p*, which guarantees that procedure p is called via the list of procedures ps that must be called from *Main* to reach procedure p. The remaining assumptions mirror those of the *Main* rules or take care that procedure p is in the procedure list *procs*.

I define *get-return-edges* to collect all edges whose target node agrees with the return information specified in the parameter call edge; if the parameter is no call edge, I return the empty set. Every call edge has

$$\frac{prog \vdash n\ -IEdge\ et \rightarrow_i n'}{prog,procs \vdash (Main,n)\ -et \rightarrow (Main,n')}\ I1$$

$$\frac{prog \vdash (\text{-}l\text{-})\ -CEdge\ (p,es,rets) \rightarrow_i n' \qquad (p,ins,outs,c) \in set\ procs}{\quad et = (\lambda cf.\ True){:}(Main,n')\hookrightarrow_p map\ (\lambda e\ cf.\ [\![e]\!]cf)\ es \quad}{prog,procs \vdash (Main,(\text{-}l\text{-}))\ -et \rightarrow (p,(\text{-}Entry\text{-}))}\ C1$$

$$\frac{prog \vdash (\text{-}l\text{-})\ -CEdge\ (p,es,rets) \rightarrow_i (\text{-}l'\text{-}) \qquad (p,ins,outs,c) \in set\ procs}{et = (\lambda cf.\ snd\ cf = (Main,(\text{-}l'\text{-})))\hookleftarrow_p(\lambda cf\ cf'.\ cf'(rets\ [{:}{=}]\ map\ cf\ outs))}{prog,procs \vdash (p,(\text{-}Exit\text{-}))\ -et \rightarrow (Main,(\text{-}l'\text{-}))}\ R1$$

$$\frac{prog \vdash n\ -CEdge\ (p,es,rets) \rightarrow_i n'}{prog,procs \vdash (Main,n)\ -(\lambda s.\ False)_{\surd} \rightarrow (Main,n')}\ F1$$

$$\frac{\begin{array}{c} c \vdash n\ -IEdge\ et \rightarrow_i n' \\ (p,ins,outs,c) \in set\ procs \qquad containsCall\ procs\ prog\ ps\ p \end{array}}{prog,procs \vdash (p,n)\ -et \rightarrow (p,n')}\ I2$$

$$\frac{\begin{array}{c} c \vdash (\text{-}l\text{-})\ -CEdge\ (p',es',rets') \rightarrow_i (\text{-}l'\text{-}) \qquad (p',ins',outs',c') \in set\ procs \\ (p,ins,outs,c) \in set\ procs \qquad containsCall\ procs\ prog\ ps\ p \\ et = (\lambda cf.\ True){:}(p,(\text{-}l'\text{-}))\hookrightarrow_{p'} map\ (\lambda e\ cf.\ [\![e]\!]cf)\ es' \end{array}}{prog,procs \vdash (p,(\text{-}l\text{-}))\ -et \rightarrow (p',(\text{-}Entry\text{-}))}\ C2$$

$$\frac{\begin{array}{c} c \vdash (\text{-}l\text{-})\ -CEdge\ (p',es',rets') \rightarrow_i (\text{-}l'\text{-}) \qquad (p',ins',outs',c') \in set\ procs \\ (p,ins,outs,c) \in set\ procs \qquad containsCall\ procs\ prog\ ps\ p \\ et = (\lambda cf.\ snd\ cf = (p,(\text{-}l'\text{-})))\hookleftarrow_{p'}(\lambda cf\ cf'.\ cf'(rets'\ [{:}{=}]\ map\ cf\ outs')) \end{array}}{prog,procs \vdash (p',(\text{-}Exit\text{-}))\ -et \rightarrow (p,(\text{-}l'\text{-}))}\ R2$$

$$\frac{\begin{array}{c} c \vdash n\ -CEdge\ (p',es',rets') \rightarrow_i n' \\ (p,ins,outs,c) \in set\ procs \qquad containsCall\ procs\ prog\ ps\ p \end{array}}{prog,procs \vdash (p,n)\ -(\lambda s.\ False)_{\surd} \rightarrow (p,n')}\ F2$$

Figure 5.21.: The formal rules to create the interprocedural CFG from the procedure CFGs

only one matching return edge, so *get-return-edges* for a call edge is a singleton.

The call frame consists (i) of a mapping from variables to values, and (ii) of the return information, i.e., the return node of the respective call. Variables that get assigned are in the *Def*, those used in assignment statements or predicates in the *Use* set. *ParamUses* is a list of sets, nonempty for call nodes, where the entry for a parameter contains all the variables that are used in the argument expression corresponding to the parameter position in the call. *ParamDefs* is a list of the variables which get assigned the return values.

Before we can instantiate the locales, we have to make sure that the program (and its procedure list) fulfils some well-formedness properties:

- the formal-in parameters of every procedure quadruple in *procs* have to be distinct, as do the formal-out parameters;

- the *Main* procedure must not occur in *procs*;

- all procedure names in *proc*'s quadruples are distinct;

- the return variables provided in a call have to be distinct;

- for every procedure call in the program the lengths of the actual parameters agree to the lengths of the formal parameters as given in the matching procedure quadruple in *procs*.

Subsuming all these properties in a predicate *wf*, I regard a program *prog* and its procedure list *procs* as well-formed, if *wf prog procs* holds.

To instantiate the locales, I regard the CFG edges as *valid-edges*; *src*, *kind* and *trg* are defined straightforwardly on them. *get-proc* applied to a CFG node – remember that these nodes are tuples of a procedure and a unique label – just returns its first element. The global entry and exit nodes are the procedure entry and exit nodes of *Main*. *lift-procs* agrees to the procedure list *procs*, but eliminates the fourth tuple entry, i.e., the procedure body, from every element in the list. These definitions, together with the ones above, i.e., *get-return-edges*, *Def*, *Use*, *ParamDefs* and *ParamUses*, are now used as parameters for the locale instantiations. The proofs that the required properties hold are easy but tedious, and done mostly by case distinction on the CFG generation rules.

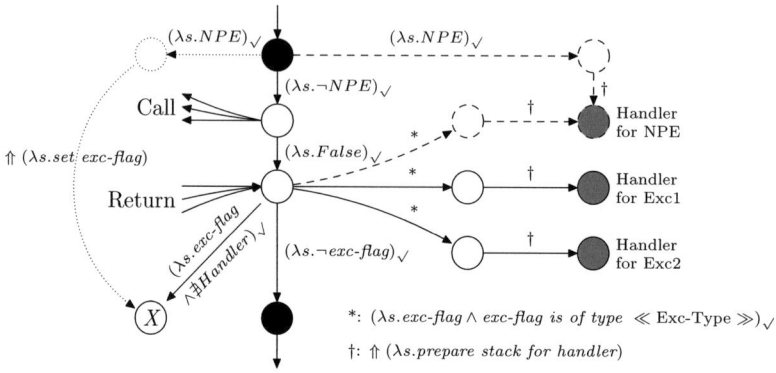

Figure 5.22.: Subgraph resulting from a single INVOKE instruction

5.4.2. Jinja VM Byte Code Interprocedural

Again, this instantiation was performed by my colleague Denis Lohner. In this subsection, I shortly sketch the differences from the intraprocedural one (see Sec. 3.4.2).

The CFG nodes are no longer identified by a call stack, which was
essential for method inlining, but by a triple consisting of class name,
method name – these two determine a procedure – and its position in
the method's instruction list. Thus, every instruction in the program
forms a node of the CFG. Still, we have to insert additional nodes (and
edges) for instructions that throw exceptions (like GETFIELD) as they
fork the control flow *and* update the state at the same time.

The changes to the CFG edges themselves are relatively small, with
the exception of the INVOKE instruction, of course. Instead of formal
rules, we use Fig. 5.22 to show the new interprocedural CFG edges of
a call, i.e., a single INVOKE. This instruction may throw an exception
either because the receiver object is `null` or the callee throws an exception. The upper black node in the figure corresponds to the entry
point of an INVOKE, the lower black node to the subsequent instruction in the method's instruction list; grey nodes are entry points for
exception handlers, the node labeled with X is the exit node of the
method. Predicate edges are given as $(\lambda s.P)_\checkmark$ where P is a predicate
over the method-local state s, and update edges are given as $\Uparrow (\lambda s.f)$
where f is a function over s. Late binding is modeled by call edges to
all statically potential call targets, using the call edge's predicate to re-

solve the dynamic target. Adding a points-to analysis, the number of call edges could be reduced and thus precision gained; future work will tackle this task. The return information contained in the call edges is the label of the call node. If the INVOKE instruction is guarded by a handler for the `NullPointerException` (NPE), the dashed nodes and edges are added to the CFG, otherwise the dotted ones. For every other exception handler guarding the INVOKE instruction there are edges from the return node to the handlers' entry points. If IN-VOKE returns in an exceptional state for which no handler is present in the current method, the exception is propagated to the method's exit node. An exceptional state contains a special flag which signals that an exception has occurred.

The actual-in parameters of a method with n parameters are always the top $n + 1$ elements of the local stack (including the callee's **this** pointer), formal-in parameters are local variables. The actual- and formal-out parameter of a method is the top element of the stack (note that in Jinja, as in Java, methods can return only one value and that a **void** method returns the dummy element *Unit*). Besides these parameters, every method also has an implicit in- and out-parameter for the heap as well as an out-parameter which signals an exception.

From this, we know that *ParamUses* must be a list of singleton sets of the form $[\{Heap\}, \{this\}, \{Stack\ (top - n + 1)\}, \dots, \{Stack\ top\}]$, if *top* denotes the index of the topmost element in the stack. Note that at every INVOKE, *this* is at position *Stack* $(top - n)$. *ParamDefs* is a list of the form $[Heap, Stack\ (top - n), Exception]$.

As Jinja byte code is a stack based language, we have to map stack positions to locations. This is done using the byte code verifier, as it guarantees for a given program point the height of the stack to be the same, regardless of the path taken. Then, the *Def* and *Use* sets are rather simple to compute, as for every instruction it is statically known which stack positions are involved. Further locations in the *Def* and *Use* sets are the heap (treated as a whole), local variables and the exception flag. Using the exception flag as location and out parameter, there is no need for multiple return edges. Thus, as in PROC, every call edge has a uniquely matching return edge.

As Jinja lacks static methods, we enrich the CFG with an artificial main method that just "calls" the actual main method. However, the **this** pointer of that method is set to `null`.

Most of the proofs for instantiating the locales are done by case distinction, some require an induction on the CFG's structure.

6

Information Flow Control via Verified Slicing

In this chapter, I present a proof that slicing can guarantee information flow noninterference. Noninterference is a standard notion in information flow control (IFC), which describes the fact that secret information in a program does not leak to public output. The most wide-spread approach for information flow noninterference are IFC type systems, e.g. see [122, 10, 58].

This noninterference proof is based on the correctness of slicing, thus reuses the results from the previous chapters. This exemplifies that the work presented here is not limited to the scope of this thesis: it forms an ideal basis to verify algorithms which use slicing as an underlying program analysis. As the proof builds on the modular slicing framework, it immediately inherits its language-independence. It holds for any language that instantiates the framework, hence we obtain a noninterference algorithm for any such language; e.g. by the results of this thesis, for a While language as well as for Jinja byte code.

I constructed a noninterference proof for both the static intra- and interprocedural case. As the proof structure is identical in both cases (yet, the proofs of the interprocedural case are much more substantial, of course), I will only show noninterference based on Horwitz-Reps-Binkley slicing in the following. Details on the intraprocedural case can be found in [132], the theories are available online [130].

6.1 Information Flow Noninterference

Language-based IFC analyzes the program source to discover security leaks, and usually aims to establish noninterference. Informally, noninterference demands that a variation in secret variables will not result in variations of public output, thus guaranteeing confidentiality. This work employs the most fundamental noninterference definition which I call *classical noninterference*; yet, other names like *low-deterministic security* [73] or *batch-job termination-insensitive noninterference* (BTINI) [5] are also common.

Let H and L be the secret (high) and public (low) confidentiality levels. For a program statement c, $[\![c]\!]$ denotes the state transformation induced by executing c in the sense of denotational semantics. Two states s and s' are low-equal, written $s \approx_L s'$, if they coincide on variables with confidentiality level L. Classical noninterference then demands that $\forall s\, s'.\, s \approx_L s' \longrightarrow [\![c]\!]s \approx_L [\![c]\!]s'$. Note that this definition only talks about the initial and final program states; classical noninterference cannot express security-relevant properties of intermediate states.

The correctness theorem proposed in this thesis can be stated as follow: if the backward slice of all low variables does not contain high variables, then classical noninterference is satisfied and hence the program is secure. In fact, it is enough to require that backward slices of *final* low variables do not contain *initial* high values, ignoring intermediate states and variables.

The converse of the theorem does not hold, because all implementations of noninterference based on program analysis, including our own, are conservative approximations; that is, they can generate false alarms. The more precise an analysis is, the less false alarms it will generate. To illustrate precision, consider the following program, which uses call-by-reference:

```
procedure swap (int x, int y) {
    int temp := y; y := x; x := temp;
}
swap (h1, h2);
swap (l1, l2);
```

It swaps two H values as well as two L values using the same auxiliary method. The program is perfectly secure in the sense of noninterference, but a context-insensitive analysis will generate a false alarm, as it does not distinguish the two calling contexts and thus erroneously reports that a H value may be assigned (i.e., leaked) to an L variable. Furthermore, most systems require an annotation for `temp` with either H or L, which generates another false alarm. Being context-sensitive, Horwitz-Reps-Binkley slicing can guarantee that this programm is indeed noninterferent. Hence, the approach presented in the following has truly additional benefit compared to standard IFC type systems, which cannot validate noninterference in this example.

Due to being flow-sensitive, slicing can prove programs like `l := h; l := 0;` noninterferent. Most type systems would reject it as unsecure as it assigns a high variable to a low variable; however, flow types as proposed from Hunt and Sands [58] eliminate this drawback. Still, while classical noninterference based on slicing produces fewer false alarms, 100% precision is impossible due to decidability problems.

6.2 The Proof

In the definitions and lemmas of this section, I sometimes abuse notation to not wear out the reader. For example, I omit conversions between CFG and SDG nodes and node sets as well as between states whose call frames contain return information and those that do not, that initial states in the noninterference theorems consist of only one call frame, etc.

6.2.1. The Assumptions

Classical IFC noninterference, a special case of a noninterference definition using partial equivalence relations (PER) [97], partitions the variables (i.e., locations) into security levels. Usually, only two levels, H for secret or high and L for public or low variables, are used. Basically, a program that is noninterferent has to fulfil one basic property: executing the program in two different initial states that may differ in the values of their H-variables yields two final states that again only differ in the values of their H-variables; thus the values of the H-variables did not influence those of the L-variables. We will now show how slicing à la Horwitz, Reps, and Binkley can guarantee that a program is noninterferent.

locale *NonInterferenceGraph* = *SDG* +
fixes H :: '*var set*
fixes L :: '*var set*
fixes (*-High-*) :: '*node*
fixes (*-Low-*) :: '*node*
assumes *HighLowDistinct*: $H \cap L = \{\}$
and *HighLowUNIV*: $H \cup L = UNIV$
and *Entry-edge-Exit-or-High*: ⟦*valid-edge a*; *src a* = (*-Entry-*)⟧
   $\implies$ *trg a* = (*-Exit-*) ∨ *trg a* = (*-High-*)
and *High-target-Entry-edge*: ∃ *a*. *valid-edge a* ∧ *src a* = (*-Entry-*) ∧
   trg a = (*-High-*) ∧ *kind a* = (λ*s*. *True*)$_{\sqrt{}}$
and *Entry-predecessor-of-High*:
   ⟦*valid-edge a*; *trg a* = (*-High-*)⟧ $\implies$ *src a* = (*-Entry-*)
and *Exit-edge-Entry-or-Low*: ⟦*valid-edge a*; *trg a* = (*-Exit-*)⟧
   $\implies$ *src a* = (*-Entry-*) ∨ *src a* = (*-Low-*)
and *Low-source-Exit-edge*: ∃ *a*. *valid-edge a* ∧ *src a* = (*-Low-*) ∧
   trg a = (*-Exit-*) ∧ *kind a* = (λ*s*. *True*)$_{\sqrt{}}$
and *Exit-successor-of-Low*:
   ⟦*valid-edge a*; *src a* = (*-Low-*)⟧ $\implies$ *trg a* = (*-Exit-*)
and *DefHigh*: *Def* (*-High-*) = H
and *UseHigh*: *Use* (*-High-*) = H
and *UseLow*: *Use* (*-Low-*) = L

Figure 6.1.: Locale fixing the assumptions for IFC noninterference by
slicing

Classical noninterference makes certain assumptions: (i) all H-variables are defined at the beginning of the program, (ii) all L-variables are observed (or used in our terms) at the end and (iii) every variable is either H or L. This security label is fixed for a variable and can not be altered during a program run. Thus, we have to extend the prerequisites of our framework accordingly in a new locale *NonInterferenceGraph*, see Fig. 6.1.

To fulfil the third assumption, we assume two variable sets H and L that partition the set of all variables; *HighLowDistinct* and *High-LowUNIV* make sure this holds. A naive approach to guarantee that assumptions (i) and (ii) hold would require (*-Entry-*) to have all H-variables in its *Def* set and (*-Exit-*) to have all L-variables in its *Use* set. Yet, remember that our framework requires that the *Def* and *Use* sets of both nodes are empty. Hence, we assume two special nodes, (*-High-*) and (*-Low-*), where the former is the only immediate successor of $(\textit{-Entry-})^1$, the latter the only immediate predecessor of (*-Exit-*); both connecting edges are labelled with no-op $(\lambda s.\ True)_{\sqrt{}}$, hence both (*-Low-*) and (*-High-*) are in procedure *Main*. All *H*-variables are contained in the *Def* set of (*-High-*) (for conformance reasons, they also have to be in its *Use* set), all *L*-variables in the *Use* set of (*-Low-*).

6.2.2. Low Equality

In classical noninterference, an external observer can only see public values, in our case the *L*-variables; moreover, he can only observe them at the beginning and end of program execution. If two states agree in the values of all *L*-variables, these states are indistinguishable for him. *Low equality* groups those states in an equivalence class using the relation $\approx_L$:

$$s \approx_L s' \equiv \forall V \in L.\ \textit{state-val } s\ V = \textit{state-val } s'\ V$$

The next lemma builds a bridge between low equal states as needed in the noninterference proof and the relevant variables of the weak simulation in the slicing correctness proof: if we have two low equal states and (*-High-*) is not in the HRB slice of n_c, then the values of the relevant variables of (*-Entry-*) are equal in both states:

Lemma 6.1 *Relating Low-Equality and Relevant Variables:*

$$\frac{s \approx_L s' \qquad (\textit{-High-}) \notin \textit{HRB-slice } n_c}{\forall V \in rv\ n_c\ (\textit{-Entry-}).\ \textit{state-val } s\ V = \textit{state-val } s'\ V}$$

6.2.3. Slicing Guarantees Noninterference

Assume a program and two low equal initial states $s \approx_L s'$ whose execution yields two final states that are not low equal. A different value in a *L*-variable in the final states can only occur due to a different value in a *H*-variable in *s* or *s'*, as traversing a CFG is deterministic. Hence, we know that at least one initial *H*-variable influenced a result *L*-variable. As (*-Low-*) uses all *L*-variables and (*-High-*) defines all *H*-variables, there is a valid path in the SDG between them due to this interference (this correlation is an implication from the correctness result in the previous chapter). Thus, the HRB slice computed for (*-Low-*) contains (*-High-*). So, to guarantee that there is no such influence, there

---

[1]This of course only holds with the exception of the special (*-Entry-*)-(*-Exit-*) edge.

may not be a valid SDG path, hence $(\textit{-High-}) \notin HRB\textit{-slice} (\textit{-Low-})$ has to hold.

The next lemma is the key to show this; its proof takes up the majority of the whole theory. It looks at the values of the variables used in (*-Low-*), which is also the slicing node, after traversing paths in the sliced graph. Assume we have two paths *as* and *as'* between *n*, a node in the *Main* procedure, and (*-Low-*). Both paths fulfill all their predicates in the sliced graph of (*-Low-*) with initial states *s* and *s'*, respectively. These two states agree on the values of all relevant variables of *n* in this sliced graph. Then the final states after traversing *as* and *as'* in the sliced CFG agree in the values of the used variables in (*-Low-*):

Lemma 6.2 *Relating Relevant and Used Variables:*

$$\frac{\begin{array}{ll} n -as \rightarrow_{\sqrt{}*} (\textit{-Low-}) & preds \ (slice\textit{-}kinds \ (\textit{-Low-}) \ as) \ s \\ n -as' \rightarrow_{\sqrt{}*} (\textit{-Low-}) & preds \ (slice\textit{-}kinds \ (\textit{-Low-}) \ as') \ s' \\ get\textit{-proc} \ n = Main & \forall V \in rv \ (\textit{-Low-}) \ n. \ state\textit{-}val \ s \ V = state\textit{-}val \ s' \ V \end{array}}{\begin{array}{c} \forall V \in Use \ (\textit{-Low-}). \ state\textit{-}val \ (transfers \ (slice\textit{-}kinds \ (\textit{-Low-}) \ as) \ s) \ V = \\ state\textit{-}val \ (transfers \ (slice\textit{-}kinds \ (\textit{-Low-}) \ as') \ s') \ V \end{array}}$$

Proof. Both *n* and (*-Low-*) are in *Main*, so *as* and *as'* are same level paths, remember their definition in Sec. 5.2.2. The above lemma is a corollary of a more general one, which draws the same conclusion but only requires suffixes of same level paths with an appropriate call edge stack. The latter can be proved by induction on *same-level-path*, where in each nonempty case we have to make sure that the following conditions on the path suffixes from the assumptions hold: (i) their lengths are equal, (ii) the leading edge of both paths is the same, and (iii) for all relevant variables in the target node of the leading edge, the values after traversing the leading edge in states *s* and *s'* agree. For call and return edges, to prove that the leading edges agree is quite simple, for an intraprocedural edge we need that the sliced graph is deterministic. Combining these conditions with the induction hypotheses, the conclusion follows directly. $\square$

For the original CFG, the final state of executing a program in an initial state *s* is *transfers (kinds as) s*, if *as* is the corresponding valid path between (*-Entry-*) and (*-Exit-*) in the CFG and *preds (kinds as) s* holds. Following the argumentation from above, assuring that *HRB-slice* of (*-Low-*) does not contain (*-High-*) suffixes in proving noninterference of a program. Thus, we state the noninterference theorem for HRB slicing as follows:

Theorem 6.3 *Path Noninterference Theorem for HRB Slicing:*

$$\frac{s \approx_L s' \quad \text{(-Entry-)} -as\rightarrow_{\surd}* \text{(-Exit-)}}{\text{(-Entry-)} -as'\rightarrow_{\surd}* \text{(-Exit-)} \quad \text{(-High-)} \notin \text{HRB-slice (-Low-)}}{\frac{preds\ (kinds\ as)\ s \quad preds\ (kinds\ as')\ s'}{transfers\ (kinds\ as)\ s \approx_L transfers\ (kinds\ as')\ s'}}$$

Proof. The trick to prove this theorem is to argue in the sliced graph of (*-Low-*). First, we split the paths *as* and *as'* into paths from (*-Entry-*) to (*-Low-*) and the no-op edges between (*-Low-*) and (*-Exit-*). Then, we apply the Fundamental Property of HRB Slicing Thm. 5.9 to both trimmed paths. Thus, the values of all variables that are used in (*-Low-*) are equal, regardless if we traversed the original or the sliced graph; this holds for both trimmed paths. Using Lem. 6.1 and Lem. 6.2, the first two premises and the paths from (*-Entry-*) to (*-Low-*), we know that these values also agree for both traversals of the sliced graph. Thus, the values of (*-Low-*)'s used variables also agree in the final states after traversing the paths in the original graph. Since traversing the edges between (*-Low-*) and (*-Exit-*) has no influence on the states, we know that the same holds for the final states after executing the whole program. As the variables used in (*-Low-*) are exactly the *L*-variables, we obtain the conclusion. □

If we have a semantically well-formed CFG, i.e., the CFG conforms to an operational semantic, we obtain a theorem that connects HRB slicing to the standard semantic definition for noninterference as a corollary from Thm. 6.3 after the following considerations.

As mentioned in Sec. 6.1, classical noninterference just considers a complete program execution, starting in the initial statement *c* that describes the program. However, the framework argues about paths, so we need to identify the initial node of program execution, i.e., the first node after (*-Entry-*) and (*-High-*). A naive approach would assume a predicate over statements *initial*, which guarantees that its parameter is indeed the initial statement, and then identify the corresponding node via $\triangleq$. Though, this does not lead to the desired initial node. Consider program $c = $ `skip; while (true) skip`. All standard small step semantics evaluate this statement in two steps to `skip; while (true) skip` again (by unfolding the loop body). Hence, this statement is identified by two different nodes, only one of them being the initial one.

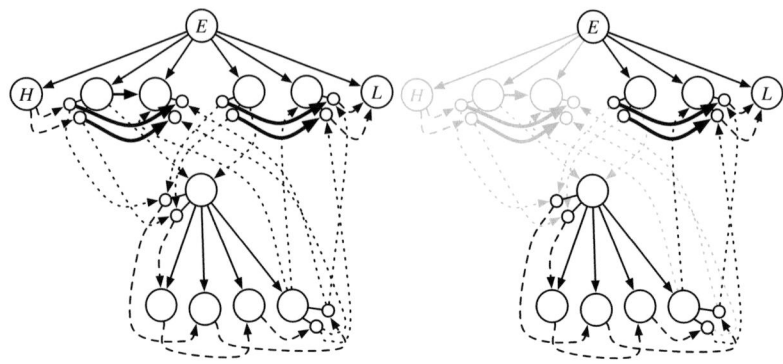

Figure 6.2.: Slicing shows the `swap` example noninterferent

However, there is a solution for this dilemma: let n be the immediate successor node of (-*High*-); since (-*Entry*-) and (-*High*-) are mere auxiliary nodes without a corresponding statement, this is the initial node that starts the program; we write this as *initial n*. If n identifies c, written $n \triangleq c$, c is the statement describing this program. Analogously, predicate *final* holds only for the node which is the immediate predecessor of (-*Low*-). The statement that it identifies is thus the fully evaluated statement. While this approach "pollutes" a semantic proof with CFG notions, it seems the only satisfying solution, since arguing solely on statements cannot work, as showed above. Then, we can lift low-deterministic correctness as follows:

Theorem 6.4 *Noninterference Theorem for HRB slicing:*

$$\frac{s_1 \approx_L s_2 \quad (\text{-}High\text{-}) \notin \textit{HRB-slice} \ (\text{-}Low\text{-}) \quad \textit{initial n}}{n \triangleq c \quad \textit{final } n' \quad n' \triangleq c' \quad \langle c, s_1 \rangle \Rightarrow \langle c', s_1' \rangle \quad \langle c, s_2 \rangle \Rightarrow \langle c', s_2' \rangle}{s_1' \approx_L s_2'}$$

Reconsider the `swap` example from Sec. 6.1. The graph on the left in Fig. 6.2 shows the SDG for this example with the necessary (-*High*-) and (-*Low*-) added, which are labelled H and L, respectively[2]. Note that x and y are in- as well as out-parameters for procedure `swap`. The HRB slice of node L includes only those nodes not greyed out in the graph on the right. As H is greyed out, it is not part of the slice and thus, no information can flow from H to L, which proves the program to be noninterferent.

---

[2]As usual, solid arrows denote control, dashed arrows data, dotted arrows call and parameter and bold arrows summary edges.

6.3 Lifting Arbitrary Framework Graphs

In general, only few CFGs that are valid in the framework will fulfil the assumptions from locale *NonInterferenceGraph*, as they do not have the required (*-High-*) and (*-Low-*) nodes. However, we can lift any arbitrary CFG from the framework such that the above requirements hold. Note that the partition in *H*- and *L*-variables must still be provided from the outside.

First, relabel the (*-Entry-*) node to (*-High-*) and the (*-Exit-*) node to (*-Low-*). Next, adapt its *Def* and *Use* set, so that (*-High-*) defines and uses all *H*-variables, (*-Low-*) uses all *L*-variables. Add two additional nodes, *NewEntry* and *NewExit*, the new entry and exit nodes of the lifted CFG, with empty *Def* and *Use* sets. They have to connect to (*-High-*) and (*-Low-*) with the required intraprocedural no-op edges. Moreover, every function assumed and defined in the original locales has to be lifted. Finally, I proved that this lifted graph instantiates locale *NonInterferenceGraph*, which contains the correctness results Thm. 6.3 and 6.4, if its original graph is a valid CFG in the slicing framework.

7

Discussion and Related Work

In this chapter I first review the formalizations in this thesis in terms of their sizes. While it may not be too important if some formalization is some lines longer than another, comparing the sizes leads to some interesting insights. The subsequent sections discuss related work. We distinguish several categories:

- works concerning semantics and type safety proofs for object-oriented languages as well as multiple inheritance,

- works on the correctness of slicing,

- some works that address similar formalization and verification issues in proof assistants, and

- works which formalize and verify information flow noninterference in proof assistants.

7.1 Formalization Sizes

Both formalizations, the CoreC++ semantics as well as the slicing framework, are substantial developments and belong to the large-scale projects in theorem provers. Fig. 7.1, Fig. 7.2, and Fig. 7.3 show the

LoC	Lemmas	Definitions	Locales
14,727	505	82	0

Figure 7.1.: CoreC++ formalization numbers

	LoC	Lemmas	Definitions	Locales
Framework				
Common subset	1,836	72	12	7
Dynamic slicing	1,653	48	8	4
Static intrapr. slicing	3,383	89	23	5
Instantiations				
WHILE	2,319	40	14	0
+ semantic well-form.	3,177	51	17	0
Jinja	2,884	57	24	0
+ semantic well-form.	5,517	100	27	0
IFC Noninterference				
Proof	558	15	2	2
CFG lifting	1,470	12	3	0
Total	14,103	333	86	18
+ semantic well-form.	17,594	387	92	18

Figure 7.2.: Dynamic and static intraprocedural slicing

size of the formalizations in terms of lines of code, lemmas, definitions (which also includes recursive and inductive ones) and locales. In the following, I focus on some interesting details.

Consider the sizes of the frameworks in Fig. 7.2 and Fig. 7.3. Although I could reuse some parts of the static intraprocedural work (i.e., common subset + static intraprocedural slicing), the size of the interprocedural framework grew by a factor of 4. This is mainly due to the complicated formalizations of SDGs with summary edges and the algorithm of Horwitz, Reps, and Binkley, as well as the new precision proof and the lifting of the correctness proof to the interprocedural case.

The proof that slicing can guarantee noninterference grew from intra- to interprocedural slicing by a factor of 3, the lifting only by 30%. In both cases, the proof is quite short compared to the framework size. Hopefully, the correctness results of the framework turn out to be a benefit in proving other slicing related issues, similar to IFC noninterference as shown here.

As for the instantiations, some surprising facts can be seen. Remember that PROC is essentially WHILE plus procedures. Adding procedures to WHILE – thus gaining PROC – resulted in an instantiation size increase by factor 2.8. However, for Jinja the migration from intra- to

	LoC	Lemmas	Definitions	Locales
Framework	18,988	579	104	12
Instantiations (w/o semantic well-form.)				
PROC	6,758	127	29	0
Jinja	3,429	64	30	0
IFC Noninterference				
Proof	1,502	20	2	2
CFG lifting	2,025	8	10	0
Total	32,702	798	175	14

Figure 7.3.: Static interprocedural slicing

interprocedural led to an increase of the instantiation size of only $\frac{1}{6}$. This is likely due to the fact that byte code languages reflect the corresponding CFG structure very well in the sense that nodes correspond to instruction positions in a rather natural way.

Is the approach of using a language independent framework to prove the correctness of slicing actually wise? In the intraprocedural case, each instantiation we showed (While and Jinja) took about 50% of the size of the framework. Now, in the interprocedural case, we were able to push this factor down to $\frac{1}{3}$ for PROC and even to $\frac{1}{5}$ for Jinja; hence, instantiating the framework with a new language is indeed much easier than redoing the whole proof.

7.2 Type Safe Semantics for C++

There is a wealth of material on formal semantics of object-oriented languages, but to our knowledge, a formal semantics for a language with C++-style multiple inheritance with type safety proof has not yet been presented. An impressive piece of work is the C++ semantics of Norrish [83], which formalizes the C++ standard [116] and sticks very close to the language implementation. While not providing a type safety proof, Norrish can handle concepts this thesis ignores, such as namespaces, templates, explicit pointers and the like.

7.2.1. Type Safety Proofs for Object-Oriented Languages

Java formed a primary target for research in semantics and type safety because of its rich and well documented type system. The work of Drossopoulou and Eisenbach [42] can be considered ground-breaking in this area: they were the first to prove an substantial object-oriented subset of Java to be type safe.

Jinja [61] was a big achievement for showing type safety of object-oriented programs, it was the first type safety proof of a relevant subset of a widely-used OO language in a theorem prover. As this project also showed type safety for Jinja byte code, verified a byte code verifier and a compiler, the whole compilation chain down to byte code has been proved correct.

In his thesis [45], Fruja showed type safety of C# and its byte code representation, the .NET CLR. The language under consideration is again a subset, however very sophisticated, as it features structs, delegates, ref- and out-parameters, and boxing and unboxing. C# uses, like Java, single inheritance, thus many of the problems considered in this thesis do not show up. To prove type safety, Fruja provides the semantics of the languages through an abstract interpreter, which is defined as an *abstract state machine* model. He shows that its execution according to the semantics of legal and well-typed methods does not lead to run-time type violations and leaves the program in a good state. To this end, the complex definite assignment analysis of variables is proved to be sound, just like the CLR byte code verifier. Yet, all proofs were done manually, they are not machine-checked.

Bruce et al. define an object-oriented language called PolyTOIL [30] and its byproduct $\mathcal{LOOM}$ [29]. The requirement for both languages was to be type safe by design. They achieve this by three design decisions: (i) classes are not types but values, (ii) a special type MyType for the this-Pointer, and (iii) a *matching* relation replacing the standard subtyping relation. This enables them to handle contravariant parameter types, parameterized types and (match-bounded) polymorphism. With the aid of a subject reduction theorem, they prove their languages type safe. However, this approach differs considerably from the object-oriented understanding used in wide-spread languages like Java and C++. Yet they were able to carry over their results to Java; the resulting language is called $\mathcal{LOOJ}$ [28].

7.2.2. Semantics of Multiple Inheritance

Cardelli [32] presents a formal semantics for a form of multiple inheritance based on structural subtyping of record types, which also extends to function types. Another early paper from Breazu-Tannen et al. [27] claims to give a semantics to multiple inheritance for a language (PCF++) with record types. It is difficult to relate the language constructs used in each of these to the multiple inheritance model of C++.

The work by Attali et al. [6] is similar to ours in spirit but treats Eiffel rather than C++, whose multiple inheritance model differs considerably. Eiffel uses shared inheritance by default; repeated inheritance is not possible, instead repeated members must be uniquely renamed when inherited.

CZ as proposed by Malayeri and Aldrich [72] tackles the problem of diamonds in multiple inheritance class hierarchies. They only regard shared inheritance, as this is "the desirable semantics" [72, Sec. 2] for multiple inheritance. Instead of the repeated inheritance problem of field copies, diamonds using shared inheritance require careful handling when initializing objects; the constructor of a shared superclass may only be called once, cf. Sec. 2.6.1. CZ tackles a well-known problem: it separates subclassing (for which it uses the keyword `extends`) from subtyping, indicated by `requires`. Subclassing diamonds are then prohibited, but subtyping diamonds are allowed. A class `A` that `requires` class `B` should not call `B`'s constructor; however, all concrete subclasses of `A` have to `extend` `B`.

Scala [84] provides a mechanism for symmetrical mixin inheritance as introduced by Bracha and Cook [26], in which a class can inherit members from multiple superclasses. If members are inherited from two mixin classes, the inheriting class has to resolve the conflict by providing an explicit overriding definition. Scala side-steps the issue of shared vs. repeated multiple inheritance by simply disallowing a class to (indirectly) inherit from a class that encapsulates state more than once (multiply inheriting from abstract classes that do not encapsulate state – called traits – is allowed, however). The semantic foundations of Scala, including a type system and soundness proof can be found in [85].

7.2.3. C++ Multiple Inheritance

Wallace [124] presents an informal discussion of the semantics of many C++ constructs, but avoids all the crucial issues. The natural semantics for C++ presented by Seligman [102] does not include multiple inheritance nor covariant return types. Most closely related to our work is [55], where some basic C++ data types (including structs but excluding pointers) are specified in PVS; an object model is "in preparation".

The complexities introduced by C++-style multiple inheritance are manifold, and have to our knowledge never been formalized adequately or completely. In the C++ standard [116], the semantics of operations such as method calls and casts that involve class hierarchies are defined informally, while several other works (see, e.g., Stroustrup [114]) discuss the implementation of these operations in terms of compiler data structures such as virtual function pointer tables ("v-tables"). Rossie and Friedman [93] were the first to formalize the semantics of operations on C++ class hierarchies in the form of a calculus of subobjects. This work forms the basis for the semantics presented in this thesis and previous work [126].

Ramalingam and Srinivasan [89] observe that a direct implementation of Rossie and Friedman's definition of member lookup can be inefficient because the size of a subobject graph may be exponential in the size of the corresponding class hierarchy graph. They present an efficient member lookup algorithm for C++ that operates directly on the class hierarchy graph. Still, like Rossie and Friedman, their definition does not follow C++ precisely in cases where static information is used to resolve ambiguities.

7.3 Correctness of Slicing

In this section, I present some key works which address the correctness of slicing, grouped in static and dynamic approaches.

7.3.1. Static Slicing

While dependence graphs are a quasi standard in slicing, it is surprising that there is no work on the correctness of interprocedural slicing based on dependence graphs; all contributions shown in the following that use this technique are intraprocedural.

Reps and Yang [92] were the first to prove static intraprocedural slicing correct using CFGs and PDGs. This work is restricted to a simple While language without procedures and standard control dependence. The correctness proof by Ball and Horwitz [7] uses a similar language and the same control dependence, but allows also non-structural control flow, e.g. jumps. While these proofs were ground-breaking, they suffer from their limited application area, e.g. for varying languages or control dependence relations.

Ranganath et al. [90] and Amtoft [3] define correctness of slicing using a weak simulation, an approach that is also used in this thesis. The former focuses on defining and using various control dependences, the latter concentrates on weak order dependence and the presentation of the correctness proof. In spite of its limitations, Amtoft's work turned out to be ideal for the slicing framework of this thesis as

(i) his code map conforms to applying the functions *kind* and *transfer* to the corresponding CFG edges in the framework, and

(ii) in the intraprocedural case, the characteristics of weak order dependence are just needed in exactly one lemma where Amtoft proves that the observable set for any node is at most a singleton; if one can show this property for another control dependence, the whole proof still holds for this new control dependence.

The work presented here goes well beyond Amtoft's work as I eliminated the concrete language as well as, in the intraprocedural case, the concrete control dependence definition. Moreover, I lifted it to the interprocedural case and to the sophisticated slicing definition of Horwitz, Reps, and Binkley [57].

In [125], Ward and Zedan model slicing as a program transformation, thereby abstracting from specific representations. In their sense, a program transformation is any operation on a program which generates a semantically equivalent program. The aim of their work, which concerns intra- and interprocedural slicing, is to provide a unified mathematical framework for sequential programs. However, it deviates considerably from the wide-spread dependence graph based slicing approach as formalized in this thesis; moreover, it relies on pen-and-paper proofs whereas my framework is fully machine-checked.

7.3.2. Dynamic Slicing

The approach for dynamic slicing as presented in this thesis relates to the work by Agrawal and Horgan [1], primarily to Approach 3, since nodes can occur multiple times in paths (e.g. in loops), my equivalent to their *execution history*. From such an execution history, they build the *Dynamic Dependence Graph*, but this graph does not correspond to the dynamic PDG computed here as the latter contains all paths, not only a selected one. Although data dependence can be computed for a single path in isolation, we need this additional information about all possible paths for computing the control dependence relation. Agrawal and Horgan also use (in their case static) PDG information to determine the control dependences in their execution history. Having all possible traces in a TCFG is only a formalization trick that is of course not applicable in algorithms really computing dynamic slices because TCFGs are potentially infinite.

The approach of Gouranton and Le Métayer [49] is similar to mine as they present a language independent framework and use it to show the correctness of dynamic slicing. Instead of graph structures, they base their work on natural semantics. The slicing itself uses annotations where program points with annotation *False* are treated as *Skip*, the same strategy I pursue with the notion of bit vectors. They also present the embedding of three different languages in their framework: an imperative, a logic programming and a functional one. As my framework is based on CFGs, instantiating it with a logic or functional language is far from trivial, but for the latter the results by Shivers [103] suggest that it may nevertheless be possible – at least for the dynamic and static intraprocedural framework.

7.4 Working with Proof Assistants

This section subsumes various areas directly associated with working in a proof assistant. It concerns (i) structuring and abstracting proofs via modularization, (ii) the formalization of flow graphs, and (iii) some results on the verification of program analyses.

7.4.1. Modularized Proofs

The ability to modularize proofs is not unique to locales in Isabelle, other theorem provers provide comparable tools, cf. parametric theories in PVS [86] and modules in Coq [35]. Similar to my work, other approaches use these means to prove properties abstracting from concrete program instances.

The Coq part in the tool KRAKATOA by Marché et al. [74] – a tool for verifying that a Java program meets its JML specification – uses the module concept to abstract from a concrete Java program. KRAKATOA ensures that the properties proven for the abstract instance, i.e., a signature representing the class structure of an arbitrary Java program, also hold for any concrete program.

7.4.2. Flow Graphs in Proof Assistants

Various works on verification in theorem provers use a notion of control flow graphs, e.g. see Leroy [68] and Blech et al. [24]. In most cases, they define control flow implicitly, i.e., as a relation, not as a real graph structure.

Lammich and Müller-Olm [67] define a parallel flow graph similar in structure to my control flow graph (but they also formalize parallelism), which is not restricted to a certain language either. While my work uses flow graphs to construct dependence graphs and to prove certain properties of them, they focus on the correctness of analyses on the flow level.

7.4.3. Machine Checked Verification of Program Analyses

Using theorem provers to verify program analyses has gained widespread acceptance, mainly for basic analyses like Kildall's workflow algorithm [60, 38, 99, 69], simple compiler optimizations [24, 119], etc. Bertot et al. [19] go one step further and provide a framework in Coq [18] for compiler optimizations such as dead code elimination and common subexpression elimination. Results for sophisticated interprocedural analyses as the one presented in this paper are rare, exceptions being the verification of a Java byte code verifier [61, 17] and a data race analyzer based on a context sensitive points-to analysis by Dabrowski and Pichardie [39].

An interesting idea is presented by Chang et al. in [34]: they introduce *certified program analyses*, whose implementation is accompanied by a checkable proof for soundness, in the sense of proof-carrying code [79]. Their approach employs code extraction from Coq, while trying to preserve the implementation structure as close as possible. Also Cachera et al. [31] use code extraction from Coq to achieve a verified dataflow analyzer in OCaml.

7.5 IFC Noninterference in Proof Assistants

Most works that formalize information flow noninterference in a proof assistant that we are aware of are information flow type systems [96]. This comes as no surprise because how to prove properties of type systems in proof assistants is well-known. However, we also discuss two other approaches: (i) formalizations of Goguen/Meseguer style noninterference, and (ii) noninterference via dynamic logic.

7.5.1. Verification of Information Flow Type Systems

Noninterference in type systems is usually defined analogously to the notion of classical noninterference of this thesis. Some IFC type systems also allow more general PER noninterference models as described in [97] by Sabelfeld and Sands. We distinguish between intra- and interprocedural approaches in the following.

Intraprocedural Type Systems

Barthe and Nieto [11] formalize an information flow type system for a concurrent while language as defined by Boudol and Castellani [25], which is an extension of the Volpano/Smith system [107]. Using Isabelle/HOL, they define a bisimulation (which allows stuttering) over the semantic rules to show noninterference. Furthermore, they also verify noninterference for scheduling programs. The sequential subset of the Volpano/Smith system was also formalized in Isabelle/HOL by Snelting and Wasserrab [110], together with a proof that it preserves classical noninterference.

   Kammüller developed a framework for using the byte code verifier of a Java-like language to show non-interference [59]. His work relates to this thesis as he uses the module concept of Coq to abstract from a specific language syntax. His framework restricts to byte code languages, whereas the framework presented here can handle source as well as byte code languages. Due to Coq, his proofs are executable as programs, i.e., they can actually run their non-interference check.

The underlying type system is not given explicitly, but seems inspired by the work of Barthe et al. [10]. The paper does not clearly state if the noninterference analysis is intra- or interprocedural, the instructions shown do not display any call or invoke rule.

Interprocedural Type Systems

The type system of Banerjee and Naumann [9] covers the sequential core of Java. They prove their system sound via simulation and indistinguishability of states. This work (omitting access control) has been formalized in theorem provers: in PVS by Naumann [78] and in Isabelle/HOL by Strecker [113].

Using Isabelle/HOL, Beringer and Hofmann [16] formalize and prove correct different type systems, starting with the Volpano-Smith-Irvine type system [122] for a while language, which they extended with an additional simple call rule to procedures without parameters. They augment this type system with Hunt's and Sand's flow types [58] and objects as covered by Barthe and Rezk in [13]. Instead of the usual noninterference definition, which compares two program runs, they use a security property which captures noninterference formally with only a single execution.

In [12], Barthe, Pichardie, and Rezk define a noninterference byte code verifier for a Java-like language. They build on an existing formalization of a Java-like byte code language in Coq, called Bicolano [36], which is quite similar to the one formalized in Jinja, but features all byte code instructions. The noninterference verifier consists of three parts: (i) a pre-analyzer which computes information to reduce the control flow graph, (ii) an analyzer for control dependence regions, and (iii) the actual information flow analyzer, which leverages Kildall's dataflow algorithm to compute for every program point its security environment. The latter two are proved correct in Coq, whereas the correctness of the pre-analyzer is assumed; integrating a machine-checked correctness proof for it, for which parts already exist [20], is left for future work.

7.5.2. Formalization of Goguen/Meseguer

In his work on noninterference, Rushby [95] focuses on security policies whose interference relation is intransitive. He formalizes the core of the Goguen/Meseguer approach to provide an "unwinding lemma", using notation that differs considerably from the original. The theorem prover EHDM, a predecessor of PVS, is used for this task.

Von Oheimb [123] uses Isabelle/HOL to extend this work with nondeterminism. Furthermore, he adds a concept for confidentiality similar to IFC, called *nonleakage*. If a program is nonleaking, data from the initial states should not be leaked, whereas Goguen/Meseguer noninterference says that the occurrence of certain events should not be observable. The combination of both, *noninfluence*, is also formalized.

7.5.3. Noninterference via Dynamic Logic

In [40], Darvas et al. formalize noninterference in dynamic logic and include it in the theorem prover KeY [2]. Noninterference is encoded in two formulas, first a formalization of classical noninterference as presented in this thesis, and second, an equivalent formula $\forall l. \exists r. \forall h. \langle p \rangle r \doteq l$. This formula states that "when starting (the terminating program) p with arbitrary values l, then the value r after executing p is independent of the choice of h." Then, they were able to prove programs like $l = h; l = l - h;$ or if $(\texttt{false})\ l = h;$ secure, which are rejected by type systems and even by slicing based approaches. They present extensions for proving insecurity and handling exceptions and (forms of) declassification. However, the examples presented in this work are very small, the authors themselves expect that this approach scales poorly to more complex programs with several high and low variables.

*We can only see a short distance
ahead, but we can see plenty
there that needs to be done.*
        A. Turing

8

Future Work

While the work in this thesis is self-contained, there are many areas in which future research is desirable or even necessary. I will focus on a few interesting problems, although there may still be other directions which could be worth some more consideration.

8.1 Extending the CoreC++ Semantics

When discussing the results of [134], I was often asked if I planned formalizing C++ templates [121]. Templates are the C++ mechanism for generic programming, but are much more powerful than Java's generics [76]. This is because they work by mere textual replacement. However, this hinders seperate type checking of templates independently from their uses, which is possible with Java generics.

Formalizing templates and showing their type safety should be realizable in the CoreC++ semantics presented in this thesis. There is already a formalization of C++ templates in Isabelle [104], however, the language presented there lacks statements and all of the object-oriented features. As these were the main focus of my work, it remains to see if this work could serve as a basis for extending the semantics.

Recent reasearch proposed means to tackle the problem of seperate type checking of templates via *concepts* [50]. It would be interesting to see how this idea works in the area of the formal CoreC++ semantics and how it would affect the type safety proof.

There is also room for extending the framework with new concepts. This has been done for arrays and threads in Jinja [70, 71], I would not expect many new insights from reimplementing such extensions.

8.2 Extending the Slicing Framework

The work in this thesis considers static intra- and interprocedural as well as dynamic slicing based on graph structures. I do not expect the framework to be adaptable for slicing algorithms that do not use dependence graphs as their basis (an example for such an algorithm is Weiser's initial slicing algorithm [136]). Hence, all of the following adaptions take dependence graphs as a basis.

Slice for a set of nodes. In slicing, it is sometimes necessary to compute the slice for a set of nodes, not just for a single slicing node. While many definitions (e.g. backward slice, *slice-kind*, the moves and the weak simulation) take the slicing node as parameter, it should be easy to adapt these definitions to a set of node: e.g. the backward slice of a set of node is basically just the union of the slices of all nodes in this set. The correctness proofs themselves should then be just a lifting of the existing ones.

Control dependences. Changing the dependence definitions should not pose a problem, when we restrict ourselves to the intraprocedural case. In Sec. 3.3.3, I showed how the framework can already be instantiated with different control dependence definitions; also changing the definition of data dependence or even incorporating new dependences like def-def should be straightforward.

In the interprocedural case, this may be not that easy. As already mentioned in Sec. 5.2.3, incorporating new control dependences in the framework can lead to non procedure-local changes: e.g. a termination sensitive dependence gives rise to new dependences in the procedure which calls this procedure, as all nodes after the call of a procedure which contains a (possibly non-terminating) loop should be control dependent on this call. Hence, incorporating new dependences in the interprocedural framework will not be as easy as in the intraprocedural case.

Concurrency. Algorithms for slicing of concurrent programs exist [63, 77, 46], so future extensions could try to include concurreny in the framework. The adaptions on the framework will be substantial, though, e.g. interference edges have to be introduced. Moreover, there are to my knowledge no correctness proofs, neither formal nor informal, for concurrent slicing. Hence, extending the framework to concurrency is no aim for the near future, but should be kept in mind as a vision.

8.3 Extracting a Verified Slicer

This thesis presents the formalization and verification of slicing algorithms in a functional style language. Naturally, the question arises if this formalization can be used to generate a verified slicer. Isabelle's recently improved code generator [51] (which replaces [15]) extracts code for the functional languages ML, Haskell, and OCaml from Isabelle theories. However, isolated code extraction from the CFG locales seems not practicable, as the graph representation is too abstract. A possible approach would be to generate code from a concrete CFG definition of an instantiating language, which restates all definition of the framework's abstract CFG; an equivalence proof then has to guarantee that these definitions coincide. This means that code extraction – even for the language-independent framework – needs to be redone for every instantiated language. Also, it remains to see if substantial code generator parts, e.g. for inductive predicates, actually work as expected in locales.

8.4 Language Instantiations

Of course, further instantiations would still increase the credibility of the framework. An instantiation with CoreC++ [134] would underline the applicability of the framework for non-trivial languages; however, as the special features in this language (i.e., multiple inheritance) are completely orthogonal to slicing, I do not expect any new basic insights from such an instantiation. Perhaps it would be more worthwile to instantiate the framework with a language whose structure (or even paradigm) differs considerably from the languages already inverstigated. For example, I would expect many insights from an instantiation with a functional language (CFGs for such languages can be built, according to Shivers [103]); however, such an instantiation will be extremely extensive and tedious.

But also in the existing instantiations there is room for improvement, e.g. in the area of precision. In the Jinja byte code instantiation (see Sec. 3.4.2 and Sec. 5.4.2), the slice size would shrink significantly if we added a points-to analysis. Some formalizations of powerful points-to analyses in theorem provers already exist, see e.g. the work of Dabrowski and Pichardie [39]. Perhaps, the instantiation can even be modularized w.r.t. a concrete points-to analysis using a locale. Then, different analyses can be "plugged-in", from the trivial that is already present (i.e., all objects on the heap are aliased) to far more sophisticated ones. One of the missions of our project "Quis custodiet" is the verification of the information flow algorithm in [52], which incorporates a points-to analysis. Hence, this area will be one central point in future work.

8.5 Information Flow Control

The work in this thesis is only the first step of our project "Quis custodiet", which aims for the verification of sophisticated information flow algorithms that use slicing. In Chap. 6, I present a first result which shows that slicing can guarantee classical noninterference. However, the slicing algorithms on which we focus (e.g. [52]) are stronger w.r.t. information flow control than can be expressed in classical noninterference.

Remember that classical noninterference only allows secret values that are fixed at the beginning of the program. It also assumes an attacker who can only view public outputs at the beginning and the end of the program run. Sophisticated noninterference algorithms, however, allow arbitrary annotations of program points as secret or public; this would not be possible in approaches that require a fixed assignment from variables to security level. Via these annotations, noninterference algorithms allow arbitrary intermediate in- and output, both secret and public. Moreover, the notion of the attacker is stronger, as he can also observe intermediate public outputs. However, classical noninterference as presented in this thesis is not strong enough to handle such annotations. Hence, before we attempt to verify those information flow algorithms, we have to find a notion of what we mean by noninterferent in their case. Actually, our group is already working on a more general noninterference definition, which can handle such arbitrary annotations, but still incorporates classical noninterference as a special case.

Beware of bugs in the above code; I have only proved it correct, not tried it.

D. Knuth

Conclusion

This thesis presented two substantial formalizations in the proof assistant Isabelle/HOL:

(i) a formal semantics and type safety proof for multiple inheritance in C++, called CoreC++, and

(ii) a language-independent modular framework for slicing based on dependence graphs with correctness proofs.

The CoreC++ formalization not only exhibited the first formal proof that C++-like multiple inheritance does not compromise type safety. It also showed that modern proof assistants nowadays are capable to handle formalizations and proofs of substantial size; an experience which increased my confidence that I could manage the subtle proofs I had in mind for the second formalization, i.e., showing a complex context-sensitive interprocedural slicing algorithm correct, using a proof assistant.

Proving slicing correct was the first step towards the objective of the "Quis custodiet" project, which aims at verifying sophisticated information flow algorithms based on slicing. While proofs for intraprocedural slicing had already existed, I detached the correctness property from a concrete language and control dependence definition. Moreover, being machine-checked, my proofs gain increased confidence compared to the existing pen-and-paper approaches.

Whereas the context-sensitive algorithm of Horwitz, Reps, and Binkley is the quasi-standard for interprocedural slicing – and its correctness beyond doubt for twenty years –, no correctness results had existed. Hence, this thesis presented the first formal proof of its correctness, be it machine-checked or on paper.

I presented two language instantiations for the slicing framework to show that I chose the abstractions and requirements in the framework sensibly. With the two languages being a simple imperative and a sophisticated object-oriented, as well as a source and a byte code one, I demonstrated the flexibility of the framework.

The correctness proof of slicing in this thesis is not only a result in itself, but can also be leveraged for further verifications. I reused it to show how slicing can safely guarantee classical noninterference. Hence, this thesis lays the ground for the upcoming verification issues in the "Quis custodiet" project.

Small Step Rules for CoreC++

$$\frac{\textit{new-Addr } h = \lfloor a \rfloor \qquad h' = h(a \mapsto (C, \{(Cs, \textit{fs}) \mid \textit{init-obj } P\, C\, (Cs, \textit{fs})\}))}{P,E \vdash \langle \texttt{new } C,(h, l)\rangle \rightarrow \langle \textit{ref } (a, [C]),(h', l)\rangle}$$

$$\frac{\textit{new-Addr } h = \textit{None}}{P,E \vdash \langle \texttt{new } C,(h, l)\rangle \rightarrow \langle \textit{THROW OutOfMemory},(h, l)\rangle}$$

$$\frac{P,E \vdash \langle e,s\rangle \rightarrow \langle e',s'\rangle}{P,E \vdash \langle \texttt{stat\_cast } C\, e,s\rangle \rightarrow \langle \texttt{stat\_cast } C\, e',s'\rangle}$$

$$P,E \vdash \langle \texttt{stat\_cast } C\, \textit{null},s\rangle \rightarrow \langle \textit{null},s\rangle$$

$$\frac{P \vdash \textit{path last Cs to C via Cs}' \qquad Ds = Cs \,@_p\, Cs'}{P,E \vdash \langle \texttt{stat\_cast } C\, (\textit{ref } (a, Cs)),s\rangle \rightarrow \langle \textit{ref } (a, Ds),s\rangle}$$

$$P,E \vdash \langle \texttt{stat\_cast } C\, (\textit{ref } (a, Cs\, @\, [C]\, @\, Cs')),s\rangle \rightarrow \langle \textit{ref } (a, Cs\, @\, [C]),s\rangle$$

$$\frac{C \notin \textit{set Cs} \qquad \neg P \vdash \textit{last Cs} \preceq^* C}{P,E \vdash \langle \texttt{stat\_cast } C\, (\textit{ref } (a, Cs)),s\rangle \rightarrow \langle \textit{THROW ClassCast},s\rangle}$$

$$\frac{P,E \vdash \langle e,s\rangle \rightarrow \langle e',s'\rangle}{P,E \vdash \langle \texttt{dyn\_cast } C\, e,s\rangle \rightarrow \langle \texttt{dyn\_cast } C\, e',s'\rangle}$$

$$P,E \vdash \langle \texttt{dyn\_cast } C\, \textit{null},s\rangle \rightarrow \langle \textit{null},s\rangle$$

$$\frac{P \vdash \textit{path last Cs to C unique} \\ P \vdash \textit{path last Cs to C via Cs}' \qquad Ds = Cs \,@_p\, Cs'}{P,E \vdash \langle \texttt{dyn\_cast } C\, (\textit{ref } (a, Cs)),s\rangle \rightarrow \langle \textit{ref } (a, Ds),s\rangle}$$

$$P,E \vdash \langle \texttt{dyn\_cast } C\, (\textit{ref } (a, Cs\, @\, [C]\, @\, Cs')),s\rangle \rightarrow \langle \textit{ref } (a, Cs\, @\, [C]),s\rangle$$

$$\frac{hp\, s\, a = \lfloor (D, S)\rfloor \qquad P \vdash \textit{path D to C via Cs}' \qquad P \vdash \textit{path D to C unique}}{P,E \vdash \langle \texttt{dyn\_cast } C\, (\textit{ref } (a, Cs)),s\rangle \rightarrow \langle \textit{ref } (a, Cs'),s\rangle}$$

$$\frac{hp\ s\ a = \lfloor(D, S)\rfloor \qquad \neg\ P \vdash \textit{path } D \textit{ to } C \textit{ unique}}{\neg\ P \vdash \textit{path last } Cs \textit{ to } C \textit{ unique} \qquad C \notin \text{set } Cs}{P,E \vdash \langle \texttt{dyn\_cast } C\ (\textit{ref } (a,\ Cs)),s\rangle \rightarrow \langle \textit{null},s\rangle}$$

$$\frac{P,E \vdash \langle e,s\rangle \rightarrow \langle e',s'\rangle}{P,E \vdash \langle e \ll\!bop\!\gg e_2,s\rangle \rightarrow \langle e' \ll\!bop\!\gg e_2,s'\rangle}$$

$$\frac{P,E \vdash \langle e,s\rangle \rightarrow \langle e',s'\rangle}{P,E \vdash \langle \texttt{Val } v_1 \ll\!bop\!\gg e,s\rangle \rightarrow \langle \texttt{Val } v_1 \ll\!bop\!\gg e',s'\rangle}$$

$$\frac{\textit{binop } (bop,\ v_1,\ v_2) = \lfloor v\rfloor}{P,E \vdash \langle \texttt{Val } v_1 \ll\!bop\!\gg \texttt{Val } v_2,s\rangle \rightarrow \langle \texttt{Val } v,s\rangle}$$

$$\frac{l\ V = \lfloor v\rfloor}{P,E \vdash \langle \texttt{Var } V,s\rangle \rightarrow \langle \texttt{Val } v,(h,\ l)\rangle}$$

$$\frac{P,E \vdash \langle e,s\rangle \rightarrow \langle e',s'\rangle}{P,E \vdash \langle V := e,s\rangle \rightarrow \langle V := e',s'\rangle}$$

$$\frac{E\ V = \lfloor T\rfloor \qquad P \vdash T \textit{ casts } v \textit{ to } v'}{P,E \vdash \langle V := \texttt{Val } v,(h,\ l)\rangle \rightarrow \langle \texttt{Val } v',(h,\ l(V \mapsto v'))\rangle}$$

$$\frac{P,E \vdash \langle e,s\rangle \rightarrow \langle e',s'\rangle}{P,E \vdash \langle e.F\{Cs\},s\rangle \rightarrow \langle e'.F\{Cs\},s'\rangle}$$

$$\frac{h\ a = \lfloor(D, S)\rfloor \qquad Ds = Cs' @_p Cs \qquad (Ds,\ fs) \in S \qquad fs\ F = \lfloor v\rfloor}{P,E \vdash \langle \textit{ref } (a,\ Cs').F\{Cs\},s\rangle \rightarrow \langle \texttt{Val } v,(h,\ l)\rangle}$$

$$P,E \vdash \langle \textit{null}.F\{Cs\},s\rangle \rightarrow \langle \textit{THROW NullPointer},s\rangle$$

$$\frac{P,E \vdash \langle e,s\rangle \rightarrow \langle e',s'\rangle}{P,E \vdash \langle e.F\{Cs\} := e_2,s\rangle \rightarrow \langle e'.F\{Cs\} := e_2,s'\rangle}$$

$$\frac{P,E \vdash \langle e,s\rangle \rightarrow \langle e',s'\rangle}{P,E \vdash \langle \texttt{Val } v.F\{Cs\} := e,s\rangle \rightarrow \langle \texttt{Val } v.F\{Cs\} := e',s'\rangle}$$

$$\frac{h\ a = \lfloor(D, S)\rfloor \qquad P \vdash \textit{last } Cs' \textit{ has least } F : T \textit{ via } Cs}{P \vdash T \textit{ casts } v \textit{ to } v' \qquad Ds = Cs' @_p Cs \qquad (Ds,\ fs) \in S}{P,E \vdash \langle \textit{ref } (a,\ Cs').F\{Cs\} := \texttt{Val } v,(h,\ l)\rangle \rightarrow}$$
$$\langle \texttt{Val } v',(h(a \mapsto (D, \{(Ds,\ fs(F \mapsto v'))\} \cup (S - \{(Ds,\ fs)\}))),\ l)\rangle$$

$$P,E \vdash \langle .F\{Cs\} := \texttt{Val } v,s\rangle \rightarrow \langle \textit{THROW NullPointer},s\rangle$$

$$\frac{P,E \vdash \langle e,s \rangle \to \langle e',s' \rangle}{P,E \vdash \langle Copt\ e\ M\ es,s \rangle \to \langle Copt\ e'\ M\ es,s' \rangle}$$

$$\frac{P,E \vdash \langle es,s \rangle\ [\to]\ \langle es',s' \rangle}{P,E \vdash \langle Copt\ (\texttt{Val}\ v)\ M\ es,s \rangle \to \langle Copt\ (\texttt{Val}\ v)\ M\ es',s' \rangle}$$

$$\frac{\begin{array}{c} h\ a = \lfloor(C, S)\rfloor \qquad P \vdash last\ Cs\ has\ least\ M = (Ts',\ T',\ pns',\ body')\ via\ Ds \\ P \vdash (C,Cs\ @_p\ Ds)\ selects\ M = (Ts,\ T,\ pns,\ body)\ via\ Cs' \\ |vs| = |pns| \qquad |Ts| = |pns| \\ bs = blocks\ (this{\cdot}pns,\ Class\ (last\ Cs'){\cdot}Ts,\ Ref\ (a,\ Cs'){\cdot}vs,\ body) \\ new\text{-}body = (case\ T'\ of\ Class\ D \Rightarrow \texttt{stat\_cast}\ D\ bs\ |\ \text{-} \Rightarrow bs) \end{array}}{P,E \vdash \langle (ref\ (a,\ Cs)).M\ (map\ \texttt{Val}\ vs),(h,\ l) \rangle \to \langle new\text{-}body,s \rangle}$$

$$\frac{\begin{array}{c} P \vdash path\ last\ Cs\ to\ C\ unique \qquad P \vdash path\ last\ Cs\ to\ C\ via\ Cs'' \\ P \vdash C\ has\ least\ M = (Ts,\ T,\ pns,\ body)\ via\ Cs' \\ Ds = (Cs\ @_p\ Cs'')\ @_p\ Cs' \qquad |vs| = |pns| \qquad |Ts| = |pns| \end{array}}{\begin{array}{c} P,E \vdash \langle (ref\ (a,\ Cs)).C{::}M(map\ \texttt{Val}\ vs),s \rangle \to \\ \langle blocks\ (this{\cdot}pns,\ Class\ (last\ Ds){\cdot}Ts,\ Ref\ (a,\ Ds){\cdot}vs,\ body),s \rangle \end{array}}$$

$$P,E \vdash \langle Copt\ null\ M\ (map\ \texttt{Val}\ vs),s \rangle \to \langle THROW\ NullPointer,s \rangle$$

$$blocks\ (V{\cdot}Vs,\ T{\cdot}Ts,\ v{\cdot}vs,\ e) = \{V{:}T;\ V := \texttt{Val}\ v;\ blocks\ (V,\ T,\ v,\ e)\}$$

$$blocks\ ([],\ [],\ [],\ e) = e$$

$$\frac{\begin{array}{c} P,E(V \mapsto T) \vdash \langle e,(h,\ l(V := None)) \rangle \to \langle e',(h',\ l') \rangle \\ l'\ V = None \qquad \neg\ assigned\ V\ e \end{array}}{P,E \vdash \langle \{V{:}T;\ e\},(h,\ l) \rangle \to \langle \{V{:}T;\ e'\},(h',\ l'(V := l\ V)) \rangle}$$

$$\frac{\begin{array}{c} P,E(V \mapsto T) \vdash \langle e,(h,\ l(V := None)) \rangle \to \langle e',(h',\ l') \rangle \\ l'\ V = \lfloor v \rfloor \qquad \neg\ assigned\ V\ e \end{array}}{P,E \vdash \langle \{V{:}T;\ e\},(h,\ l) \rangle \to \langle \{V{:}T;\ V := \texttt{Val}\ v;\ e'\},(h',\ l'(V := l\ V)) \rangle}$$

$$\frac{\begin{array}{c} P,E(V \mapsto T) \vdash \langle e,(h,\ l(V \mapsto v')) \rangle \to \langle e',(h',\ l') \rangle \\ l'\ V = \lfloor v'' \rfloor \qquad P \vdash T\ casts\ v\ to\ v' \end{array}}{P,E \vdash \langle \{V{:}T;\ V := \texttt{Val}\ v;\ e\},(h,\ l) \rangle \to \langle \{V{:}T;\ V := \texttt{Val}\ v'';\ e'\},(h',\ l'(V := l\ V)) \rangle}$$

$$P,E \vdash \langle \{V{:}T;\ \texttt{Val}\ u\},s \rangle \to \langle \texttt{Val}\ u,s \rangle$$

$$\frac{P \vdash T\ casts\ v\ to\ v'}{P,E \vdash \langle \{V{:}T;\ V := \texttt{Val}\ v;\ \texttt{Val}\ u\},s \rangle \to \langle \texttt{Val}\ u,s \rangle}$$

$$\frac{P,E \vdash \langle e,s \rangle \to \langle e',s' \rangle}{P,E \vdash \langle e;\ e_2,s \rangle \to \langle e';\ e_2,s' \rangle} \qquad P,E \vdash \langle \texttt{Val}\ v;\ e_2,s \rangle \to \langle e_2,s \rangle$$

$$\frac{P,E \vdash \langle e,s \rangle \to \langle e',s' \rangle}{P,E \vdash \langle \text{if } (e) \; e_1 \text{ else } e_2,s \rangle \to \langle \text{if } (e') \; e_1 \text{ else } e_2,s' \rangle}$$

$$P,E \vdash \langle \text{if } (\textit{true}) \; e_1 \text{ else } e_2,s \rangle \to \langle e_1,s \rangle$$

$$P,E \vdash \langle \text{if } (\textit{false}) \; e_1 \text{ else } e_2,s \rangle \to \langle e_2,s \rangle$$

$$P,E \vdash \langle \text{while } (b) \; c,s \rangle \to \langle \text{if } (b) \; (c; \; \text{while } (b) \; c) \text{ else } \textit{unit},s \rangle$$

$$\frac{P,E \vdash \langle e,s \rangle \to \langle e',s' \rangle}{P,E \vdash \langle \text{throw } e,s \rangle \to \langle \text{throw } e',s' \rangle}$$

$$P,E \vdash \langle \text{throw } \textit{null},s \rangle \to \langle \textit{THROW NullPointer},s \rangle$$

$$\frac{P,E \vdash \langle e,s \rangle \to \langle e',s' \rangle}{P,E \vdash \langle e \cdot es,s \rangle \; [\to] \; \langle e' \cdot es,s' \rangle} \qquad \frac{P,E \vdash \langle es,s \rangle \; [\to] \; \langle es',s' \rangle}{P,E \vdash \langle \text{Val } v \cdot es,s \rangle \; [\to] \; \langle \text{Val } v \cdot es',s' \rangle}$$

$$P,E \vdash \langle \text{dyn\_cast } C \; (\textit{Throw } r),s \rangle \to \langle \textit{Throw } r,s \rangle$$

$$P,E \vdash \langle \text{stat\_cast } C \; (\textit{Throw } r),s \rangle \to \langle \textit{Throw } r,s \rangle$$

$$P,E \vdash \langle \textit{Throw } r \; \ll bop \gg e_2,s \rangle \to \langle \textit{Throw } r,s \rangle$$

$$P,E \vdash \langle \text{Val } v_1 \; \ll bop \gg \textit{Throw } r,s \rangle \to \langle \textit{Throw } r,s \rangle$$

$$P,E \vdash \langle V := \textit{Throw } r,s \rangle \to \langle \textit{Throw } r,s \rangle$$

$$P,E \vdash \langle \textit{Throw } r.F\{Cs\},s \rangle \to \langle \textit{Throw } r,s \rangle$$

$$P,E \vdash \langle \textit{Throw } r.F\{Cs\} := e_2,s \rangle \to \langle \textit{Throw } r,s \rangle$$

$$P,E \vdash \langle \text{Val } v.F\{Cs\} := \textit{Throw } r,s \rangle \to \langle \textit{Throw } r,s \rangle$$

$$P,E \vdash \langle \textit{Copt } (\textit{Throw } r) \; M \; es,s \rangle \to \langle \textit{Throw } r,s \rangle$$

$$\frac{es = \textit{map } \text{Val } vs \; @ \; \textit{Throw } r \cdot es'}{P,E \vdash \langle \textit{Copt } (\text{Val } v) \; M \; es,s \rangle \to \langle \textit{Throw } r,s \rangle}$$

$$P,E \vdash \langle \{V{:}T; \; \textit{Throw } r\},s \rangle \to \langle \textit{Throw } r,s \rangle$$

$$\frac{P \vdash T \textit{ casts } v \textit{ to } v'}{P,E \vdash \langle \{V{:}T; \; V := \text{Val } v; \; \textit{Throw } r\},s \rangle \to \langle \textit{Throw } r,s \rangle}$$

$$P,E \vdash \langle \textit{Throw } r; \; e_2,s \rangle \to \langle \textit{Throw } r,s \rangle$$

$$P,E \vdash \langle \text{if } (\textit{Throw } r) \; e_1 \text{ else } e_2,s \rangle \to \langle \textit{Throw } r,s \rangle$$

$$P,E \vdash \langle \text{throw } (\textit{Throw } r),s \rangle \to \langle \textit{Throw } r,s \rangle$$

B

Constructor Eliminating Algorithm Example

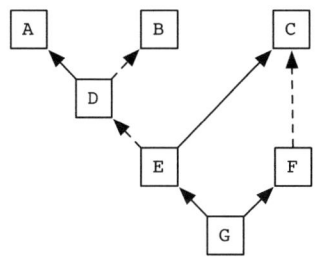

Class hierarchy of the example program

Original program:

```
class A {
public:
  int xa;
  A() {xa = 0;}
  virtual int f() {
    return xa;
  }
};
```

Program with eliminated constructors:

```
class A {
public:
  int xa;
  A() {};
  A* initA_L() {
    xa = 0; return this;
  }
  A* initA() {return initA_L();}
  virtual int f() {return xa;}
};
```

```
class B {                    class B {
public:                      public:
  int xb;                      int xb;
  B() {xb = 0;}                B() {}
};                             B* initB_L() {
                                 xb = 0; return this;
                               }
                               B* initB() {return initB_L();}
                             };

class C {                    class C {
public:                      public:
  int xc;                      int xc;
  C() {xc = 0;}                C() {}
};                             C* initC_L() {
                                 xc = 0; return this;
                               }
                               C* initC() {return initC_L();}
                             };

class D: public A,           class D: public A,
  public virtual B {           public virtual B {
public:                      public:
  int xd;                      int xd;
  D() {xd = 0;}                D() {}
};                             void initD_S() {D::initB_L();}
                               D* initD_L() {
                                 initA_L(); xd = 0; return this;
                               }
                               D* initD() {
                                 initD_S(); return initD_L();
                               }
                             };
```

```
class E: public C,            class E: public C,
  public virtual D {            public virtual D {
public:                       public:
  int xe;                       int xe;
  E() {xe = 0; f();}            E() {}
  virtual int f() {             void initE_S() {
    return xe;                     D::initB_L(); E::initD_L();
  }                              }
};                              E* initE_L() {
                                  initC_L(); xe = 0;
                                  E::f(); return this;
                                }
                                E* initE() {
                                  initE_S(); return initE_L();
                                }
                                virtual int f() {return xe;}
                              };

class F:                      class F: public virtual C {
  public virtual C {          public:
public:                         int xf;
  int xf;                       F() {}
  F() {xf = 0;}                 void initF_S() {F::initC_L();}
};                              F* initF_L() {
                                  xf = 0; return this;
                                }
                                F* initF() {return initF_L();}
                              };
```

APPENDIX B. CONSTRUCTOR ELIMINATING ALGORITHM EXAMPLE

```
class G: public E,          class G: public E,
  public F {                  public F {
public:                     public:
  int xg;                     int xg;
  G() {xg = 0; f();}          void initG_S(){
  virtual int f() {             D::initB_L(); E::initD_L();
    return xg;                  F::initC_L();
  }                           }
};                            G* initG_L(){
                                initE_L(); initF_L();
                                xg = 0; G::f(); return this;}
                              G* initG() {
                                initG_S(); return initG_L();
                              }
                              virtual int f() {return xg;}
                            };

int main(){                 int main(){
  G* g = new G();             G* g = (new G())->initG();
}                           }
```

Bibliography

[1] Hiralal Agrawal and Joseph R. Horgan. Dynamic program slicing. In *Proceedings of the ACM SIGPLAN 1990 conference on Programming language design and implementation (PLDI)*, pages 246–256. ACM, 1990.

[2] Wolfgang Ahrendt, Thomas Baar, Bernhard Beckert, Richard Bubel, Martin Giese, Reiner Hähnle, Wolfram Menzel, Wojciech Mostowski, Andreas Roth, Steffen Schlager, and Peter H. Schmitt. The KeY tool – integrating object oriented design and formal verification. *Software and Systems Modeling*, 4(1):32–54, 2005.

[3] Torben Amtoft. Slicing for modern program structures: a theory for eliminating irrelevant loops. *Information Processing Letters*, 106(2):45–51, 2008.

[4] Paul Anderson, Thomas Reps, and Tim Teitelbaum. Design and implementation of a fine-grained software inspection tool. *IEEE Transactions on Software Engineering*, 29(8):721–733, 2003.

[5] Aslan Askarov, Sebastian Hunt, Andrei Sabelfeld, and David Sands. Termination-insensitive noninterference leaks more than just a bit. In *Computer Security – ESORICS 2008*, volume 5283 of *LNCS*, pages 333–348. Springer, 2008.

[6] Isabelle Attali, Denis Caromel, and Sidi Ould Ehmety. A natural semantics for Eiffel dynamic binding. *ACM Transactions on Programming Languages and Systems*, 18(6):711–729, 1996.

[7] Thomas Ball and Susan Horwitz. Slicing programs with arbitrary control-flow. In *Automated and Algorithmic Debugging – AADEBUG 1993*, volume 749 of *LNCS*, pages 206–222. Springer, 1993.

[8] Clemens Ballarin. Locales and locale expressions in Isabelle/Isar. In Stefano Berardi, Mario Coppo, and Ferruccio Damiani, editors, *Types for Proofs and Programs – TYPES 2003*, volume 3085 of *LNCS*, pages 34–50. Springer, 2004.

[9] Anindya Banerjee and David A. Naumann. Secure information flow and pointer confinement in a Java-like language. In *Proceedings of the 15th IEEE Computer Security Foundations Workshop (CSFW)*, pages 239–253. IEEE, 2002.

[10] Gilles Barthe, Amitabh Basu, and Tamara Rezk. Security types preserving compilation. In *Verification, Model Checking, and Abstract Interpretation – VMCAI 2004*, volume 2937 of *LNCS*, pages 2–15. Springer, 2004.

[11] Gilles Barthe and Leonor Prensa Nieto. Secure information flow for a concurrent language with scheduling. *Journal of Computer Security*, 15(6):647–689, 2007.

[12] Gilles Barthe, David Pichardie, and Tamara Rezk. A certified lightweight non-interference Java bytecode verifier. In *16th European Symposium on Programming – ESOP 2007*, volume 4421 of *LNCS*, pages 125–140. Springer, 2007.

[13] Gilles Barthe and Tamara Rezk. Non-interference for a JVM-like language. In *Proceedings of the 2005 ACM SIGPLAN international workshop on Types in languages design and implementation (TLDI)*, pages 103–112. ACM, 2005.

[14] Samuel Bates and Susan Horwitz. Incremental program testing using program dependence graphs. In *Proceedings of the 20th ACM SIGPLAN-SIGACT symposium on Principles of programming languages (POPL)*, pages 384–396. ACM, 1993.

[15] Stefan Berghofer and Tobias Nipkow. Executing Higher Order Logic. In P. Callaghan, Z. Luo, J. McKinna, and R. Pollack, editors, *Types for Proofs and Programs – TYPES 2000*, volume 2277 of *LNCS*, pages 24–40. Springer, 2002.

[16] Lennart Beringer and Martin Hofmann. Secure information flow and program logics. In *Proceedings of the 20th IEEE Computer Security Foundations Symposium (CSF)*, pages 133–148. IEEE, 2007.

[17] Yves Bertot. Formalizing a JVML verifier for initialization in a theorem prover. In *Computer Aided Verification – CAV 2001*, volume 2102 of *LNCS*, pages 14–24. Springer, 2001.

[18] Yves Bertot and Pierre Castéran. *Interactive Theorem Proving and Program Development - Coq'Art: The Calculus of Inductive Constructions.* Springer, 2004.

[19] Yves Bertot, Benjamin Grégoire, and Xavier Leroy. A structured aproach to proving compiler optimizations based on dataflow analysis. In *Types for Proofs and Programs – TYPES 2004*, volume 3839 of *LNCS*, pages 66–81. Springer, 2006.

[20] Frédéric Besson, Thomas Jensen, and David Pichardie. Proof-carrying code from certified abstract interpretation and fixpoint compression. *Theoretical Computer Science*, 364(3):273–291, 2006.

[21] David Binkley. Semantics guided regression test cost reduction. *IEEE Transactions on Software Engineering*, 23(8):498–516, 1997.

[22] David Binkley, Nicolas Gold, and Mark Harman. An empirical study of static program slice size. *ACM Transactions on Software Engineering and Methodology*, 16(2):8, 2007.

[23] David Binkley and Mark Harman. A large-scale empirical study of forward and backward static slice size and context sensitivity. In *Proceedings of the International Conference on Software Maintenance (ICSM)*, page 44. IEEE, 2003.

[24] Jan Olaf Blech, Lars Gesellensetter, and Sabine Glesner. Formal verification of dead code elimination in Isabelle/HOL. In *Proceedings of the 3rd IEEE International Conference on Software Engineerings and Formal Methods (SEFM)*, pages 200–209. IEEE, 2005.

[25] Gérard Boudol and Ilaria Castellani. Noninterference for concurrent programs and thread systems. *Theoretical Computer Science*, 281(1-2):109–130, 2002.

[26] Gilad Bracha and William Cook. Mixin-based inheritance. In *Proceedings of the European conference on object-oriented programming on Object-oriented programming systems, languages, and applications (OOPSLA/ECOOP)*, pages 303–311, 1990.

[27] Val Breazu-Tannen, Carl A. Gunter, and Andre Scedrov. Computing with coercions. In *Proceedings of the 1990 ACM conference on LISP and functional programming (LFP)*, pages 44–60. ACM, 1990.

[28] Kim B. Bruce and J. Nathan Foster. $\mathcal{LOOJ}$: Weaving $\mathcal{LOOM}$ into Java. In *ECOOP 2004 – Object-Oriented Programming*, volume 3086 of *LNCS*, pages 390–414, 2004.

[29] Kim B. Bruce, Leaf Petersen, and Adrian Fiech. Subtyping is not a good "match" for object-oriented languages. In *ECOOP 1997 – Object-Oriented Programming*, volume 1241 of *LNCS*, pages 104–127. Springer, 1997.

[30] Kim B. Bruce, Angela Schuett, Robert van Gent, and Adrian Fiech. PolyTOIL: A type-safe polymorphic object-oriented language. *ACM Transactions on Programming Languages and Systems*, 25(2):225–290, 2003.

[31] David Cachera, Thomas Jensen, David Pichardie, and Vlad Rusu. Extracting a data flow analyser in constructive logic. In *Programming Languages and Systems – ESOP 2004*, volume 2986 of *LNCS*, pages 385–400. Springer, 2004.

[32] Luca Cardelli. A semantics of multiple inheritance. *Information and Computation*, 76(2-3):138–164, 1988.

[33] Luca Cardelli. *The Computer Science and Engineering Handbook*, chapter Type Systems, pages 2208–2236. CRC Press, 2nd edition, 2004.

[34] Bor-Yuh Evan Chang, Adam Chlipala, and George C. Necula. A framework for certified program analysis and its applications to mobile-code safety. In *Verification, Model Checking, and Abstract Interpretation – VMCAI 2006*, volume 3855 of *LNCS*, pages 174–189. Springer, 2006.

[35] Jacek Chrzaszcz. Implementing Modules in the Coq System. In David Basin and Burkhart Wolff, editors, *Theorem Proving in Higher Order Logics – TPHOLs 2003*, volume 2758 of *LNCS*, pages 270–286. Springer, 2003.

[36] Mobius Consortium. Deliverable 3.1: Bytecode specification language and program logic, 2006. Available online from `http://mobius.inria.fr`.

[37] James C. Corbett, Matthew B. Dwyer, John Hatcliff, Shawn Laubach, Corina S. Păsăreanu, Robby, and Hongjun Zheng.

Bandera: extracting finite-state models from Java source code. In *Proceedings of the 22nd international conference on Software engineering (ICSE)*, pages 439–448. ACM, 2000.

[38] Solange Coupet-Grimal and William Delobel. A uniform and certified approach for two static analyses. In *Types for Proofs and Programs – TYPES 2004*, volume 3839 of *LNCS*, pages 115–137. Springer, 2006.

[39] Frédéric Dabrowski and David Pichardie. A certified data race analysis for a Java-like language. In *Theorem Proving in Higher Order Logics – TPHOLs 2009*, volume 5674 of *LNCS*, pages 212–227. Springer, 2009.

[40] Ádám Darvas, Reiner Hähnle, and David Sands. A theorem proving approach to analysis of secure information flow. In *Security in Pervasive Computing – SPC 2005*, volume 3450 of *LNCS*, pages 193–209. Springer, 2005.

[41] Karl Driesen and Urs Hölzle. The direct cost of virtual function calls in C++. In *Proceedings of the 11th annual ACM SIGPLAN conference on Object-oriented programming systems, languages, and applications (OOPSLA)*, pages 306–323. ACM, 1996.

[42] Sophia Drossopoulou and Susan Eisenbach. Java is type safe — probably. In *ECOOP 1997 – Object-Oriented Programming*, volume 1241 of *LNCS*, pages 389–418. Springer, 1997.

[43] Maryam Emami, Rakesh Ghiya, and Laurie J. Hendren. Context-sensitive interprocedural points-to analysis in the presence of function pointers. In *Proceedings of the ACM SIGPLAN 1994 conference on Programming language design and implementation (PLDI)*, pages 242–256. ACM, 1994.

[44] Jeanne Ferrante, Karl J. Ottenstein, and Joe D. Warren. The program dependence graph and its use in optimization. *ACM Transactions on Programming Languages and Systems*, 9(3):319–349, 1987.

[45] Nicu G. Fruja. *Type Safety of C# and .NET CLR*. PhD thesis, ETH Zurich, 2006.

[46] Dennis Giffhorn and Christian Hammer. Precise slicing of concurrent programs - an evaluation of static slicing algorithms for concurrent programs. *Journal of Automated Software Engineering*, 16(2):197–234, 2009.

[47] Michael J. C. Gordon. *Mechanizing programming logics in higher order logic*, pages 387–439. Springer, 1989.

[48] Michael J. C. Gordon and Tom F. Melham, editors. *Introduction to HOL: a theorem proving environment for higher order logic*. Cambridge University Press, 1993.

[49] Valerie Gouranton and Daniel Le Métayer. Dynamic slicing: a generic analysis based on a natural semantics format. *Journal of Logic and Computation*, 9(6):835–871, 1999.

[50] Douglas Gregor, Jaako Järvi, Jeremy Siek, Bjarne Stroustrup, Gabriel Dos Reis, and Andrew Lumsdaine. Concepts: linguistic support for generic programming in C++. In *Proceedings of the 21st annual ACM SIGPLAN conference on Object-oriented programming systems, languages, and applications (OOPSLA)*, pages 291–310. ACM, 2006.

[51] Florian Haftmann. *Code Generation from Specifications in Higher Order Logic*. PhD thesis, Institut für Informatik, Technische Universität München, 2009.

[52] Christian Hammer and Gregor Snelting. Flow-sensitive, context-sensitive, and object-sensitive information flow control based on program dependence graphs. *International Journal of Information Security*, 8(6):399–422, December 2009.

[53] Thomas A. Henzinger, George C. Necula, Ranjit Jhala, Grégoire Sutre, Rupak Majumdar, and Westley Weimer. Temporal-safety proofs for systems code. In *Computer Aided Verification – CAV 2002*, volume 2404 of *LNCS*, pages 382–399. Springer, 2002.

[54] C. A. R. Hoare. An axiomatic basis for computer programming. *Communications of the ACM*, 12(10):576–580, 1969.

[55] Michael Hohmuth and Hendrik Tews. The semantics of C++ data types: Towards verifying low-level system components. In D. Basin and B. Wolff, editors, *Theorem Proving in Higher Order*

Logics: Emerging Trends – TPHOLs 2003, pages 127–144, 2003. Tech. Rep. 187.

[56] Susan Horwitz, Jan Prins, and Thomas Reps. Integrating non-interfering versions of programs. In *Proceedings of the 15th ACM SIGPLAN-SIGACT symposium on Principles of programming languages (POPL)*, pages 133–145. ACM, 1988.

[57] Susan Horwitz, Thomas Reps, and David Binkley. Interprocedural slicing using dependence graphs. *ACM Transactions on Programming Languages and Systems*, 12(1):26–60, 1990.

[58] Sebastian Hunt and David Sands. On flow-sensitive security types. In *Proceedings of the 33rd ACM SIGPLAN-SIGACT symposium on Principles of programming languages (POPL)*, pages 79–90. ACM, 2006.

[59] Florian Kammüller. Formalizing non-interference for a simple bytecode language in Coq. *Formal Aspects of Computing*, 20(3):259–275, 2008.

[60] Gerwin Klein and Tobias Nipkow. Verified bytecode verifiers. *Theoretical Computer Science*, 298(3):583–626, 2003.

[61] Gerwin Klein and Tobias Nipkow. A machine-checked model for a Java-like language, virtual machine and compiler. *ACM Transactions on Programming Languages and Systems*, 28(4):619–695, 2006.

[62] Jens Krinke. Evaluating context-sensitive slicing and chopping. In *Proceedings of the International Conference on Software Maintenance (ICSM)*, page 22. IEEE, 2002.

[63] Jens Krinke. Context-sensitive slicing of concurrent programs. *ACM SIGSOFT Software Engineering Notes*, 28(5):178–187, September 2003.

[64] Jens Krinke. *Handbook of Software Engineering and Knowledge Engineering, Vol. 3: Recent Advances*, chapter Program Slicing, pages 307–332. World Scientific Publishing, 2005.

[65] Jens Krinke. Effects of context on program slicing. *Journal of Systems and Software*, 79(9):1249–1260, 2006.

[66] Sébastien Labbé and Jean-Pierre Gallois. Slicing communicating automata specifications: polynomial algorithms for model reduction. *Formal Aspects of Computing*, 20(6):563–595, 2008.

[67] Peter Lammich and Markus Müller-Olm. Precise fixpoint-based analysis of programs with thread-creation and procedures. In L. Caires and V T. Vasconcelos, editors, *Concurrency Theory – CONCUR 2007*, volume 4703 of *LNCS*, pages 287–302. Springer, 2007.

[68] Xavier Leroy. Formal certification of a compiler back-end or: programming a compiler with a proof assistant. In *Proceedings of the 33rd ACM SIGPLAN-SIGACT symposium on Principles of programming languages (POPL)*, pages 42–54. ACM, 2006.

[69] Xavier Leroy. A formally verified compiler back-end. *Journal of Automated Reasoning*, 43(4):363–446, 2009.

[70] Andreas Lochbihler. Type safe nondeterminism – a formal semantics of Java threads. In *International Workshop on Foundations of Object-Oriented Languages (FOOL)*, 2008.

[71] Andreas Lochbihler. Verifying a compiler for Java threads. In *European Symposium on Programming (ESOP'10)*, volume 6012 of *LNCS*, pages 427–447. Springer, 2010.

[72] Donna Malayeri and Jonathan Aldrich. CZ: multiple inheritance without diamonds. In *Proceeding of the 24th ACM SIGPLAN conference on Object-oriented programming systems languages and applications (OOPSLA)*, pages 21–40, 2009.

[73] Heiko Mantel, Henning Sudbrock, and Tina Kraußer. Combining different proof techniques for verifying information flow security. In *Logic-Based Program Synthesis and Transformation – LOPSTR 2006*, volume 4407 of *LNCS*, pages 94–110, 2006.

[74] Claude Marché, Christine Paulin-Mohring, and Xavier Urbain. The KRAKATOA tool for certification of Java/JavaCard programs annotated in JML. *Journal of Logic and Algebraic Programming*, 58:89–106, 2004.

[75] Andrew C. Myers. JFlow: practical mostly-static information flow control. In *Proceedings of the 26th ACM SIGPLAN-SIGACT*

symposium on Principles of programming languages (POPL), pages 228–241. ACM, 1999.

[76] Maurice Naftalin and Philip Wadler. *Java generics and collections*. O'Reilly, 2006.

[77] Mangala Gowri Nanda and S. Ramesh. Interprocedural slicing of multithreaded programs with applications to Java. *ACM Transactions on Programming Languages and Systems*, 28(6):1088–1144, 2006.

[78] David A. Naumann. Verifying a secure information flow analyzer. In *Theorem Proving in Higher Order Logics – TPHOLs 2005*, volume 3603 of *LNCS*, pages 211–226. Springer, 2005.

[79] George C. Necula. Proof-carrying code. In *Proceedings of the 24th ACM SIGPLAN-SIGACT symposium on Principles of programming languages (POPL)*, pages 106–119. ACM, 1997.

[80] Flemming Nielson, Hanne Riis Nielson, and Chris Hankin. *Principles of Program Analysis*. Springer, 1999.

[81] Tobias Nipkow, Lawrence C. Paulson, and Markus Wenzel. *Isabelle/HOL — A Proof Assistant for Higher-Order Logic*, volume 2283 of *LNCS*. Springer, 2002.

[82] Michael Norrish. C formalised in HOL. Technical Report UCAM-CL-TR-453, University of Cambridge, 1998.

[83] Michael Norrish. A formal semantics for C++. Technical report, NICTA, 2008.

[84] Martin Odersky, Philippe Altherr, Vincent Cremet, Burak Emir, Sebastian Maneth, Stéphane Micheloud, Nikolay Mihaylov, Michel Schinz, Erik Stenman, and Matthias Zenger. An overview of the Scala programming language. Technical Report LAMP-REPORT-2006-001, École Polytechnique Fédérale de Lausanne, Lausanne, Switzerland, 2004.

[85] Martin Odersky, Vincent Cremet, Christine Röckl, and Matthias Zenger. A nominal theory of objects with dependent types. In *ECOOP 2003 – Object-Oriented Programming*, volume 2743 of *LNCS*, pages 201–224. Springer, 2003.

[86] Sam Owre and Natarajan Shankar. Theory Interpretation in PVS. Technical Report SRI-CSL-01-01, SRI International, April 2001.

[87] Benjamin C. Pierce. *Types and Programming Languages*. The MIT Press, 2002.

[88] Andy Podgurski and Lori A. Clarke. A formal model of program dependences and its implications for software testing, debugging, and maintenance. *IEEE Transactions on Software Engineering*, 16(9):965–979, 1990.

[89] G. Ramalingam and Harini Srinivasan. A member lookup algorithm for C++. In *Proceedings of the ACM SIGPLAN 1997 conference on Programming language design and implementation (1997)*, pages 18–30. ACM, 1997.

[90] Venkatesh Prasad Ranganath, Torben Amtoft, Anindya Banerjee, John Hatcliff, and Matthew B. Dwyer. A new foundation for control dependence and slicing for modern program structures. *ACM Transactions on Programming Languages and Systems*, 29(5):27, 2007.

[91] Thomas Reps, Susan Horwitz, Mooly Sagiv, and Genevieve Rosay. Speeding up slicing. In *Proceedings of the 2nd ACM SIGSOFT symposium on Foundations of software engineering (SIGSOFT)*, pages 11–20. ACM, 1994.

[92] Thomas W. Reps and Wuu Yang. The semantics of program slicing and program integration. In Josep Díaz and Fernando Orejas, editors, *TAPSOFT 1989*, volume 352 of *LNCS*, pages 360–374. Springer, 1989.

[93] Jonathan G. Rossie, Jr. and Daniel P. Friedman. An algebraic semantics of subobjects. In *Proceedings of the tenth annual conference on Object-oriented programming systems, languages, and applications (OOPSLA)*, pages 187–199. ACM, 1995.

[94] Jonathan G. Rossie, Jr., Daniel P. Friedman, and Mitchell Wand. Modeling subobject-based inheritance. In *ECOOP 1996 – Object-Oriented Programming*, volume 1098 of *LNCS*, pages 248–274. Springer, 1996.

[95] John Rushby. Noninterference, transitivity, and channel-control security policies. Technical Report CSL-92-02, SRI International, 1992.

[96] Andrei Sabelfeld and Andrew C. Myers. Language-based information-flow security. *Journal on Selected Areas in Communications*, 21(1):5–19, 2003.

[97] Andrei Sabelfeld and David Sands. A PER model of secure information flow in sequential programs. *Higher Order Symbolic Computation*, 14(1):59–91, 2001.

[98] Mooly Sagiv, Thomas Reps, and Reinhard Wilhelm. Parametric shape analysis via 3-valued logic. *ACM Transactions on Programming Languages and Systems*, 24(3):217–298, 2002.

[99] Alexandru Sălcianu and Konstantine Arkoudas. Machine-checkable correctness proofs for intra-procedural dataflow analyses. In *Proceedings of the Fourth International Workshop on Compiler Optimization meets Compiler Verification (COCV)*, pages 53–68. Elsevier, 2005.

[100] Nobert Schirmer. *Verification of Sequential Imperative Programs in Isabelle/HOL*. PhD thesis, Technische Universität München, 2006.

[101] Fred B. Schneider and Greg Morrisett. A language-based approach to security. In Reinhard Wilhelm, editor, *Informatics*, volume 2000 of *LNCS*, pages 86–101. Springer, 2001.

[102] Adam Seligman. FACTS: A formal analysis for C++. Master's thesis, Williams College, 1995. Undergraduate thesis.

[103] Olin Shivers. *Control-flow analysis of higher-order languages :–or Taming Lambda*. PhD thesis, Carnegie Mellon University, May 1991.

[104] Jeremy Siek and Walid Taha. A semantic analysis of C++ templates. In *ECOOP 2006 – Object-Oriented Programming*, volume 4067 of *LNCS*, pages 304 – 327. Springer, 2006.

[105] Vincent Simonet. Flow Caml in a nutshell. In *Proceedings of the first APPSEM-II workshop*, pages 152–165, 2003.

[106] Saurabh Sinha, Mary Jean Harrold, and Gregg Rothermel. Inter-procedural control dependence. *ACM Transactions on Software Engineering and Methodology*, 10(2):209–254, 2001.

[107] Geoffrey Smith and Dennis Volpano. Secure information flow in a multi-threaded imperative language. In *Proceedings of the 25th ACM SIGPLAN-SIGACT symposium on Principles of programming language (POPL)*, pages 355–364. ACM, 1998.

[108] Gregor Snelting. Combining slicing and constraint solving for validation of measurement software. In *Proceedings of the Third International Symposium on Static Analysis (SAS)*, volume 1145 of *LNCS*, pages 332–348. Springer, 1996.

[109] Gregor Snelting, Torsten Robschink, and Jens Krinke. Efficient Path Conditions in Dependence Graphs for Software Safety Analysis. *ACM Transactions on Software Engineering and Methodology*, 15(4):410–457, 2006.

[110] Gregor Snelting and Daniel Wasserrab. A correctness proof for the Volpano/Smith security typing system. In Gerwin Klein, Tobias Nipkow, and Lawrence Paulson, editors, *The Archive of Formal Proofs*. http://afp.sf.net/entries/VolpanoSmith.shtml, September 2008. Formal proof development.

[111] Manu Sridharan, Stephen J. Fink, and Rastislav Bodik. Thin slicing. In *Proceedings of the 2007 ACM SIGPLAN conference on Programming language design and implementation (PLDI)*, pages 112–122. ACM, 2007.

[112] Bjarne Steensgaard. Points-to analysis in almost linear time. In *Proceedings of the 23rd ACM SIGPLAN-SIGACT symposium on Principles of programming languages (POPL)*, pages 32–41. ACM, 1996.

[113] Martin Strecker. Formal analysis of an information flow type system for MicroJava (extended version). Technical report, Technische Universität München, July 2003.

[114] Bjarne Stroustrup. Multiple inheritance for C++. *Computing Systems*, 2(4):367–395, 1989.

[115] Bjarne Stroustrup. *The Design and Evolution of C++*. Addison Wesley, 1994.

[116] Bjarne Stroustrup. *The C++ Standard: Incorporating Technical Corrigendum No. 1*. John Wiley, 2nd edition, 2003.

[117] Frank Tip. A survey of program slicing techniques. *Journal of Programming Languages*, 3(3):121–189, 1995.

[118] Frank Tip. Personal communication, August 2005.

[119] Jean-Baptiste Tristan and Xavier Leroy. Verified validation of lazy code motion. In *Proceedings of the 2009 ACM SIGPLAN conference on Programming language design and implementation (PLDI)*, pages 316–326. ACM, 2009.

[120] Rob J. van Glabbeek. Branching bisimulation as a tool in the analysis of weak bisimulation. Available at `ftp://boole.stanford.edu/pub/DVI/tool.dvi.gz`.

[121] David Vandevoorde and Nikolai M. Josuttis. *C++ Templates: The Complete Guide*. Addison-Wesley, 2003.

[122] Dennis Volpano, Geoffrey Smith, and Cynthia Irvine. A sound type system for secure flow analysis. *Journal of Computer Security*, 4(2-3):167–187, 1996.

[123] David von Oheimb. Information flow control revisited: Noninfluence = Noninterference + Nonleakage. In P. Samarati, P. Ryan, D. Gollmann, and R. Molva, editors, *Computer Security – ESORICS 2004*, volume 3193 of *LNCS*, pages 225–243. Springer, 2004.

[124] Charles Wallace. The semantics of the C++ programming language. *Specification and Validation Methods*, pages 131–164, 1995.

[125] Martin Ward and Hussein Zedan. Slicing as a program transformation. *ACM Transactions on Programming Languages and Systems*, 29(2):7, 2007.

[126] Daniel Wasserrab. Formale Semantik einer C++-ähnlichen Sprache mit Fokussierung auf Mehrfachvererbung. Master's thesis, Technische Universität München, 2004. In german.

[127] Daniel Wasserrab. CoreC++. In Gerwin Klein, Tobias Nipkow, and Lawrence Paulson, editors, *The Archive of Formal Proofs*. http://afp.sf.net/entries/CoreC++.shtml, September 2006. Formal proof development.

[128] Daniel Wasserrab. Towards certified slicing. In Gerwin Klein, Tobias Nipkow, and Lawrence Paulson, editors, *The Archive of Formal Proofs*. http://afp.sf.net/entries/Slicing.shtml, September 2008. Formal proof development.

[129] Daniel Wasserrab. Backing up slicing: Verifying the interprocedural two-phase Horwitz-Reps-Binkley slicer. In Gerwin Klein, Tobias Nipkow, and Lawrence Paulson, editors, *The Archive of Formal Proofs*. http://afp.sf.net/entries/HRB-Slicing.shtml, September 2009. Formal proof development.

[130] Daniel Wasserrab. Information flow noninterference via slicing. In Gerwin Klein, Tobias Nipkow, and Lawrence Paulson, editors, *The Archive of Formal Proofs*. http://afp.sf.net/entries/InformationFlowSlicing.shtml, March 2010. Formal proof development.

[131] Daniel Wasserrab and Andreas Lochbihler. Formalizing a framework for dynamic slicing of program dependence graphs in Isabelle/HOL. In Outmane Ait Mohamed, César Muñoz, and Sofiène Tahar, editors, *Theorem Proving in Higher Order Logics – TPHOLs 2008*, volume 5170 of *LNCS*, pages 294–309. Springer, 2008.

[132] Daniel Wasserrab, Denis Lohner, and Gregor Snelting. On PDG-based noninterference and its modular proof. In *Proceedings of the 4th Workshop on Programming Languages and Analysis for Security (PLAS)*, pages 31–44. ACM, June 2009.

[133] Daniel Wasserrab, Tobias Nipkow, Gregor Snelting, and Frank Tip. An operational semantics and type safety proof for C++-like multiple inheritance. Technical Report RC23709, IBM, 2005.

[134] Daniel Wasserrab, Tobias Nipkow, Gregor Snelting, and Frank Tip. An operational semantics and type safety proof for multiple inheritance in C++. In *Proceedings of the 21st annual ACM*

SIGPLAN conference on Object-oriented programming systems, languages, and applications (OOPSLA), pages 345–362. ACM, 2006.

[135] Mark Weiser. *Program slices: formal, psychological, and practical investigations of an automatic program abstraction method.* PhD thesis, University of Michigan, 1979.

[136] Mark Weiser. Program slicing. *IEEE Transactions on Software Engineering*, 10(4):352–357, 1984.

[137] Markus Wenzel. *Isabelle/Isar — A Versatile Environment for Human-Readable Formal Proof Documents.* PhD thesis, Institut für Informatik, Technische Universität München, 2002.

[138] Glynn Winskel. *The Formal Semantics of Programming Languages. An Introduction.* MIT Press, 1993.

[139] Michael Joseph Wolfe. *High Performance Compilers for Parallel Computing.* Addison-Wesley, 1995.

[140] Andrew K. Wright and Matthias Felleisen. A syntactic approach to type soundness. *Information and Computation*, 115(1):38–94, 1994.

[141] Fangjun Wu and Tong Yi. Slicing Z specifications. *SIGPLAN Notices*, 39(8):39–48, 2004.

[142] Xiangyu Zhang, Neelam Gupta, and Rajiv Gupta. A study of effectiveness of dynamic slicing in locating real faults. *Empirical Software Engineering*, 12(2):143–160, 2007.

Index